Information Trapping

Real-Time Research on the Web

TARA CALISHAIN

New Riders

Information Trapping
Real-Time Research on the Web
Tara Calishain

New Riders
1249 Eighth Street
Berkeley, CA 94710
510/524-2178
800/283-9444
510/524-2221 (fax)
Find us on the Web at: newriders.com
To report errors, please send a note to errata@peachpit.com
New Riders is an imprint of Peachpit, a division of Pearson Education

Project Editor: Nancy Davis
Editor: Jill Marts Lodwig
Production Editor: Becky Winter
Proofreader: Ted Waitt
Compositor: Danielle Foster
Indexer: Emily Glossbrenner
Cover Design: Charlene Will

ISBN 0-321-49171-8
9 8 7 6 5 4 3 2 1
Printed and bound in the United States of America

Dedication

To my husband, Phil, with all my love and affection.

Acknowledgements

Many thanks to Mary Ellen Bates and Kathy Biehl, who took an initial look at the manuscript and provided invaluable feedback. Many thanks to Nancy Davis and Jill Lodwig for finally pinning down this book and getting it on track to paperdom. Thanks also to Becky Winter, for her production expertise and for helping me track all those crazy little details, and Danielle Foster, for her layout talents.

A heartfelt thanks goes out to my family and coworkers, who are always patient when I'm in the middle of writing a book and my brain is off playing with search engines.

And a big thanks to all the readers of ResearchBuzz, who constantly inspire me with their questions, ideas, suggestions, and feedback.

Contents

1

What Is Information Trapping?

For a long time—and especially around 1994, when the World Wide Web was just getting its jumpstart—the Internet appeared to many as a vast pool of information just sitting in cyberspace. People who used the Internet for research "cast their nets" by entering queries into a search engine, and then pulled in "fish," in the form of information. Once they had the information they needed, they didn't bother to repeat the search, unless enough time lapsed and the information changed.

Nowadays the Internet is in a constant state of flux. No longer a static repository of information, Web content changes minute by minute. From bloggers posting their thoughts online and news sources adding timely stories, to Flickr users showing off their latest photographs and the explosion of online video and podcasts, information is being added at a breathtaking rate.

This continuous flow of information provides an opportunity to not only conduct Web searches of relatively constant information, such as a phone number or the capital of Idaho, but to continuously monitor live information, such as the expansion of area codes or the population growth of Idaho over time, to stay abreast of topics that are of interest.

This idea of using ongoing information "trapping"—constant information gathering that's as automated as possible—instead of relying only on static, single instances of Web searching is what this book is all about. And as you'll discover, many tools are available for trapping information.

The Benefits of Information Trapping

Picture this: You get up in the morning and go to your office. You're in the middle of a project on online retail sales. Before information trapping was a reality, you would spend some time visiting various specialty magazines and conducting online news searches, looking for more retail statistics. With information trapping, you initially set up information-gathering traps for information and statistics about online retail sales, and then each morning you simply open your RSS feed reader and/or e-mail application, sit back, and read through the information your traps have found. You can save and organize whatever data you want. As you move on to the other work you need to accomplish, your information traps are busily scanning the Internet to provide you updated information the next time you do your research.

The primary benefit of information trapping, versus running a static search every time you need up-to-date information, is saved time. Once you've set up the traps, information flows to you and into an infrastructure you have organized; you no longer need to go out and seek it. This puts you in a better position to gather information and learn about your topic than if you simply ran searches on search engines whenever you had the time.

The usual process for getting information from the Web looks something like this:

1. Run a search on a search engine.

2. Evaluate the results.

3. Refine the query.

4. Repeat this process until you get the information you need.

This process works fine when you need basic information, or you're searching for information that you will need only once. However, when you're trying to get information about something for which you have an ongoing interest, performing these steps over and over can get tedious.

Compare this process to the process of information trapping:

1. Consider your subject and carefully develop search queries.

2. Evaluate possible resources to search.

3. Set up your queries.

4. Receive and evaluate the results.

The downside to information trapping is that setting up your traps takes more time initially than just running a single query on a search engine. The reason? Once you've created a search term or set of resources to be monitored, you don't have the ability to refine your queries, so you have to do your tweaking in advance. However, once they're established, information traps run just fine on their own, and you don't have to continually remember to keep running queries to stay abreast of your topic. You'll receive results for as long as you're interested in getting them—days, weeks, months, or possibly even years. And over time, you can refine your search as your interests change or as the topic itself changes.

Information-Trapping Scenarios

Setting up information traps is a large investment in time and thought, and you might be wondering if it's worth it for your topic. Consider these scenarios:

Example #1: You're a PR professional. You have ten clients whose names you want to monitor in the context of their appearances, getting coverage in the media, and so forth. You have ten easy candidates for information trapping.

Example #2: A member of your family has cystic fibrosis. They have very good medical care but you want to monitor news, medical, and governmental resources for updates and information about advances in the care of people with cystic fibrosis.

Example #3: You're an avid collector of old woodworking tools. For your own interest and to enhance a hobby site you've put together, you want to monitor news, discussion groups, and hobby blogs for information about old woodworking tools.

All these examples are valid, whether they're related to hobbies, personal interests, or professional pursuits. Information trapping doesn't have to be related to the stock market or a professional endeavor to provide useful results.

Asking the Right Questions

I'm going to spend a lot of time in this book talking about techniques, resources, sites, and software—the stuff you'll need to make your information traps a reality. But before I get to that I want you to be aware that one of the most important tools for effective information trapping is your own brain. Your brain is what guides the process and determines the kind of content you actually want to see. It's essential that you ask the right questions before you begin.

This section details the questions you should ask yourself each and every time you design an information trap.

Why trap for this particular topic?

There are literally millions of topics that are suitable candidates for information trapping, but you still need to think about why you want to trap a particular one. Being able to answer why you want to trap it influences the resources you choose and the way you organize your information. Are you maintaining a Web site on a subject and you need to monitor the Internet for new sites and information that will help you generate content? Are you trying to get publicity for something and need to monitor the Web for similar stories? Are you trying to keep up to date with a certain health condition? Having a sense of why you want to set up information trapping will help you design a better information trap.

What sources do you want to search?

A wide variety of sites on the Internet are available for trapping—they vary in scope, kind of material, and credibility. What kind of information do you want? Do you want to limit yourself to highly credible sources? In that case, you'll probably want to search just government resources and news search engines. Don't mind less credible results? Then you could expand your results to search engines in general. Want to hear what people think about a topic? Then you could monitor discussion lists or blogs. There are many different types of resources available to monitor; choosing the best resources for your needs is one of the things I'll show you in this book.

Where do you want to search?

Answering where you want to search overlaps with the previous "what sources?" question. If you answered that question sufficiently, you're well on your way to answering the "where" question, which addresses the geographical factor you need to consider for your research. Many search resources these days let you narrow your search results to a particular region, country, state, or city. Not all topics require geographic restriction, but sometimes it's useful. Say you want to create an information trap on a sports star. Unfortunately, he has a very common name, but by setting up the trap to include the name of his team's city, and perhaps even his own hometown, the information you receive in your traps is more likely to be focused only on him.

How often do you want to receive results?

If you've created a series of information traps, and you can handle the flow (or deluge) of information that comes back to you, you may want to see results each day. If you're in a rush, you may even want the results on an hourly basis. On the other hand, you may have only a certain amount of time to devote to your research, so you might elect to receive updates only once a week. When answering this question, it's important to consider how much time you have to devote to your information trap. If you're uncertain, be a little conservative. It's easier to turn up your frequency than to dig yourself out from under a pile of information.

How do you want to receive your results?

Not too long ago, if you wanted to monitor information online, you had one choice for delivery—good ol' e-mail. Nowadays, you can still use e-mail, but you've got other choices, including RSS feeds (which I discuss a lot in this book) and SMS ("short message service," which a growing number of mobile phones support). You don't have to limit yourself to only one delivery type. You may decide that you want to get most of your results by e-mail, but there's one important topic—about which you want to be alerted immediately— where SMS is the better choice.

You've probably heard a lot about RSS, and you might even have heard some people say that "e-mail is dead" or something like that. Trust me: E-mail is not going anywhere. The important thing is that you choose a delivery method that's comfortable for you. If you're not comfortable with RSS, use e-mail. Or use SMS. If alerts were available by carrier pigeon, I'd tell you to use those if that's what you like best.

Take a few minutes and muse on the questions above; we'll explore some of the answers you might have—and how to use those answers to implement well designed information traps—later in the book. If you already have a topic in mind and you have solid answers to the questions above, you're well on your way to setting up your first information trap!

Getting Practical

This chapter hopefully rewired your brain a little bit so that you now think of the Internet as a dynamic pool of data from which you can harness and automatically cull certain types of information that interest you on an ongoing basis, without having to fetch it yourself.

In addition to learning how to think about the Internet in new ways and understanding its potential, you're also going to need to expand your Internet toolbox. Sure, you'll be using your familiar Web browser, but you're also going to be learning about and using RSS, page monitors, and e-mail alerts. Let's get started!

2

RSS Basics

To do static, one-time searches on the Web, you use one type of tool—a Web browser. (You may not think of your copy of Firefox as a tool, but it is!) To do information trapping, you need a whole other set of tools. Your browser will still come in handy, but its main function is to help you set your traps.

You also need to know about a technology called RSS, which stands for either Rich Site Summary or RDF Site Summary, depending on who you ask. And it helps to know a little bit about page monitors, for those occasions when RSS won't do.

This chapter and the next take a close look at what these tools are and how they work. Before diving into the creation of information traps, which you'll do in Chapter 5, take some time to explore the resources presented in this chapter and Chapter 3, and try some experimenting on your own. When you're finished, you'll be fully prepared for integrating the tools into a set of basic information traps in Chapter 5.

For now, let's focus on RSS and what you can do with it—including even the weird things!

What Is RSS?

RSS is a type of XML. That's the short answer. But unfortunately, the short answer is not always the most useful one. The long answer is more helpful—it's important to understand a little about XML in order to fully appreciate the value of RSS.

XML holds the key

Web pages are often written in HyperText Markup Language, or HTML. The "markups" are computer code that looks `<like this>` and specifies how certain characters, words, and sections of a page should look. An HTML file is simply a text file formatted so that your browser displays it in a certain way.

HTML is just one way to format a text file. Another method is to use eXtensible Markup Language, or XML. Like HTML, an XML file looks like a text file that's formatted a certain way, but it specifies a lot more than plain, old HTML.

In HTML, the markup tells you what the title of the page is, and there are ways to tell what the keywords and description of the page are. And that's where it pretty much ends. There is no way to delineate specific information within the content of the page. Take, for example, an HTML page of information about birds. While someone might easily be able to scan the page for information about bird migration, a search engine could not. That's because the page simply is not formatted in a way for search engines to look at it and determine what part of the content is migration information.

You might do a keyword search for words relevant to migration, but the search engine finding your results might find the keywords anywhere—in the header of a page, in menus, or even in the copyright statement! There's no way that the search can be restricted to the area of the HTML page concerned with migration. HTML pages simply aren't structured to allow a search engine to break down the information they hold.

XML takes care of this problem by allowing for additional ways to delineate the information contained in the pages. With XML, you can have a formatting style for a page to display information about birds, so both people and search engines can read it. Why is this important? Because a computer can read not only this particular page about birds, but also ten million *other* pages about birds formatted in XML. Then from this gathered information, it can build a useful, searchable, outlined chunk of information about birds.

To take this scenario one step further, imagine that a search engine indexed 10,000 pages about birds from several different sites that were formatted in XML. Because of the XML format, you could search for all birds that migrated in November, or all birds that eat seeds. With HTML, you'd have to do keyword searches using words like `migration November cardinal` and you'd just have to hope you get useful results.

RSS feeds: a type of XML

So how does RSS relate to XML?

RSS is a type of text file, a particular type of XML for page and story summaries that is formatted so that the data is delineated very clearly, and broken down far more than it would be on a regular HTML page. There are more extensive types of RSS that carry all kinds of data, including sound and video files, but this book focuses on basic RSS text files. (Once you begin to trap multimedia, you'll notice plenty of examples of RSS feeds that carry data in addition to text.)

You've probably heard the term *RSS feed* bantered about. An RSS file is called a feed in the same way that an HTML file is called a Web page. RSS feeds carry summary data about the latest articles on or additions to a Web site. (So in essence, a nicely structured RSS feed summarizes new content that's often made available in chaotic, unstructured HTML pages.)

The data in an RSS feed is broken down by title and summary, and contains additional information, including when the summary was generated, where it came from, who the author is, what language it's in, and so on. Some RSS feeds carry only headlines of new information, while others carry summaries—the title of a new article and maybe the first 20 words of that article—while still others are called "full feeds" that contain all the text (and sometimes multimedia) available from a Web site. In other words, you can read the content of a site without having to visit the site at all (**Figure 2.1**)!

Figure 2.1

The International Herald Tribune offers a bevy of feeds that provides content without your having to visit the Web site.

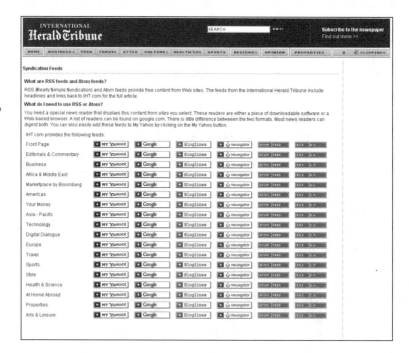

What about Atom?

As you're looking for RSS feeds, you may read about of a different file format called *Atom*. Atom does the same thing that RSS does, for the most part. There don't seem to be as many Atom feeds as RSS feeds, however. Most feed readers that support RSS also support Atom, so don't worry about the differences between the two formats.

Anatomy of an RSS Feed

I just described to you what a feed looks like, but let's consider an actual example.

You're used to HTML pages, which can look like pretty much anything, limited only by the creativity of the designer. But RSS feeds are much more uniform.

Here's a part of an RSS feed, a summary of an article that was published on the Book Standard (bookstandard.com). I'm showing you the code of it, which looks very much like the source of an HTML page:

```
<item>
<title>Piracy Threat on the Horizon?</title>
<link>http://www.thebookstandard.com/bookstandard/news/publisher/
article_display.jsp?vnu_content_id=1000963039</link>
<description>The Book Standard, June 16, 2005. An overview of how
piracy is impacting American publishers, including this scary
little stat: "U.S. publishers lost an estimated $571 million to
the illegal activity in 2004, according to the International
Intellectual Property Alliance." The article also raised the
question of why piracy wasn't more of an issue at the BEA, and how
outsourcing may be driving some of the problem.
</description>
<pubDate>Mon, 20 Jun 2005 22:22:20 GMT</pubDate>
</item>
```

How this information is displayed for you depends on your RSS reader. Browsers all display RSS feeds a little bit differently, just like they display HTML pages a little bit differently (**Figures 2.2** and **2.3**).

Even without the fancy display, you can see by reading through the example feed item that it is quite a capsule of information. It has a title, a link, a description, and a publishing date. And this is a very basic item; far more information can be added. Having the information broken out like this makes it very easy for a search engine to organize content by date or title—a nifty capability for information trappers.

Figure 2.2

The ResearchBuzz RSS feed, which you can view in a Web browser.

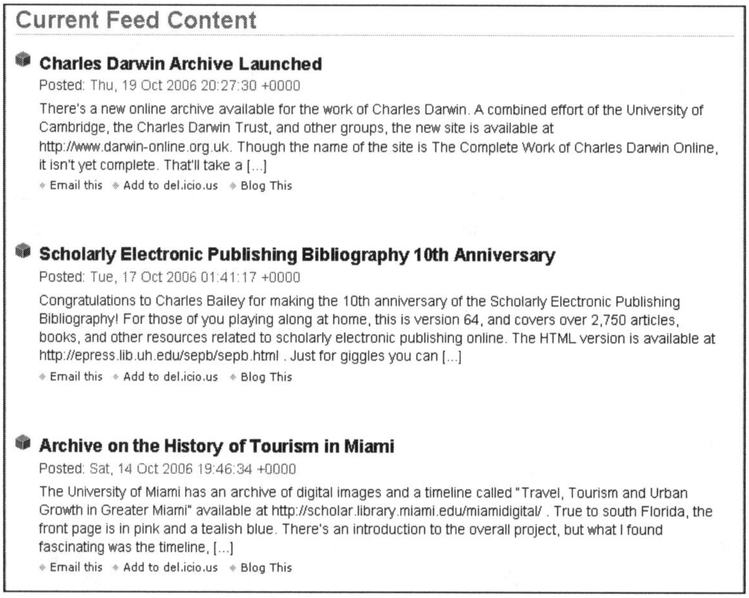

Current Feed Content

Charles Darwin Archive Launched

Posted: Thu, 19 Oct 2006 20:27:30 +0000

There's a new online archive available for the work of Charles Darwin. A combined effort of the University of Cambridge, the Charles Darwin Trust, and other groups, the new site is available at http://www.darwin-online.org.uk. Though the name of the site is The Complete Work of Charles Darwin Online, it isn't yet complete. That'll take a [...]

Email this · Add to del.icio.us · Blog This

Scholarly Electronic Publishing Bibliography 10th Anniversary

Posted: Tue, 17 Oct 2006 01:41:17 +0000

Congratulations to Charles Bailey for making the 10th anniversary of the Scholarly Electronic Publishing Bibliography! For those of you playing along at home, this is version 64, and covers over 2,750 articles, books, and other resources related to scholarly electronic publishing online. The HTML version is available at http://epress.lib.uh.edu/sepb/sepb.html . Just for giggles you can [...]

Email this · Add to del.icio.us · Blog This

Archive on the History of Tourism in Miami

Posted: Sat, 14 Oct 2006 19:46:34 +0000

The University of Miami has an archive of digital images and a timeline called "Travel, Tourism and Urban Growth in Greater Miami" available at http://scholar.library.miami.edu/miamidigital/ . True to south Florida, the front page is in pink and a tealish blue. There's an introduction to the overall project, but what I found fascinating was the timeline, [...]

Email this · Add to del.icio.us · Blog This

Figure 2.3

Other RSS feeds can be tough to read in a Web browser, and require a feed reader.

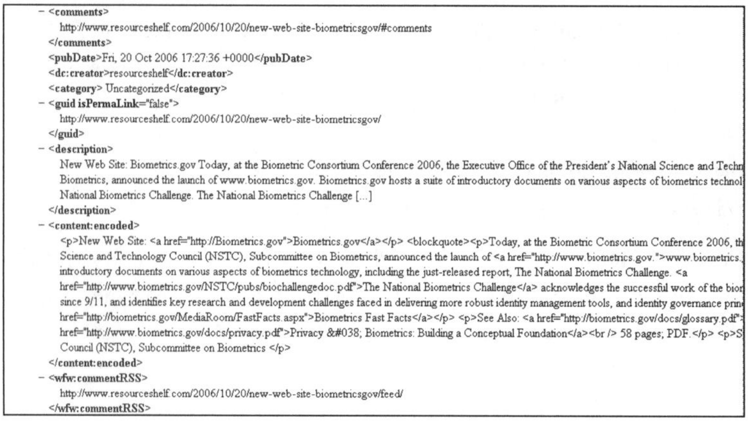


```
- <comments>
    http://www.resourceshelf.com/2006/10/20/new-web-site-biometricsgov/#comments
  </comments>
  <pubDate>Fri, 20 Oct 2006 17:27:36 +0000</pubDate>
  <dc:creator>resourceshelf</dc:creator>
  <category> Uncategorized</category>
- <guid isPermaLink="false">
    http://www.resourceshelf.com/2006/10/20/new-web-site-biometricsgov/
  </guid>
- <description>
    New Web Site: Biometrics.gov Today, at the Biometric Consortium Conference 2006, the Executive Office of the President's National Science and Techn
    Biometrics, announced the launch of www.biometrics.gov. Biometrics.gov hosts a suite of introductory documents on various aspects of biometrics technol
    National Biometrics Challenge. The National Biometrics Challenge [...]
  </description>
- <content:encoded>
    <p>New Web Site: <a href="http://Biometrics.gov">Biometrics.gov</a></p> <blockquote><p>Today, at the Biometric Consortium Conference 2006, th
    Science and Technology Council (NSTC), Subcommittee on Biometrics, announced the launch of <a href="http://www.biometrics.gov.">www.biometrics.
    introductory documents on various aspects of biometrics technology, including the just-released report, The National Biometrics Challenge. <a
    href="http://www.biometrics.gov/NSTC/pubs/biochallengedoc.pdf">The National Biometrics Challenge</a> acknowledges the successful work of the bior
    since 9/11, and identifies key research and development challenges faced in delivering more robust identity management tools, and identity governance prin
    href="http://biometrics.gov/MediaRoom/FastFacts.aspx">Biometrics Fast Facts</a></p> <p>See Also: <a href="http://biometrics.gov/docs/glossary.pdf"
    href="http://www.biometrics.gov/docs/privacy.pdf">Privacy &#038; Biometrics: Building a Conceptual Foundation</a><br /> 58 pages; PDF.</p> <p>S
    Council (NSTC), Subcommittee on Biometrics </p>
  </content:encoded>
- <wfw:commentRSS>
    http://www.resourceshelf.com/2006/10/20/new-web-site-biometricsgov/feed/
  </wfw:commentRSS>
```

The Big "So What?"

If you've read *Web Search Garage*, my book on general Internet searching, you know I have a "So What" test: whenever I hear about a new technology or trend I say, "So what?" The So What is the payoff, or what it's going to do for me as a searcher. If it's just nifty technology, that's fine, but I don't want to spend too much time playing with technologies that aren't going to make my searching, exploring, and teaching easier. There's just too much new technology out there!

The So What for you, in the case of RSS, is saved time. Instead of visiting several Web sites to get their latest articles, you can have an RSS feed reader do it for you and provide a summary or list of site updates. Furthermore, some RSS feeds give you lists of search engine results based on the queries you specify—these are called "keyword-based RSS feeds," which are very important. (You'll learn more about these later in the chapter.) So instead of having to run the same search over and over again (on an hourly, daily, or weekly basis), the RSS feed will automatically update itself and provide you with updated results and new content.

Let's look at a real-life, full-blown RSS feed scenario. I use NewsGator Online (newsgator.com) as my RSS feed reader. An RSS feed reader, like an HTML Web browser (such as Internet Explorer or Firefox), formats RSS feeds so that people, as well as computers, can read them. My RSS feed reader has about 100 RSS feeds—summary information about new additions to content on about 100 Web sites.

Can you imagine how long it would take me to visit every last one of those sites to see what new content it had? With RSS feeds and the online feed reader, however, I can skim through these sites in an hour or so.

RSS can save you lots and lots of time by showing you only new and updated content from Web sites.

TIP

Many blogs run on services like Blogger, or use content-management software like Movable Type. Many of these software packages and services can automatically create RSS feeds for their users. This is good for you (the trapper) in that there are lots and lots of feeds out there; it's bad for you because many of the feeds are from blogs and, therefore, aren't primary, credible sources. Don't fret: there are many primary-source RSS feeds available: and many blog feeds do link to primary-source content.

NOTE

Some RSS feed readers are client-based—that is, they're installed on your computer. Others are Web-based; you access them by visiting a Web site. (NewsGator is a Web-based feed reader.) Still others are installed as part of your Web browser. Which you use depends on your situation; we'll look at your options later in the chapter.

RSS is the cornerstone of any information-trapping strategy. RSS feeds are compact, focus on content, and contain a lot of clearly delineated information—the essential parts of the data flow you monitor. There will be times when you have to look at the content of entire Web pages and Web sites instead of using an RSS feed—sometimes RSS feeds aren't available for the materials in which you're really interested. But whenever possible, you should use RSS feeds. How to find an RSS feed, and what options you have to read them, is the subject of the rest of this chapter.

Finding RSS Feeds

Of course, you can't use an RSS feed until you find one. Fortunately, you've got several places to look! There are three major places: on RSS-enabled pages themselves, in RSS feed directories (which often allow for extensive searching), and in searchable subject indexes of RSS feeds (which allow for less searching but have feed listings broken down into detailed subcategories).

Keyword-based RSS feeds, which we'll look at in more detail later in the chapter, are usually created as the result of a search; therefore, there's not really a place to find them. Instead, you have to investigate the RSS feed sources you come across and see if they have keyword-based RSS feeds available, or use a tool that generates keyword-based RSS feeds.

On the site itself

Many Web sites advertise the fact that they have RSS feeds. Look for either a link that says "RSS feed" or, more commonly, an orange button that says XML on it. There is also a small square orange button that's getting popular (**Figure 2.4**).

Figure 2.4

This orange button is becoming a popular way to denote RSS feeds.

Yahoo's My Yahoo portal feature offers support for RSS feeds, so you might see a My Yahoo button in addition to an RSS Feed button. Many RSS feed readers also have their own style of buttons, which makes it easy to add a feed to that reader with one click. So you might see a plain XML button, and then half-a-dozen of the ones listed for individual feed readers (**Figure 2.5**). People really like promoting their RSS feeds!

If you already have a particular set of resources in mind that you want to monitor, then I recommend that you visit those sites first to see if they provide RSS feeds. If you don't have any resources in mind yet, start by looking in RSS feed directories.

Figure 2.5

Many RSS feeds give you multiple ways to subscribe.

RSS feed directories

RSS feed directories are—surprise!—directories of RSS feeds. Despite the fact that RSS has been getting a lot of press for some time, the technology has been going strong for a lot longer, and there are literally millions of feeds out there. You can get RSS feeds from four different sources, beginning with two search engines designed exclusively for RSS feeds.

Feedster

Feedster (feedster.com) is a search engine that indexes RSS feeds. Therefore, any pages you find on Feedster will be connected with an RSS feed.

If your particular interest is fairly obscure or narrowly focused, try searching Feedster first. In the query box, just enter a few keywords that describe your interest. For example, let's say I'm interested in collecting action figures. I'd plug **"action figures"** into Feedster.

Look at an example of Feedster's search results (**Figure 2.6**). Notice it includes a title, source, number of words, and when the information was actually published. (It can include an exact date of publication because an RSS feed notes that information in a format that a search engine can understand. Three more cheers for RSS!)

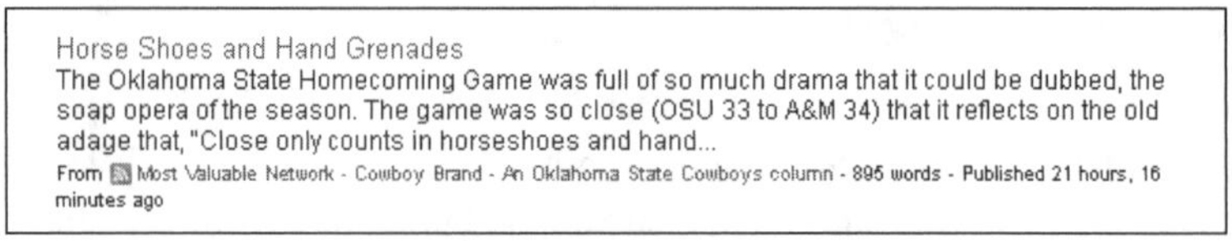

Figure 2.6

Feedster's results give you just enough content to allow a little preview of the blog itself.

> Horse Shoes and Hand Grenades
> The Oklahoma State Homecoming Game was full of so much drama that it could be dubbed, the soap opera of the season. The game was so close (OSU 33 to A&M 34) that it reflects on the old adage that, "Close only counts in horseshoes and hand...
> From ⟨R⟩ Most Valuable Network - Cowboy Brand - An Oklahoma State Cowboys column - 895 words - Published 21 hours, 16 minutes ago

Notice, too, that the source of the result is shown at the bottom underneath the "snippet" of the search result. (The snippet usually contains at least one of the keywords for which you were searching.) You might skim the snippet and decide you immediately want to subscribe to the RSS feed. In that case, you can click the orange button just to the right of the word *From* at the bottom of the entry.

There's your RSS feed. Sometimes you won't want to subscribe to that feed, but you may want to read some of the articles on the feed and see what sites the articles refer to. This takes some extra time, but it can pay off by pointing you to sources of information you might not find otherwise.

What Should You Do with These Resources?

We're going through these resources and I'm teaching you how to search for and find things, but I'm not teaching you what to do with them...yet. So what should you do with them? Should you make an attempt to gather RSS feeds now, or just do example searches now and come back later?

If you're starting from square one, you can either try a few example searches now and come back and do the real searches a little later on, or start a text file and paste in the URLs of any RSS feeds you find interesting that you want to come back to. If you're a little more advanced and already have a favorite feed reader set up, go ahead and add your feeds to it.

Syndic8

Syndic8 (syndic8.com) is a bit geekier than Feedster, and is designed only for finding RSS feeds instead of searching for information from RSS feeds. For this reason, Syndic8 provides a lot of information about the feeds it lists.

Look for the Search for Feed query box on the front page (**Figure 2.7**).

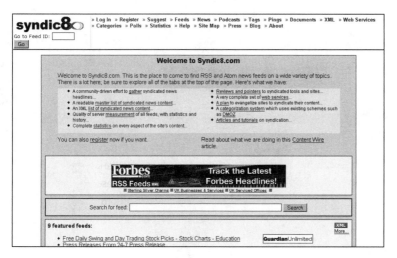

Figure 2.7

Syndic8's home page.

Here you can do a keyword search just like you could using Feedster's query box.

Let's do the same search on Syndic8 that we did with Feedster—for **"action figures"** (**Figure 2.8**).

I received 17 results, ranging from "toy news" to information on character figures. The information includes the language of the feeds (not very useful to get an Italian RSS feed if you don't speak Italian!). You can also view when the feed was created and when it was changed. In general, if a feed is fairly old (fairly old in Internet terms is a couple of years) and it's changed in the last few days, you've probably found an active feed.

You can get more information about the feed by clicking on the Feed ID number (don't click on the feed name, which takes you to the feed's Web site). There's also information about the last time the feed was "polled" (checked by Syndic8), its RSS version, its status, whether it contains metadata, and so on. A lot of these terms may sound like Greek to you—but rest assured, by the time you're finished reading this book, RSS parlance will come naturally to you!

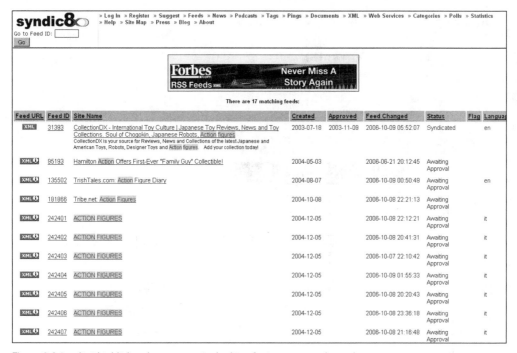

Figure 2.8 Syndic8 highlights the term you're looking for in your search results.

Pay attention to the dates on the search results page—an older feed that's still active usually contains good data, as I mentioned earlier. Be aware of "ghost feeds" that haven't been updated in years. There are a lot of people out there who enthusiastically start a site, offer RSS feeds, and realize a few months down the road that regularly updating a site requires time and effort. So they give up. You want to be using feeds that are up to date. You won't often encounter ghost feeds when searching in Feedster, since Feedster lists search results by date. (The feeds that have updated more recently appear at the top of Feedster's search results.) With Syndic8, however, you want to pay more attention.

You can also see the last entries in the RSS feed (**Figure 2.9**). Scroll down to the very bottom of the feed information page, and notice there's a list of the most recent entries and enough of the content to get a good sense of what the feed is about.

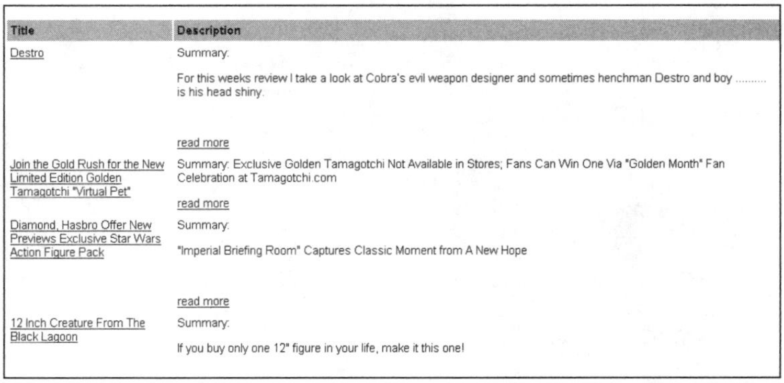

Title	Description
Destro	Summary:
	For this weeks review I take a look at Cobra's evil weapon designer and sometimes henchman Destro and boy .... is his head shiny.
	read more
Join the Gold Rush for the New Limited Edition Golden Tamagotchi "Virtual Pet"	Summary: Exclusive Golden Tamagotchi Not Available in Stores; Fans Can Win One Via "Golden Month" Fan Celebration at Tamagotchi.com
	read more
Diamond, Hasbro Offer New Previews Exclusive Star Wars Action Figure Pack	Summary:
	"Imperial Briefing Room" Captures Classic Moment from A New Hope
	read more
12 Inch Creature From The Black Lagoon	Summary:
	If you buy only one 12" figure in your life, make it this one!

Figure 2.9

Syndic8's feed information pages also include a list of recent additions to the RSS feed.

If you take the time now to vet the feed, making sure it covers your topic of interest, you'll save yourself from having to remove the feed from all your traps later.

NewsIsFree

NewsIsFree (newsisfree.com) could be considered a combination of Syndic8 and Feedster. You can search sources, like Feedster, but you can also browse sources, like Syndic8. The direct URL for browsing sources is newsisfree. com/sources/bycat.

Take a close look and notice the channels are broken out by category, from Top News to blogs (**Figure 2.10**).

Pick a category, and you get a list of RSS feed sources, with the most popular ones at the top and the rest listed alphabetically. The category listing gives the name of the feed, category, language, and a brief description. Click on the name of the feed and you get some additional information. At the top of the page, you can see the name of the feed, and there is also an orange XML button on the page—that's right, a link to the RSS feed (**Figure 2.11**).

Figure 2.10

NewsIsFree offers RSS feed listings in a variety of categories.

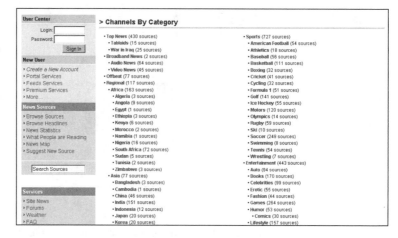

Figure 2.11

Finding the RSS feeds for items listed in NewsIsFree.

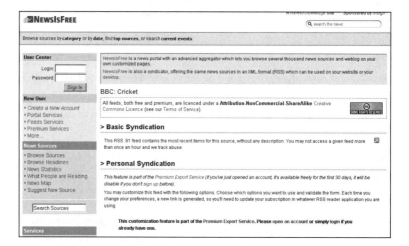

I'm mentioning this because the rest of the page can be a bit confusing and you may think that you have to pay to get a link to the RSS feed (which is not the case).

Notice that on the left side of a feed information page there's a search form for searching the sources of the news on the site (instead of searching the items within the sources).

A search for **"action figure"** on NewsIsFree brought no results—you might find you have to stick with Syndic8 or Feedster for more specific searches. That's because NewsIsFree doesn't seem to have as many sources as Feedster or Syndic8. However, I've included it here because it has been around a long time, it offers a unique way of looking at what's available, and it's an invaluable resource for keeping up with newly available feeds, which is a topic we return to when we discuss pruning, reevaluating, and adding sources.

Technorati's Blogfinder

Technorati has a service called Blogfinder (technorati.com/blogs/), which at this writing is still in beta, but you can use it to find RSS feeds as well. (Most blog-creation software nowadays automatically generates RSS feeds.)

Technorati lets you search for blogs using "tags," which are simply keywords describing the blog. This type of tag search means you need to use more general search words than you might use to search the full content of a blog. **"Action figures"** is general enough, and you'll probably get some results. **Figure 2.12** shows what those search results look like.

Figure 2.12

Using Technorati's Blogfinder, you can sort your results two different ways. The Freshness option works well if you're looking for frequently updated blogs for your information traps.

When I conducted my search, I received eight results, with a name of and a link to the blog, a brief description, the tags associated with the blog, and a note about when the blog was last updated (remember, you don't want to monitor ghost feeds!). You also get a link that lists who is linking to that blog, and sometimes you'll see a list of tags at the top of the search results that are related to the one you searched for (in this case, for example, related tags are for Vintage Toys and Star Wars).

Pulling the RSS feeds from the found blogs involves revisiting the site to look for the orange RSS logos or one of the personalized RSS logos from My Yahoo or another site. It takes a little extra work; on the other hand, the tag system makes searching for blogs/RSS feeds on more general subjects easier than using a full-text search engine.

Specialty RSS Feed Directories

RSS is popular enough at this point that specialized listings of feeds are becoming available. Here are a couple that might help you in your information trapping:

- **Corporate feeds.** Nooked (http://dir.nooked.com/home.dir) provides corporate RSS feeds only. You can search the feeds by keyword or browse for them by category. There's a brief description of each feed, and some entities have multiple feeds available (press releases, products, and so forth). This resource isn't 100 percent comprehensive, but it is considerable.

- **Newspaper feeds.** The Media Drop (themediadrop.com/archives/003699.php) is a list of U.S. newspapers, broken out by state, that have RSS feeds. If you're interested in non-US newspaper content, check out the list of UK papers that have RSS feeds, available at http://dave.org.uk/newsfeeds/.

RSS in Searchable Subject Indexes

There are many searchable subject indexes of RSS feeds. A searchable subject index is a directory set up into categories (**Figure 2.13**).

The categories also have subcategories and sometimes they go into astonishing detail. In addition to being set up into categories, such a directory is also searchable by keywords (think Yahoo Directory). There are literally dozens of searchable subject indexes for RSS feeds—I discuss just a couple of them here.

Figure 2.13

2RSS, a searchable subject index for RSS feeds.

2RSS

2RSS (2rss.com) goes beyond RSS feeds to offer RSS tools and other RSS-related information. It begins with the directory of RSS feeds, divided into several categories. There are blog and news feeds here, yes, but there are also business feeds, regional feeds, and lists for feeds that were recently added, as well as feeds that are recommended. If you want to get a sense of what RSS feeds look like, try the feed reader (2RSS Reader, at the top of the page)—you don't have to log in to use it; just choose a feed from the pull-down menu or enter the URL of a feed.

RSS Network

RSS Network (rss-network.com/) offers a directory of RSS feeds, but divides the feeds into several unusual categories, including real estate, shopping, classified, and animal. When browsing results, you can view the RSS feed as a Web page to get a preview of the content, or go straight to the "raw" RSS feed or to the Web site for the feed content.

For 90 percent of your RSS discovery needs, search engines and feed directories will do the trick. There are many of them and the biggest ones frequently add new feeds.

Six Weird Things You Can Do with RSS Feeds

So far you may have gotten the impression that RSS feeds are good for nothing but delivering news and article updates from Web sites. Not so! RSS feeds are all about delivering information—many different kinds of information. With that in mind, here are six weird—or at least unexpected—things you can do with an RSS feed.

- **Track a UPS package** (simpletracking.com/). Want to track a FedEx or DHL package but don't want to keep going back to the shipper's Web site and hitting refresh? Enter a package number on this form (it supports USPS numbers too!) and it generates a handy RSS feed for you.

- **Search Amazon** (oxus.net/amazon). Yes, you can use the tool on this page to keep up with your favorite authors or book subjects, but you can also use it to keep up with additions to other Amazon stores. Want to look for classical music, new DVDs, or even new games on that latest platform? This is the way to do it. There's another good Amazon RSS feed generator at onfocus.com/amafeed/.

- **Clip Coupons** (valpak.com/vpcol/searchRSS.do). Now that snail mail envelope full of goodies is available in RSS format. Just enter a zip code or your city and state, and Valpak generates RSS feeds for coupons in your area, or coupons based on product category.

- **Get Hurricane Information** (nhc.noaa.gov/aboutrss.shtml). If you live in the southeastern part of the United States, I'm sure you know all about when hurricane season is, especially after the last few years. The National Hurricane Center keeps you up to date with three different RSS feeds for hurricane activity in different oceans.

- **Access Library Services** (public.iastate.edu/~CYBERSTACKS/RSS.htm). As you might imagine, with all the different services they already offer, libraries are getting into RSS big time to communicate with their users about what they have to offer. This site lists several libraries and the services they offer via RSS, from announcements to databases, to new books, and more.

- **Get MTA service advisories** (robotpolishers.com/subway). Things like service advisories are most useful when reading RSS feeds on the go. I discuss this in more detail later in the book. Of course, this particular site is most useful if you're in New York, because this tool (Disorient Express) gives you service advisories for the New York City transit system.

Types of RSS Feeds

So far we've been looking at where you can find static RSS feeds—RSS feeds that Web sites make available to provide information about their site or about certain sections of their site. And these static feeds are very useful. But your secret weapon as an information trapper is not the static feed, but the keyword-based feed.

This section is all about the "So what?" I discussed earlier in the chapter. Which type of RSS feed you use can save you gobs and gobs of time and make you look like an information-gathering wizard!

Static feeds

Static feeds are just what they sound like: feeds a site offers that you can't customize with keywords—what we've been talking about up to this point in the chapter. A site may have one static feed available, or hundreds. My Web site ResearchBuzz (researchbuzz.org/wp) has a couple of main feeds with the potential for a feed for each category, which amounts to over 200 feeds—but they're all static. Static feeds are not the customizable timesavers that keyword-based feeds are, but they're essential to providing you with general overviews of a topic, or for providing you with information when your interests are too broad for a keyword search.

Static feeds are your starting point. You build your monitoring process by first setting a few information traps of general interest to make sure you get a full sweep of the topic you're interested in. However, you don't want to set too many! The idea is to create a manageable flow of information, which you can filter and redirect in whatever way you need.

Keyword-based feeds

Keyword-based feeds are feeds that are generated based on a search. This search can be done on any resource (most people do them on news search engines). The advantage is that you can create your own feeds based on the keywords you're interested in, feeds that are as narrowly focused as you like. Although most likely you can find RSS feeds that broadly address the topic you're interested in, a keyword-based RSS feed can help you coax out narrowly focused information. The rest of this chapter talks about where to find keyword-based feeds and what to do with them once you find them.

I hear you out there saying, "So what?" Okay, let's look at an example: You're interested in molybdenum mining. You might be able to find RSS feeds about mining, minerals, elements, or chemistry, but I'm pretty sure there's no *Molybdenum Mining Gazette* out there. But you could search Yahoo News for `molybdenum mining`, sort your results by date, and generate a constantly updated RSS feed of molybdenum mining news.

There might not be much news about such a topic, and that's the entire point. Instead of having to go through more general, very active feeds that change several times a month or possibly several times a day, you'd be reading a feed that might change only a couple times a month. That would be okay, however, because it would be bringing very specific, very focused news to you—the exact news you want.

In later chapters, as we dive further into RSS feeds and where they can be found, we'll get up close and personal with keyword-based RSS feeds. For now, let's return to a resource we discussed earlier in the chapter to get a better sense of how this type of feed can help you.

Remember Feedster? Feedster locates static RSS feeds. But it's also a source of keyword-based RSS feeds. Say you're a customer-service executive with Pizza Hut, and you want to know what people are saying about Pizza Hut stores. You visit Feedster, and after some experimentation, you settle on the search phrase `"pizza hut" "thin crust"`. Your search results may look like **Figure 2.14**.

Unless one of the blogs you find is called "My Diary of Going to Pizza Hut Every Day," you're probably not going to want to monitor each of these blogs. Instead, you can get an RSS feed of Feedster's results: a keyword-based RSS feed that refreshes every time Feedster finds a new entry in its index that matches `"pizza hut" "thin crust"`. (Look for the "Subscribe to this search" link at the top of the results page.) Feedster is monitoring the part of the blogging world that goes to Pizza Hut so you don't have to!

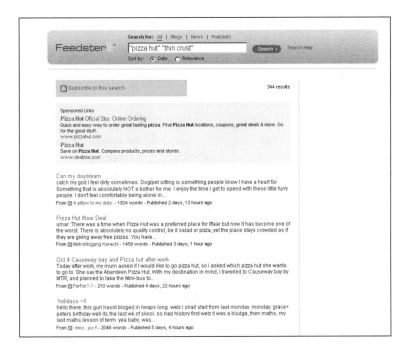

Figure 2.14

Looking for Pizza Hut experiences at Feedster.

Which feed to use and when

How specific can you get when you're generating an RSS feed? For example, if you're interested in the New York Giants, there must be a few players or staff members that are of particular interest. The names of those people would be excellent candidates for keyword-based RSS feeds.

If you're interested, say, in search engines, you could probably stick with the huge number of static RSS feeds devoted to search engines. But maybe you want a keyword-based feed for Teoma, a lesser-known search engine ?

If you're interested in digital archives, you might want to start with a couple of static feeds from archive mailing lists, and then use keyword-based RSS feeds for the rest of your traps, searching Yahoo News for **"information mining"**, for example, or **"online archives"**.

Or say you have a very specific interest, like archives about Pablo Picasso. In this case, you might want to forego static feeds entirely (though there might be one or two about modern art that stir your interest) and use only keyword-based feeds.

Obviously, the fewer traps you have, the easier it is to monitor information flow. At the same time, the fewer traps you have, the more difficult it is to make sure that most of the results are as relevant as possible to your interests (I won't say *all* of the results should be as relevant as possible because *all* is an impossible, and therefore inappropriate, quest).

I am most comfortable when I see some repeated stories in the traps I've set—say 5 percent to 10 percent. This rate assures me that I'm covering my bases and getting most of what I can possibly get, without having too many repeats that make it difficult to monitor and act on the data in my traps.

So aim for having just enough overlap between your static feeds, keyword-based feeds, and monitored pages (more about those in the next chapter). "Comprehensive but manageable" is my mantra, as you'll see in later chapters.

Now that you've found all these feeds, you have another problem: reading them. What can you use to actually look at RSS feeds? Well, your Web browser probably has the chops to read an individual feed, but you want a power tool—something that lets you comfortably review dozens (possibly hundreds) of feeds at a time.

RSS Reader Tools

RSS readers fall into two broad categories: tools that let you merely read a single feed (reformatting it so that a person can comfortably read it) and tools that let you read and organize several feeds at a time. Your browser may have the potential to do the first, and many resources are available for doing the second.

RSS readers for many different platforms are available: palmtops and cell phones—and even iPods! You can learn more about options for information trapping on the go by registering your copy of this book at peachpit.com/title/0321491718 (see the related Tip below), but for now let's stick with Windows-based and Mac-based options.

> **TIP**
>
> By registering your copy of this book at peachpit.com/title/
> 0321491718, you can access additional chapters on mobile information trapping, RSS tools, keeping up with your traps, and more.

Browser tools: Firefox

Which browser do you use? Depending on which one it is, you may have a built-in RSS reader. Eventually all the major browsers will have an easy way to read multiple RSS feeds, but at the moment that's not the case.

If your browser doesn't support RSS feeds, let me introduce you to one that does: Firefox.

Firefox, which is available at mozilla.com/firefox/, has many advantages: it's free, it runs on many different operating systems, it has extensive RSS support, and did I mention it's free? Firefox also offers many different "extensions," which allow you to do even more things with RSS, but let's start with the basics.

Basic RSS on Firefox

Firefox offers a feature called a Live Bookmark, which actually contains an RSS feed that updates periodically. Instead of displaying the entire feed, it displays a list of links to stories within the RSS feed. For example, when Firefox visits a site that has an RSS feed it recognizes, it gives you a little symbol in the address bar, as shown in Figure 2.4.

Click on that link, and you have the option of subscribing to the RSS feed as a Live Bookmark. The Live Bookmark has a symbol beside it, and displays a list of feed items when you hold your cursor over it. **Figure 2.15** shows a Live Bookmark for ResearchBuzz. You can click on any of the items to be taken to the ResearchBuzz story for that item.

Figure 2.15

A Live Bookmark for ResearchBuzz.

Sometimes Firefox runs into an RSS feed that it doesn't recognize as an RSS feed, in which case you can manually make a Live Bookmark out of it. Here's how:

1. Click the Bookmarks item on your browser menu, and then click the Manage Bookmarks option. The Bookmarks Manager File menu provides the option to add a Live Bookmark.

2. Add any RSS feed you want.

Firefox extensions

Firefox supports additions to the Firefox program that give it additional functionality. There are places to download these extensions all over the Web, but I recommend you get them directly from the Firefox site: https://addons.mozilla.org.

Here I discuss just a couple of useful Firefox extensions related to RSS. For a full overview of all the cool things you can do with Firefox and its extensions, I heartily recommend *Firefox and Thunderbird Garage*, by John Hedtke, Chris Hofmann, and Marcia Knous.

As of this writing, there are several different RSS extensions on Firefox (probably even more will have been added by the time this book goes to press):

Wizz RSS. I like Wizz RSS, which you can check out at https://addons.mozilla.org/extensions/moreinfo.php?id=424. Once installed (and it's a quick install), Wizz RSS lets you read and manage RSS feeds. You can access it from the Tools option on Firefox's main menu or by pressing Alt + W. It looks a little like a page frame (**Figure 2.16**). I recommend this solution when you have a low or moderate number of RSS feeds you want to monitor—perhaps you want to put your most critical feeds here so you always have them at hand.

I don't want to give you a huge tutorial on Wizz RSS, but let me make a few points that may not be obvious.

There's a public and private list in the Wizz RSS panel, which you open by clicking one of the two icons that look like monitor screens in the Wizz toolbar. In order to use the private list, though, you'll need to have a Wizz account, which you can create from the Options Etc menu on the Wizz toolbar (**Figure 2.17**).

Figure 2.16 Reading RSS with Wizz in Firefox.

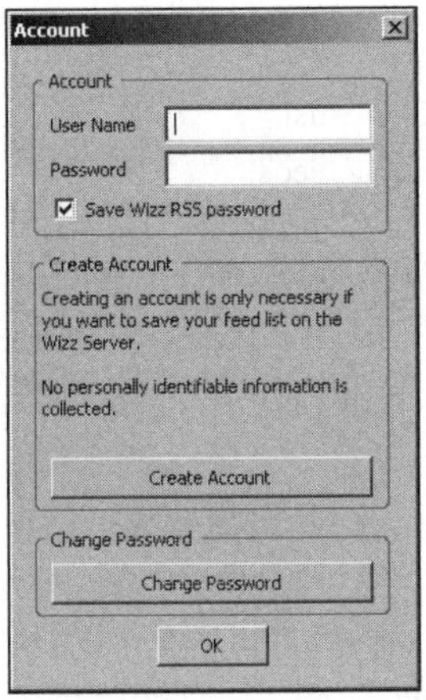

Figure 2.17

Setting up private lists does give you a little protection for sensitive data, but you'll have to establish a user name and password first.

The private list requires you to create an account using only a user name and password. This level of security is basic at best, so don't put anything ultra-sensitive in the private list, where you create your categories of RSS feeds and then populate them with individual feeds.

Once you've created a list of feeds you want to monitor, you navigate through this list on the left. When you see an interesting item, click on it, and it appears in the Web page on the right.

When you right-click on the title of an item, you have the option of sharing it via e-mail. To take advantage of this, you need to add your e-mail settings to Wizz RSS. You can add those by accessing Account Options.

Wizz RSS isn't the most full-featured RSS reader you can use, but it's simple to integrate into Firefox. And if you already use Firefox, it gives you the ability to use RSS without having to add another tool to your toolbox.

Sage. Another RSS reader for Firefox, Sage is even simpler than Wizz RSS. You can get more information about it at https://addons.mozilla.org/extensions/moreinfo.php?id=77.

Once installed, Sage looks a little like Wizz RSS (**Figure 2.18**). However, it doesn't require an account to add RSS feeds. Adding feeds is as simple as right-clicking and choosing New Bookmark—if you've used Firefox's bookmarks at all, it should be very intuitive for you.

Sage is integrated with online-resource Technorati, so you can see what other sites are linking to stories you find interesting. In addition, Sage's options let you toggle a feature to search for feeds (it hooks right into Feedster) and use a custom style sheet for rendering if you don't use the one Sage provides. I recommend Sage for lightweight feed-wrangling, especially if you don't want to bother with the account setup requirements for Wizz RSS.

RSS feed readers that integrate with your browser are good because they save you a step. You don't have to worry about another software package to install or another site to keep up with. On the other hand, they're not as robust as standalone RSS readers. I recommend them only if you don't have an extensive number of sites to watch, or if there's a small, critical number of feeds you want to keep close watch over. Having them right in your browser keeps them close at hand when you need them.

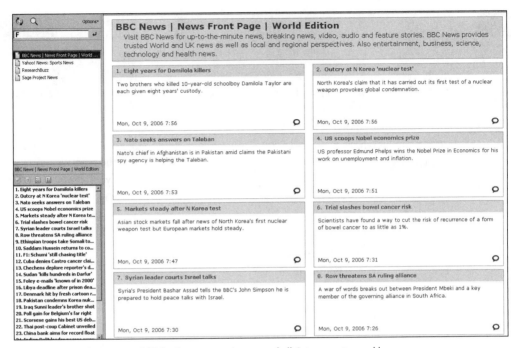

Figure 2.18 Sage lays out an RSS feed, content snippets and all, into easy-to-read boxes.

If you're a Mac user, you might want to check out Safari, Apple's browser for Mac OS X. Safari 2.0 can automatically detect RSS feeds and save them as bookmarks, letting you know when they've been updated. To learn more about Safari's offerings, check out apple.com/macosx/features/safari/.

Web-based RSS feed readers

A Web-based RSS feed reader is one that you access via a Web site.

> **TIP**
>
> Yes, they're called RSS feed readers, but for the most part they also handle the "Atom" feed type as well, so don't worry about finding an Atom feed reader.

Standalone vs. Web-Based RSS Feed Readers?

Whether you use a standalone or Web-based RSS feed reader is up to you. If you use the same computer all the time—a desktop you have at home or a laptop you carry with you everywhere—a client-side RSS reader would work fine because you'd always have the computer with the software on it. If you don't use the same computer all the time, and instead shuttle between laptop and desktop, or home and office computers, then I recommend a Web-based RSS feed reader. With this type of feed reader, as long as you can get on the Web, you can get to your collection of RSS feeds.

Bloglines

Bloglines (bloglines.com) is my favorite Web-based RSS feed reader. But be forewarned: it has an overwhelming number of options. You power users out there will probably jump up and do a little dance. Non-power users may find yourselves just wanting to get on with reading your RSS feeds.

You have to register to use this site. Once you do, and then respond to the confirmation e-mail, it's time to set up your feeds. Check out My Feeds in the upper left part of the page (**Figure 2.19**) and notice that there's already one feed there—for Bloglines itself. You can click Add to add more feeds to the list.

You can also browse Bloglines' directory by clicking the Directory tab on the main part of the page. The directory lets you search by keyword and view a list of the most popular and newest feeds. There's also a list of all the feeds available in alphabetical order, but because Bloglines has thousands and thousands of feeds, this isn't particularly useful.

When you do a keyword search, notice you get two kinds of results—RSS feeds for blogs themselves, and results for entries within blog feeds. So, for example, if you search for **Starbucks**, you might find that there are only a dozen or so blogs with the word Starbucks in their description or title, but thousands and thousands of entries which mention going to Starbucks, their favorite Starbucks drink, etc.

Bloglines can handle hundreds and hundreds of RSS feeds for you. Once you've set up the feeds, notice that it looks like a framed page. Your feed lists are on the left. Click on a feed and its content shows up on the right.

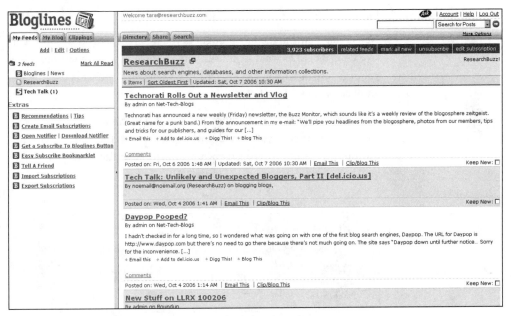

Figure 2.19 Your Bloglines account starts with a feed already in place—
for Bloglines News.

From here the possibilities are almost endless, especially for information trappers who are always out to expand their sources. For instance, look at each entry and notice they have individual "Email This" and "Clip/Blog This" links. The "Email This" link does what you'd expect: it gives you a pop-up window where you can fill out an e-mail address to send the entry to and write a message about it. The "Clip/Blog This" link it gives you another pop-up window with an area in which to "clip" the information from the story that you want. After clipping, you can publish it to a "Clip Blog" available at Bloglines, or you can file it in a Bloglines-based clipping file if you want to save it for later.

All of this discussion barely scratches the surface of Bloglines. It's a sturdy RSS reader—you can cram a lot of feeds into it, it lets you do a lot with those feeds, and it also incorporates extensive feed discovery tools in with the feed reading. If you have a moderate-to-heavy amount of RSS research you want to keep up with, and you use different computers, I can't recommend Bloglines enough. It's a great feed reader.

Newsburst

Newsburst (newsburst.com), brought to you by CNET, is a little more intrusive than Bloglines (that is, it asks you a couple of extra questions when you register), but if you can get past that then you'll probably find that it's another useful feed reader.

Once you've registered, Newsburst presents you with a few feeds apparently based on the zip code you provided when registering. The Add Source tab at the top of the page gives you a way to manually enter RSS feeds you want to read and search for new ones (**Figure 2.20**).

Figure 2.20

You can either search for additional sources in Newsburst or add your own.

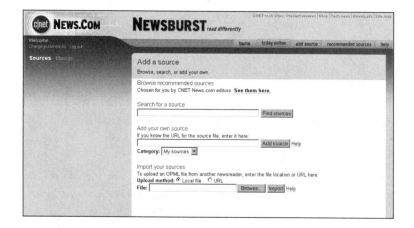

Newsburst gives advanced users who have been using another feed reader the option of uploading an OPML file. An OPML file is a specifically formatted XML file that instead of containing content items from a single RSS feed, contains information about several RSS feeds with no content items. OPML files allow you to import or export lists of RSS feeds from feed readers very quickly.

The default feed display that appears when you first log in to Newsburst is called a "dashboard," in which all the feed entries are laid out in multiple columns. In contrast, Bloglines' feed display is called a "stream"—all the feed entries are laid out in one vertical list. You can opt to have either kind of display in Newsburst by clicking Change Preferences on the left side of the screen and then indicating your choice. If you have a smaller number of feeds, you might find that the dashboard display is easier to review and absorb quickly. If you have lots of feeds, you might want the simple, one-at-a-time option of a stream.

> ### TIP
>
> You may have realized that the layouts on these RSS feed readers are very similar, with feed lists located on the left, and feed entries on the right. In the same way that browsers' look and feel have become more similar over time, RSS feed readers, too, have stabilized. Once you've played with Bloglines and these other readers for a bit, you can easily learn your way around other feed readers.

My Yahoo

Yahoo has been a major supporter of RSS feeds in the past, so it's no surprise that the My Yahoo page supports RSS feeds (my.yahoo.com/s/about/rss/index.html). My Yahoo is a little awkward to use if you want to look at a lot of RSS feeds, but if you already use the site anyway and you're not planning to subscribe to more than a dozen RSS feeds, it's hands-down the best choice. If you don't already use My Yahoo, you can register at my.yahoo.com for free.

My Yahoo has many more formatting options than the other readers we've discussed so far. You can set up your personalized page to show your local weather forecast. You can display the comic strips you want to read every day. You can set the "theme" for your page (but be careful—you want to choose the one that makes the text easiest to read). You can play around for a while until your page looks the way you want it to—after all, if everything goes well you'll be visiting your page often to check your traps.

Once you've finished setting up your page, you can add some RSS feeds to the page by clicking the Add Content tab (**Figure 2.21**). You can search for feeds by keyword, add feeds by URL, or check out the most popular feeds and add those. My Yahoo makes this extremely easy—just go to the RSS add page, paste in the URL of the RSS feed you want, click the Add button, and the feed is added to your page.

For the most part, My Yahoo uses a stream layout (vertical lists), and as you add feeds the representation of the page on your left gets longer and longer. After throwing a few dozen feeds at My Yahoo, I was unable to discover a limit to the number of feeds it can handle. If you don't mind a really long page (or a long load time), you can stack up lots of RSS feeds here.

The advantage of using My Yahoo as an RSS feed reader is that Yahoo has gone out of its way to make the feed reader pleasant and easy-to-use. And if you're using the site anyway, it's easy to seamlessly integrate reading your RSS feeds into your usual routine.

There are some drawbacks, however. Yahoo seems to list only five entries from an RSS feed at a time, and lists only the titles, not the descriptions of the articles. So while you may see a lot of entries on the My Yahoo page, they won't be as informative as smaller pages, which include entry descriptions and more than five feed entry titles at one time.

Figure 2.21

You can browse for, search for, or add your own RSS feeds to My Yahoo.

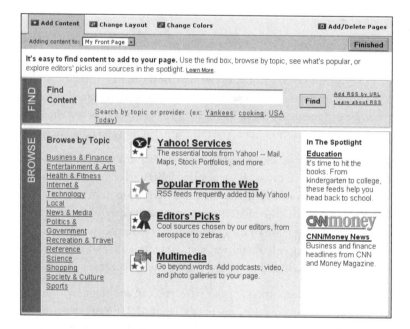

Client-side RSS feed readers

If you work mainly on one computer and you don't want to trust your feeds to a Web-based application, then a standalone, or "client-based" RSS feed reader, is the better choice. A standalone RSS feed reader is software that doesn't integrate or extend a program—instead it "stands alone" to deliver RSS feed managing and reading.

I have two suggestions for a client-based RSS feed reader: one for Windows and one for Mac.

NewzCrawler

NewzCrawler (newzcrawler.com/) is a standalone RSS feed reader. However, it relies on Internet Explorer for some of its features, so it's best for computers that run on Windows. As you're installing NewzCrawler, you have the option of installing an RSS Autodiscovery Module, which makes it easier for you to find feeds. But because most Web sites make it quite obvious where their feeds are, and you've learned several techniques for finding RSS feeds in this book, you can skip installing the module if you like.

After you've finished installing NewzCrawler and started running it for the first time, notice that it already has several RSS feeds installed in that lovely "Feeds located on the left, feed items displayed on the right" structure that you're probably very used to by now (**Figure 2.22**). Actually it's a little bit different. The panel on the right is divided into two parts. The top part shows you a summary of items, while the lower part shows the story from the item itself. From the lower part you can also visit the story on the Web.

> ## TIP
> NewzCrawler uses Internet Explorer by default to visit Web sites. Because this browser has had more than its share of security issues, make sure your copy of Internet Explorer has the latest patches and updates and that its security settings are turned all the way up. NewzCrawler also gives you the option of viewing the links from RSS feeds in the browser of your choice, which you might find more secure.

You may find that you don't want all of the RSS feeds that NewzCrawler automatically adds to your list. If you want to get rid of them, it's easy. Just right-click on the feed you want to delete (you can also click the plus sign beside the folders to open the folders and show the feeds) and you'll be presented with several options. Delete, of course, gets rid of the feed. Catch Up marks all the feed stories that have been read. Many other options are available, but I won't go into detail here.

To add feeds to NewzCrawler, right-click on any of the items, and at the top of the pop-up menu, choose New. You have the option of adding new folders or new feed items. To update your list, click the green Play button at the

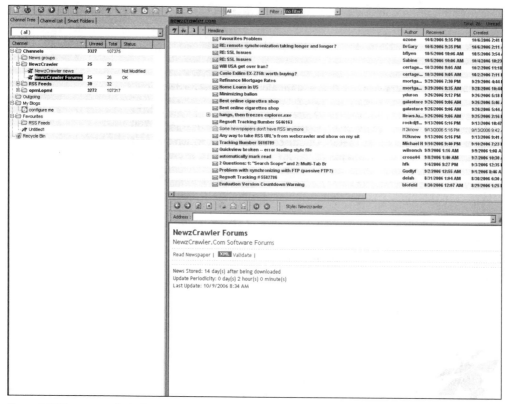

Figure 2.22 You can read RSS feeds and monitor Web pages from NewzCrawler.

top of the page, and all the feeds update. NewzCrawler has a free, two-week trial offer. It costs $24.95 after that.

If you're not using Windows, you have other options.

NetNewsWire

NetNewsWire (ranchero.com/netnewswire/) requires Mac OS X 10.2.8 but is compatible with Mac OS X 10.4. It has a typical three-panel layout, like many of the other feed readers we've looked at in this chapter, with feeds on the left (it comes preloaded with a bunch of Apple-related feeds), headlines on the top right (double-clicking on the headline takes you straight to the page with the full story), and content (either full-article or snippet) on the bottom right. A "sites drawer" provides a list of RSS feeds to which you may subscribe, while another tool lets you post to a Web log (**Figure 2.23**).

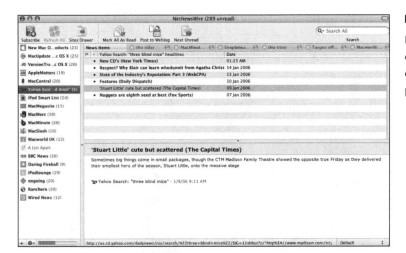

Figure 2.23

NetNewsWire comes with a lot of Mac-oriented, preinstalled feeds.

In addition to the regular RSS feeds, NetNewsWire also provides a way to subscribe to special headlines, which essentially are keyword-based RSS feeds that we've already discussed. There aren't many options available for keyword-based feeds, but there are a few available for experimentation. Another option, a Smart List, lets you group together all the feed entries that match certain conditions—all the feeds that contain the word "iPod" in the title, for example, or all the feeds that contain the word "medical" in the description. In these cases, you're conducting keyword searches of only those RSS feeds that you've subscribed to!

You'll also find a Dinosaurs option in the Window menu that shows you a list of feeds that haven't been updated in at least 30 days—a handy feature you may want to use when the number of feeds you're using is getting overwhelming. While you may want to keep those really specific keyword-based feeds that aren't supposed to update that often anyway, blog feeds that aren't updated at least once a month can be less than useful. Goodbye, empty information traps!

RSS feeds should be the cornerstone of your information trapping strategy. But not all resources you want to monitor have RSS feeds. What do you do at that point? You use another tool: a page monitor. Read on!

3

Page Monitors

In the last chapter, we looked at RSS feeds, which are easy-to-read and easy-to-follow sources of site changes and content updates. I wish I could tell you that RSS feeds are the only source you'll ever need to use when setting up information traps, but that wouldn't be true.

Why not? Because many sites still don't provide RSS feeds. Although RSS has been around for quite some time, it hasn't gained the prominence you might think it would. Some site operators don't have the time or interest to integrate another technology into their site. Others provide alternative ways for site visitors to keep up with their site's content (such as e-mail alerts) and don't feel the need to offer RSS feeds. Still others want you to actually visit their site and see their ads, rather than receive content via RSS feeds. The list goes on. So in your search for information, you more than likely will come across pages you want to continually monitor that don't have RSS feeds. What's an information trapper to do?

Use a page monitor! This chapter discusses the various kinds of page monitors that are available, walks you through how to set one up, and shows you how to limit the number of insignificant page updates you receive.

Nuts and Bolts

A page monitor simply watches HTML pages for changes and then reports them to you. Generally, the monitoring program grabs the page, then returns to the same page later, grabs a new copy of the page, and then compares the two. Any new information that's added to the page is reported to you.

At first, this sounds great. But unfortunately there's a downside: too many "false positives." For example, if a page changes its date every day, this date change may trigger a false positive to the change monitor, and the change monitor may incorrectly alert you to the new content. If a page has a visitor counter that gets updated, those updates could also trigger an alert or false positive. Even tiny things that are updated, such as a corrected spelling error, can trip the page monitor. Not good!

However, if you're careful about the pages you pick and use the page monitors to best advantage, you can minimize the number of times information traps trigger without providing any useful information.

Why use a page monitor?

There are two instances in which you'd want to use a page monitor:

▶ **You need the content, but you can't get it via RSS.** I already touched on this in the introduction to this chapter—you may want to keep up with a news source or with a page of information content, such as press releases, for example, but the information isn't offered via RSS. In this case, you can use a page monitor on the appropriate pages.

Say you're monitoring the Events page of your favorite band. You want to be updated when and where they're touring so that you're sure not to miss them when they're in town. Or maybe you want to monitor a page that contains information on a company's board of directors. You want to see when information about that group changes, something that might be more difficult to do with an RSS feed.

▶ **When you need just a tiny bit of information**. There may be some data point that you're interested in that is too small to be the subject of an RSS feed. You may want to know when a number changes, for example, or when a date changes. In that case, monitoring the page for changes makes more sense than trying to set up an RSS feed.

Just make sure you're not reinventing the wheel. If you're looking for a common small bit of data, like a stock quote or a temperature, there are services that can provide you with that information via e-mail alerts. (I cover e-mail alerts in the next chapter.)

Types of page monitors

There are two kinds of page monitors:

▶ **Web-based.** Some page monitors are Web services. You go to the site, enter the pages you want to monitor, and receive page updates via e-mail (**Figure 3.1**).

These services can be either free or fee-based. The advantage with Web service page monitors is that you can access them anywhere and receive the alerts on any device in which you are able to receive an e-mail (including cell phone, PDA, and so forth). The downside is that they're often limited in their configurability and sometimes show far more false-positive alerts than you would like. They'll also start costing you some serious money if you want to monitor more than a few dozen pages at a time.

Figure 3.1

Trackle, a Web-based
monitoring service,
sends out plain-text
update notices of the
pages it monitors.

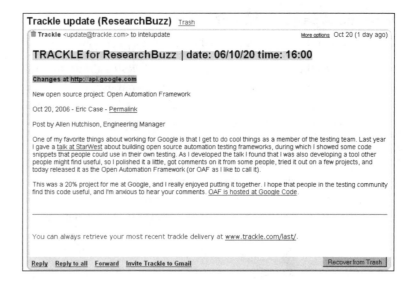

> ▶ **Client-side.** Client-side page monitoring software is installed on your
> computer and keeps copies of the pages it grabs on your computer for
> comparison purposes. The downside with this type of page monitor
> is that if you're not at your computer or have alternative access to
> it, you're not going to be able to access your page changes. Another
> downside is that unless you're connected to the Internet 24/7 with
> broadband (and you really need a broadband connection if you're
> going to monitor any number of pages), you might not get around
> to doing regular scanning. On the upside, client-side software lets
> you easily manage large numbers of monitored pages (several thou-
> sand in my case), whereas it can be cost-prohibitive to do that with
> an online service. Finally, client-side page monitors are usually much
> more configurable than Web-based ones, and can often avoid false-
> positive page change alerts.

Within these two categories, there are dozens of page monitors available,
with varying functionality. The rest of this chapter provides an overview of
some monitors I like and recommend.

Web-Based Page Monitors

If you're monitoring a minimal number of pages—less than two dozen—and you want to watch the pages you monitor from several different computers, the flexibility of a Web-based page monitor will be ideal for you.

WatchThatPage

WatchThatPage (watchthatpage.com) is a free service that lets you specify a list of pages and then monitors them for changes.

You must register to use WatchThatPage with your name, e-mail address, and a password. When you register, you have the option of specifying your time zone, how often you want to receive updates, and so on. WatchThatPage won't provide updates more than once a day.

Once you've registered, you can add pages and even folders (**Figure 3.2**). If you're planning to cover several different topics, it makes sense to set up folders for each of your interests—and setting them up just after you register makes it that much easier to administer the sites later. If you have some pages you want to monitor for changes every day, and others you want to monitor every week, you can set up different channels.

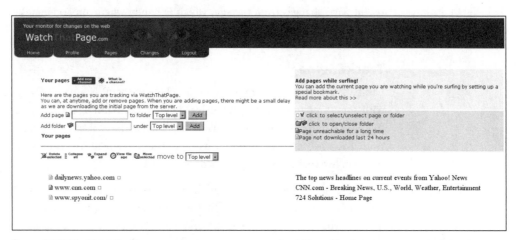

Figure 3.2 With WatchThatPage, you can group your pages by folder and select pages as you're browsing using a special bookmark called a *bookmarklet*.

What's a Bookmarklet?

A *bookmarklet* is like a bookmark, except it has a little bit of JavaScript in it that enables it to do things like query a search engine or connect to resources like WatchThatPage (**Figure 3.3**).

Figure 3.3

Bookmarklets can do simple things like tell you how recently a page has been updated.

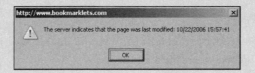

Bear in mind that if you have JavaScript turned off in your browser, bookmarklets won't work.

For security reasons, make sure you stick to using bookmarklets that are offered by services you're using, such as TrackEngine and WatchThatPage, or by legitimate Web sites, such as bookmarklets. com, rather than ones that have been e-mailed to you or you've accessed in some other way.

WatchThatPage provides page alerts via e-mail. However, you can also view recent page changes from the site, which is handy when you accidentally delete some updates but still want to see them.

TrackEngine

Unlike WatchThatPage, TrackEngine (trackengine.com) is a paid service, with some free functionality available. Registration with TrackEngine is free, and requires a name, company name, email address, user name, password, country/time zone, and a terms-of-service agreement. You can monitor up to five sources before you need to pay a fee.

TrackEngine offers a nifty bookmarklet button you can add to your browser toolbar. When you're surfing the Internet and you find a page you want to monitor, you simply click the bookmarklet button on your toolbar, and that page is automatically added to TrackEngine.

When you add a page, you are asked to provide the following: the page's URL, a title for the page (something that's easy for you to remember), and how often you want to track this page, whether it's daily, every two days, every three days, or weekly (**Figure 3.4**). You also have the option of being notified of updates containing only the keywords you specify.

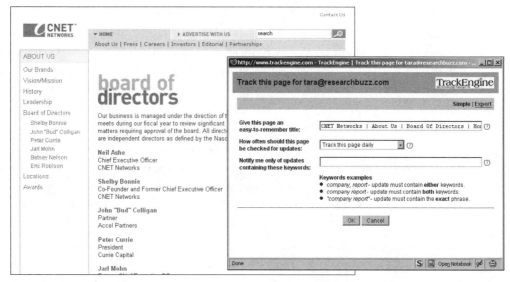

Figure 3.4 TrackEngine's bookmarklet pops open a window allowing you to add a page you're viewing to your list of monitored URLs.

> **TIP**
>
> The notification option can save you buckets of time! If there's an easy keyword that encompasses the kind of information you're looking for, such as a company name, person's name, or technology name, by all means use it! It helps eliminate a lot of the false positives you can get when trivial information on the page changes.

You can get reports about page updates from the front page once you're logged in. Unfortunately, TrackEngine doesn't allow you to monitor more than five pages at a time, which is not much, unless you have a very small monitoring job. If you want to monitor more, you have to upgrade. Monitoring 10 bookmarks costs $19.95 a year, or you can pay $4.95 a month to monitor up to 50 bookmarks.

When to Pay?

Lots of the resources you're going to see in this book are either free, with the option to pay for additional services (like TrackEngine), or available for a fee only. If you're doing information trapping for a company, you'll have to see if your company will foot the bill to pay for page-monitoring or other services. If you're on your own, you are probably wondering how much money you should pay for your traps.

Almost every resource mentioned in this book has a free trial available or a limited offering. For those that provide a free trial, it's a good idea to give it a go first, and see how you like it. Test, test, and test some more. If you have fairly limited needs, you might be able to get by with a limited, free offering. Or maybe you'll use several different free services. The rest of the services mentioned in this book are inexpensive enough that you can add at least a few of them to your toolbox without spending an excessive amount of money.

The page monitors that you pay for have a couple of big advantages. First of all, they're usually more stable in monitoring the pages you've set up, and who wants their information traps to vanish? Second, they tend to have better customer support. When you're paying for something, you want to make sure you're getting your money's worth, right? You don't have as much leverage when a service you don't pay for goes plotz.

That said, I still don't recommend paying for a Web-based page monitor unless you will be monitoring fewer than 100 pages. If you will be monitoring more than that, it makes sense to buy a client-side page monitor, because for less than $50 you can get WebSite-Watcher and monitor literally thousands of pages, as I have done for years.

InfoMinder

InfoMinder (infominder.com/webminder) combines two types of tools—it tracks both pages and RSS feeds. It's a fee-based service, but a 30-day free trial is available. (The trial version is limited to 10 pages/feeds.)

Once you've registered for the trial (and confirmed your registration) you get—well, nothing but a blank page! But that's okay. Look for the Add Page option, and then find and use the Advanced Form, because for an information trapper, the basic form doesn't amount to much (**Figure 3.5**).

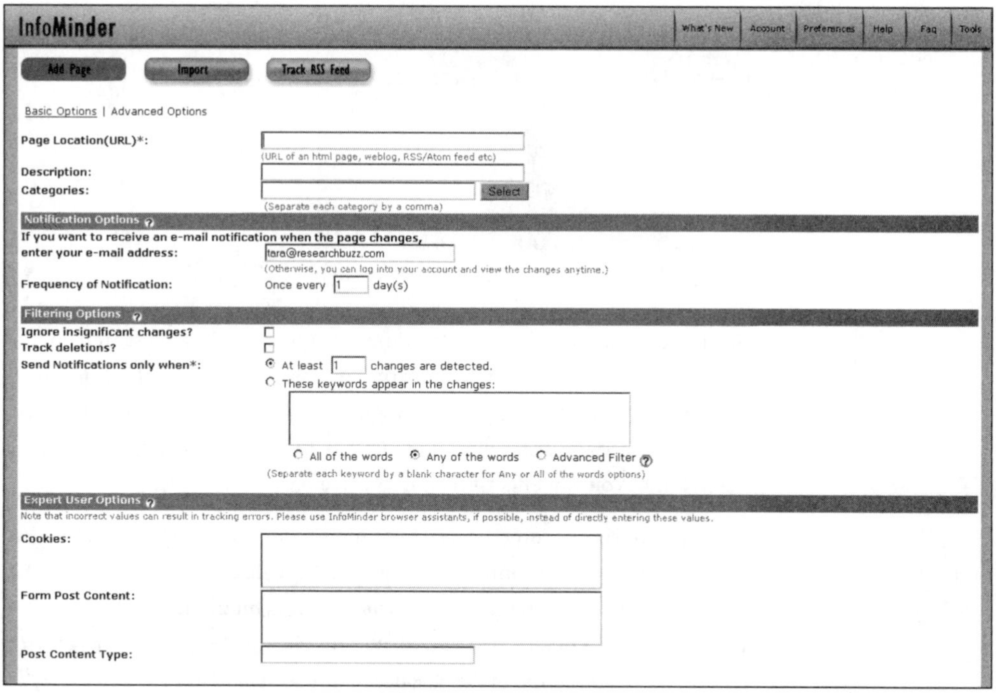

Figure 3.5 The advanced form for adding a URL to track gives you lots of options.

The Advanced Form lets you first specify the URL of the page you want to track, of course. But it also lets you specify whether you want to track insignificant changes (like dates, number changes, etc.), and the threshold for sending notices about changes (either after a certain number of changes or when certain keywords are detected, if what you're tracking makes the keyword option useful). You can also specify how often notices about changes are sent to you (every x number of days). There are also some other advanced options at the bottom involving cookies and form posting and content posting, but I wouldn't change those; it's too easy to mess up your notifications if you get a setting wrong.

At the top of the advanced search page, you're asked to provide the URL of the page you wish to search, a description, and the categories into which the page fits. Once you've provided those categories, you get a pop-up window displaying the available categories (which are very broad) and your categories (**Figure 3.6**). You can put your categories into the already-existing categories and use them later.

Figure 3.6

InfoMinder's categories are very broad.

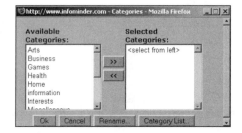

What are good category considerations? If you're monitoring search engine news, you might want to enter **"Search Engines"**, or if you only want information on one search engine, you might want to enter **Google**, **Teoma**, **Yahoo**, or whatever. Make sure what you enter is easily recognized, and specific enough that you can effectively narrow in a particular topic.

Once you've set up some pages to monitor, your login page displays a list of pages that you're monitoring (**Figure 3.7**). Click on a page URL and a framed version of the page displays with changes highlighted. The date that the changes were detected is also displayed. Having a copy of the page with the changes highlighted makes it easier to see the changes than when they're mailed to you, but the mailed changes, encapsulated in a single text e-mail, are also very useful. I recommend using both modification alert types.

There's one more thing you have to do to make sure you're ready to use InfoMinder as your page monitor: Use Preferences to choose how you want the changed information sent to you (via text or e-mail) and how you want the changed information on the pages highlighted. Once you do that, you're set.

Search Pages						Go

InfoMinder   What's New   Account   Preferences   Help   Faq   Tools

➕ Add Page(s)   ❎ Delete Checked   ▶ Share Checked   View List

Total Minders: 7

	Edit	Page Location (URL)	Description	Changes ▼	Created On
☐	Edit	www.cnn.com/ 🆕	CNN.com	58	12 Jul 2005
☐	Edit	www.ebay.com/ 🆕	eBay - New & used electronics, cars, apparel, ...	2	12 Jul 2005
☐	Edit	dubiousquality.blogspot.com/ 🆕	Dubious Quality	2	12 Jul 2005
☐	Edit	www.yahoo.com/	Yahoo!	0	12 Jul 2005
☐	Edit	www.google.com/	Google	0	12 Jul 2005
☐	Edit	www.studiob.com/studiob.rss	News and information about computer books, publish...	0	12 Jul 2005
☐	Edit	www.researchbuzz.com/	Internet news and views	0	12 Jul 2005

Figure 3.7 New icons make it easy to see which pages have changed on your InfoMinder control panel.

The 30-day free trial lets you track up to 10 URLs. The paid service varies from $9 a year, to track up to 20 URLs, to $179 a year, to track up to 1,000 URLs. There's also a Premium edition that monitors your pages for updates multiple times a day; it costs anywhere from $299 to $499 a year, depending on how many pages you track. Now do you see how after a certain number of URLs, using Web-based change detection services gets expensive?

For large companies or enterprises, there's also a server edition available; you install the software on your own server and get more control over the results and the ability to track huge numbers of pages. Contact InfoMinder for pricing information.

ChangeDetect

The free registration that ChangeDetect (changedetect.com) requires as of this writing also requires you to provide an address and phone number. If that's not a problem for you, then you'll probably discover that Change-Detect offers some very precise features in a presentation that isn't all that different from InfoMinder.

However, the free trial only allows you to monitor five pages. But Change-Detect includes a nifty option called Bulk Monitors that lets you enter several pages to monitor at a time.

Once you've set up pages to be monitored, you'll see a page that resembles InfoMinder's interface, except that it provides more controls (**Figure 3.8**). In fact, it looks a little cryptic until you get into it further. The options on the front page let you go straight to the page being monitored, view the monitor, modify the monitor, delete the monitor, test the monitor, and see when the pages were last changed.

The options for modification are extensive and worth a look. You can provide thorough descriptions of pages you're monitoring (useful if you're sharing the monitoring chores), specify how you want change information delivered to you (you can get an e-mail alert about the page changing or you can get an e-mail with the changes in it), and choose how often you want the page to be checked (every 12 hours, every day, every week, or every month).

Figure 3.8

ChangeDetect's control panel looks a little cryptic until you get used to it.

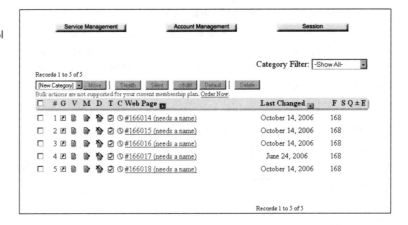

If you're using the fee-based version of the service, you also get the option to use a user name and password (for monitored pages that require validation). And don't forget to check out the advanced options at the bottom of the page. You can set the monitor to trigger when the page changes by a certain number of bytes, when a word or phrase does (or doesn't!) appear, or when one of a series of keywords appears. (There's a regular expression content filter, but it's available only for advanced users.)

ChangeDetect is available in three flavors: Personal (up to 10 pages monitored, $1.95 a month), Plus (up to 100 pages monitored, $14.95 a month), or Professional (up to 500 pages monitored, $39.95 a month). An enterprise version is also available.

Trackle

I use Trackle (trackle.com) and like it a lot for pages that I know will change on a regular basis, and for pages for which I don't need anything but plain text updates.

Trackle offers a free 14-day trial available. Once you sign up (this requires only a user name, password, and e-mail address), a one-page form displays that allows you to enter a list of URLs (up to 25) and which hours of the day you want to monitor them (up to 24, though once or twice is usually enough). Then just click the Update/Activate button and you're set (**Figure 3.9**).

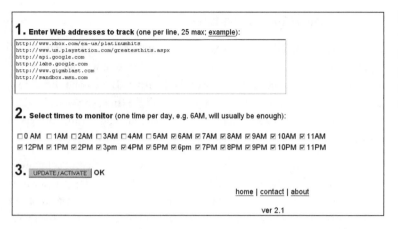

Figure 3.9

Trackle's simple
interface lets you
specify page URLs to
monitor and when you
want to monitor them.

While Trackle has a handy place on its Web site that shows you the results of your last set of updates, it's mostly a mail delivery service. It delivers the updates of specified URLs as plain text, but keeps the URLs of an update clickable. This works well if you're trying to monitor something that will provide coherent updates—say, a blog that doesn't have an RSS feed (there are still plenty of these around!) or a page of press release notes. On the other hand, if you're trying to monitor something that doesn't have coherent updates, such as a list of numbers or book names or something that won't make much sense without the context of the rest of the page around it, Trackle isn't a good solution.

Trackle costs $1.95 a month or $19.95 a year to monitor up to 25 pages. It's a lot cheaper than the other services I've mentioned so far in this chapter, but on the other hand, it doesn't offer some of the advanced features of the other services, including the ability to look for specific keywords, ignore changes below a certain page size, and so on.

Even though Trackle is the cheapest of the services I've covered here, for the number of pages it covers, it's still expensive. If you get to the point that you want to cover more than 100 pages or so, you're into "$75 or more" territory. At that point, it's best to use a client-side monitor to keep track of page changes.

Client-Side Page Monitors

There are a few major disadvantages to using client-side monitors for the Web pages you want to track. The first is that a client-side monitor is only available from your computer, not from all over the Internet. The second disadvantage is that unless you leave your computer on all the time, you won't be able to automate how often your bookmarks are checked. And if your computer crashes or has a problem, you'll need to make sure you have backups.

But there are advantages too! Because you're using software on your computer, you can have more detailed control over the kinds of monitoring you do. You can monitor pages as often as you like, even every 5 minutes if you want to. And you can monitor huge numbers of pages—200, 500, even over 1,000. You can do that with online services, of course, but at a terrific expense.

Can't possibly imagine wanting to monitor *that many pages*? Believe me, once you've been doing information trapping for a while, you'll see how much time it can save you, compared to hunting down information manually all the time. And then you'll begin to discover how many of your everyday searching chores can be turned into traps, and gradually you'll find yourself wanting to monitor more and more pages!

Page monitors for Windows

For Windows page monitoring, there's one program I adore and can't recommend enough. I've been using it for years and it's amazing: WebSite-Watcher.

By all rights, WebSite-Watcher (aignes.com) should have its own book. It's powerful, inexpensive, amazingly feature-rich, and an indispensable tool for Windows-based information trappers. There's no way I can do justice to all its features in part of a chapter. So I'm going to hit the highlights and encourage you to download it (a free trial is available), play with it, and if you like it, add it to your toolbox!

When you first launch WebSite-Watcher, a screen displays that looks like **Figure 3.10**.

There are two ways you can organize your pages to be monitored. You can monitor everything in one big file, or you can set up different files to monitor different topics in which you're interested. For example, I have a file for

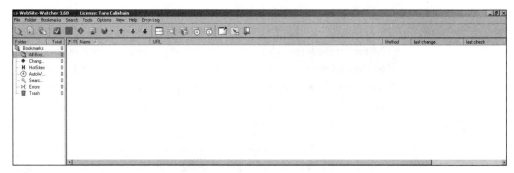

Figure 3.10 WebSite-Watcher's basic page.

monitoring pages relevant to ResearchBuzz, and I have another file set up to monitor pages relevant to some topics in another job I have. Since I want to review these two types of information with different frequency, I keep them in different files. That way I can open one of them, monitor pages, and save the other pages to monitor for later.

Whether you use one file or multiple files, you'll need to add pages to be monitored. You can do that by clicking Bookmarks/New Bookmarks. A multi-tabbed input box with options displays, as shown in **Figure 3.11**.

Figure 3.11

Using WebSite-Watcher's many options will help eliminate false-positive page changes.

Don't worry if all of these options seem overwhelming. The important parts are the title and the URL, as well as the content filtering checkboxes at the bottom of the screen (leave them on default). If you want to be able to filter by the appearance of certain keywords, click the Keywords tab. If you frequently want to check a particular URL, click the AutoWatch tab. Remember that WebSite-Watcher can only check a URL when your computer is on and connected to the Internet.

These are the basic options. Once you've gotten a set of bookmarks, you check them by choosing Bookmarks/Check all Bookmarks (or the F9 key). WebSite-Watcher scrolls through the bookmarks and checks them all. How long this takes depends on the speed of your computer and the speed of the Web sites you're checking. When the pages are all checked, you'll see a framed page that shows the lists of the URLs you're monitoring and monitored pages, with the changes highlighted as shown in **Figure 3.12**.

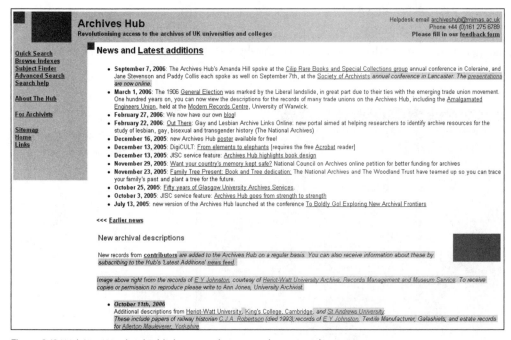

Figure 3.12 WebSite-Watcher highlights page changes so they pop right out at you.

As you can see, it's really simple to view the pages that have changed using WebSite-Watcher. You can also go to the current version of the page, compare the current version with previously changed pages, and use other options to make sure you're getting every nuance of changed information on a page.

I've just skimmed the surface of WebSite-Watcher, but the important things you need to know are adding, checking, and viewing URLs. If you want to monitor more than 20 or so pages and you use Windows, I strongly recommend WebSite-Watcher.

Page monitors for Mac

There aren't as many page monitors available for the Mac as there are for the PC, but you still have at least one good option in Web Watcher. And if you want to monitor a minimum number of pages, you can always use a Web-based monitoring service. Then it won't matter what kind of computer you're using!

Web Watcher (chaoticsoftware.com/ProductPages/WebWatcher.html) is a shareware program for Mac that costs $20, with a $200 site license and $500 multi-site license available. You may try the software for free for 15 days, however.

Web Watcher is very easy to use. When you first start the program, a list of Watchpoints displays, which will be an empty list until you populate it. To add a Watchpoint, click the Add button at the bottom of the window. A screen displays that looks like **Figure 3.13**.

Fill out the name of the page you want to monitor, as well as the URL, username and password (if it's required), and specify how often you want to check the page (you can check pages as frequently as every x seconds, which I don't recommend, to every x days). You can check for changes to a page's size, date, and whether or not its URL is accessible.

You also have several different notification options. You can request that Web Watcher play a beep, display an alert, show the URL in your Web browser, or send a notification by e-mail. You can e-mail up to three addresses and have custom text for each alert. You may also specify if you want to copy the watched URL or its contents—or both—into the notification e-mail. Be sure to add your mail server and a reply-to address using Web Watcher's Preferences window if you want to send e-mail alerts!

Figure 3.13

Web Watcher's options
are not as extensive as
WebSite-Watcher's,
but far easier to
understand.

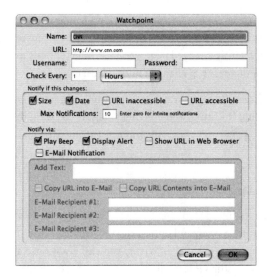

If you want to monitor for page changes often (several times a day or even several times an hour), I recommend setting them up to display in the browser. However, if you want to check pages less frequently—say, once a week—I recommend having the page changes sent in an e-mail, from which you can visit the monitored page itself and see if you find anything intriguing.

4

E-Mail Alerts

In Chapters 2 and 3, we looked at both new-school ways to monitor for information (RSS feeds) and decidedly old-school ways (Web page monitors). Smack in the middle of those two technologies are e-mail alerts.

An e-mail alert is a service provided by a Web site that sends you an e-mail whenever content on the site matches a topic or keyword in which you have expressed an interest. For example, the Web site PubMed has a service that sends an e-mail whenever new content is published about a particular disease you may be interested in.

This chapter discusses the benefits of e-mail alerts and how to find e-mail alert offerings that are relevant to your interests, as well as provides an overview of some of the more general and popular e-mail alert services. Later chapters explain how you can filter your e-mail to best manage these incoming alerts.

Advantages of E-Mail Alerts

Right now you might be thinking, "So what? Why not just use one of the more advanced Web page monitors when you want to find out when a site matches one of the keywords in which you're interested?" There are a couple reasons.

First, Web sites offering e-mail alerts don't update you with false positives. In other words, you're not going to get an alert about new content on a site unless new content is really there.

Second, most e-mail alert services monitor entire sites, not just pages. If you sign up for an alert from CNN, for instance, you get information about content added throughout CNN's Web site, rather than only from the front page. There are some Web sites, however, that provide e-mail alerts only when Web content changes, as opposed to when content based on keywords changes. I don't recommend those. If you only want to be informed when a page changes, a page monitor is a better solution, being more flexible and often more customizable.

OK, so you know when and why you might use e-mail alerts instead of Web page monitors, but what about RSS feeds? Why not use an RSS feed instead of e-mail alerts?

Again, because e-mail alerts don't update you with false-positive content, they sometimes provide more useful content than RSS feeds provide. (See Chapter 2 for more information on false positives and RSS feeds.) Another reason why e-mail alerts can sometimes be more useful is the technology on your end. You may want to get content update alerts sent somewhere other than your computer—say, your cell phone. Your cell phone may be able to receive e-mail, but it may not be able to handle RSS feeds. In this case, an e-mail alert service is a better choice.

So part of the reason for using e-mail alerts is practical: they're far less likely to give you false positives, sometimes they're all that's available, and they can cover an entire site rather than just a page. And part of the reason has to do with you. Sometimes RSS feeds and monitoring services don't mesh with the tools you've already got in your toolbox, like a cell phone that can get e-mail but can't run an RSS feed reader.

Finding E-Mail Alert Services

E-mail alert services exist for just about everything. I use alert services that let me scan for mentions of companies, find out about the latest scientific research in autism, and check eBay for different kinds of inventory. Unfortunately, this book doesn't have room to discuss all of the e-mail alert services available, so we'll start by looking at some search engine strategies that are useful for finding them, and then proceed to some of the more useful general e-mail alert services.

To find e-mail alert services, you can begin by using Google and entering the simple query **"e-mail alerts"** or **"email alerts"**. As of this writing, Google returned over 117 million results for such a search, so it's not that useful. It's better to narrow the search by including topics.

For instance, if you're interested in science, you could try **science ("e-mail alerts" OR "email alerts")**. This search produced over 32 million results, which is still too many. You'll have to get more specific.

Maybe you're interested in autism, like I am. So you could try **autism ("e-mail alerts" | "email alerts")**, which—when I did the search—returned 62 results. While that's an improvement, it's still a lot of results, so you could try different combinations of keywords in an effort to narrow your results further.

As you've most likely already guessed, finding e-mail alert services via a search engine is challenging. You have to use keywords that are general enough to snag what you're looking for but specific enough that you don't get, say, 28 million results.

Take the time to experiment. When you go searching like this, you will find lots of relevant resources that you probably didn't even know existed, which is good for you and good for your information traps.

Useful E-Mail Alert Services

There are lots of specific e-mail alert services out there that will help you in your quest to monitor the Internet for information, but unfortunately you'll have to do some mining in Google or another full-text search engine to find them. (Unfortunately since e-mail alerts tend to be features of a site, but not a highlight of the site itself, it's difficult to find topical e-mail alert services in searchable subject indexes like the Yahoo Directory.) If you're interested in more general services, we have enough room in this book to look at half-a-dozen of them.

Yahoo Alerts

Yahoo offers many different kinds of alerts, including Amber Alerts for missing children, auctions, weather, and stocks. But the ones that likely will be of most interest to information trappers are news and the breaking news alerts. The other alerts are useful on a day-to-day basis, but unless you're trapping weather topics, they're more like the "basic bits of data" discussed in Chapter 1. The news alerts, on the other hand, offer fresh data that you'd want to trap anyway, delivered to you in a timely manner (**Figure 4.1**).

To use Yahoo's alerts (alerts.yahoo.com), you need a Yahoo account (the same kind of account you use to get a My Yahoo portal page, or Yahoo's RSS feed reader). If you've got that, you're ready to go.

Let's walk through setting up an alert. Choose, say, Breaking News first, and then the kind of news you want. The second page gives you options (**Figure 4.2**). Do you want breaking news from the Associated Press or Associated Press bulletins? (Bulletins provide fewer alerts, since they're more "breaking news" type stories.)

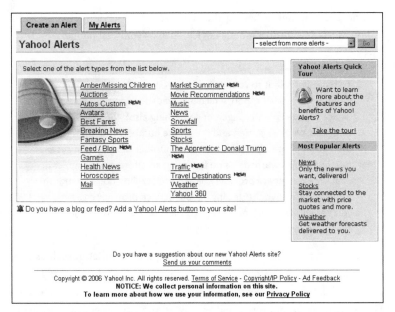

Figure 4.1

Yahoo Alerts is constantly adding new types of information to monitor, but for information trapping you'll likely find the most useful ones are breaking news, news, and possibly feeds and blogs.

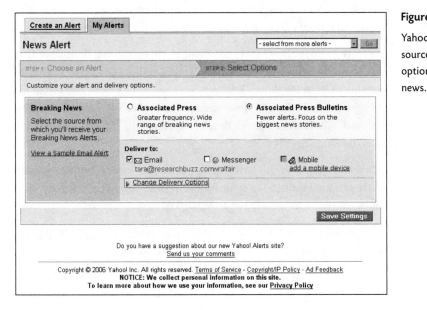

Figure 4.2

Yahoo Alerts offers source and delivery options for breaking news.

You have the option of having the alerts sent to your e-mail address, to Yahoo Messenger, or to a mobile device, such as your cell phone.

> **TIP**
>
> To have alerts sent to your cell phone, you must register your mobile device with Yahoo, which involves specifying the type of device it is (cell phone, pager, or something else), the manufacturer, the wireless carrier, and the phone number. Yahoo gives you the option of specifying the maximum number of alerts you get a day, but be forewarned: it's no fun being an information trapper if your wireless service provider charges you a zillion dollars a month for all the alerts you're getting. If your service provider charges you per wireless alert, make sure you severely limit the number of alerts Yahoo can send you per day.

If you're interested in a topic that may precipitate a bulletin, such as politics, international relations, and so on, you may find the breaking news alerts useful. (Be sure to get the bulletins, which will minimize your alerts.) However, if you're more into old woodworking equipment or treatments for shingles, breaking news may be of minimal interest to you. In cases like these, you'll want regular news alerts.

When you choose News from the main alerts menu, you'll discover that you have three types of news alerts available: breaking news (you've already seen the options for those), keyword news, or a daily news digest. Go for the keyword news. Again, e-mail alerts are best when you can filter them by keyword. You won't save much time in your trapping if you're looking over an entire daily digest's worth of news.

When choosing keyword-based news alerts, you won't be able to specify where you want the news to come from, but you will be able to specify what keywords you want included and excluded from your queries.

Once you've specified the words, you're set up to receive alerts. You can go back and add more alerts or review what you already have set up (**Figure 4.3**).

If these alert options aren't specific enough for you, and you have no objections to RSS feeds, consider Yahoo News RSS feeds instead. They have many more options, including allowing you to search categories of stories and specify the language of stories that you're searching. We'll look at more Yahoo options in later chapters.

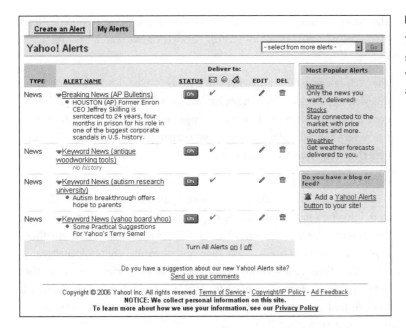

Figure 4.3

The My Alerts summary tab shows what you're monitoring and recent matches.

Google Alerts

Google Alerts (google.com/alerts) offers several different kinds of monitoring—not as many as Yahoo—but it is still a relevant option for many information trappers. Unfortunately, it only delivers via e-mail: there is no option to send alerts to your mobile phone or via an instant-messaging program. Some of the alerts Google Alerts provides include News, Web, News & Web combined, and Groups (**Figure 4.4**).

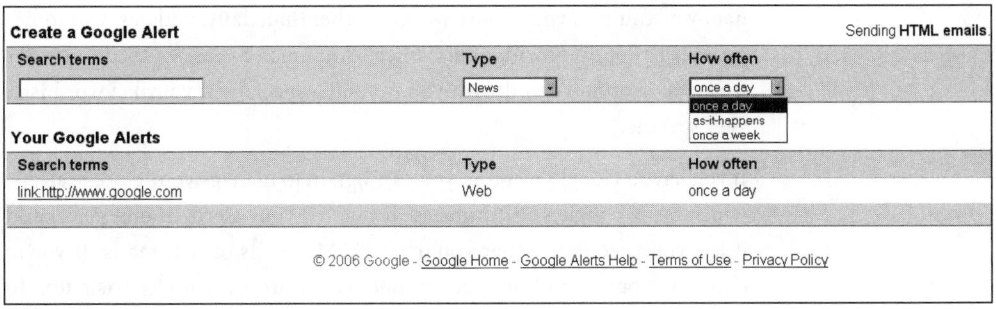

Figure 4.4 Google Alert's options.

The News category monitors the stories made available at Google News (news.google.com). As of this writing, Google's news search has over 4,500 sources.

The Web category monitors what you'd expect—Google's Web index. As of this writing, Google's Web index has over 8 billion pages. (Google doesn't even announce anymore how many pages it has in its index.) So unless you're very careful and very specific, you're going to get more search results here than you know what to do with.

Because it's hard to generate a specific query, and because it's not clear when Google indexes (or re-indexes) a page compared to when it's actually created, I don't do much monitoring of general Web pages for new additions. (For this same reason, I wouldn't use the News & Web alert option either.) If you really want to use it, make sure you use really, really specific search terms for things that you might not find in news stories, like under-the-radar online services. (I monitor for `"online museum"`, for example, which tends to find personal and new collections that haven't come to the attention of mainstream media.)

The Groups category monitors Google Groups, which is Google's index of mailing lists and discussion groups. If you're interested in monitoring things that might be discussed in groups or lists, such as political situations, technology hacks, or software support, this is an important category. Bear in mind that discussions are going to be heavy on opinion, and lighter on verified facts. Consequently, this is not a reliable source for your medical research, though it could be useful if you were looking for anecdotal information on medical treatment or "support group" type discussions.

Google Alerts provides a few options. You can get updates to your alerts once a day, as they happen, or once a week. I find the Once a Day option a happy medium. If you choose weekly, rather than daily, updates, you sometimes get a lot of information at once—too much to easily process. The As It Happens option can drown you in mail, especially if your keyword isn't very specific.

If you have a Google account, you can sign in to manage your Google alerts, which has a couple of advantages. It puts all your alerts in one place, and it lets you specify whether you'll get HTML mails or text mails. If you're checking your e-mail on a cell phone, you'll probably prefer basic text to fancy HTML that your cell phone might not be able to handle.

Yahoo and Google are useful services because they come straight from search engines. But there are some third party services that are also quite good.

Third-party e-mail alert services

Third-party e-mail alert services can offer greater flexibility and a larger range of monitored services than some e-mail alert services affiliated with individual Web sites.

Google Alert

Why, you may wonder, is there a third-party service providing Google Alerts when Google does it already? The best explanation is that third-party provider Google Alert (googlealert.com) came first! Google's own service came along a bit later. A second reason is that Google Alert offers both search options and output options that are a bit different from Google's. It's well worth a look.

Google Alert has a paid version available, but the basic, free version is very useful. You have to register, of course. Once you've registered, a page displays with a list of query boxes into which you can put searches that you want to track in Google's Web index (**Figure 4.5**).

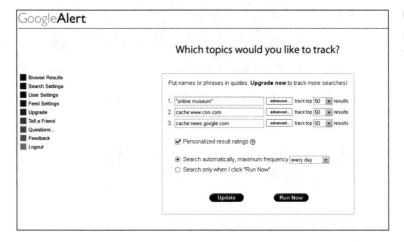

Figure 4.5

Setting up notifications with Google Alert.

I can hear the cool kids in the back of the room reminding me that earlier in this chapter I said that I don't do much monitoring of general Web pages for new additions. I did say that. However, the advanced search options make Google Alert worth looking at. Google Alert filters search results and checks them in a way that Google doesn't.

On the page that lets you create the topics you want to track, you'll find a More Options button at the bottom of the screen. Click it, and an Advanced Search form appears beside each query box (**Figure 4.6**).

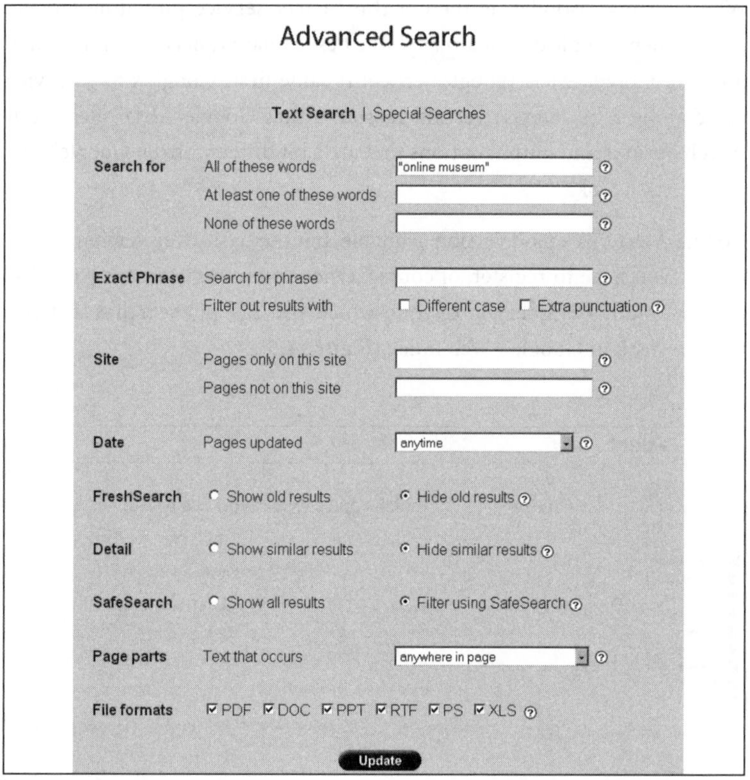

Figure 4.6

Wow, that's a lot of additional options!

There are huge numbers of additional options here. You can specify an exact capitalization for Google Alert to search for. (This is handy if, say, you want pages about Windows CE so you want to find **WinCE** instead of the word **wince**). You can filter out similar pages. You can even filter out older results. So if you've got a search that could use some extra filtering, especially for punctuation and capitalization, I urge you to try Google Alert.

> ### TIP
>
> How is Google Alert able to offer advanced searching options that Google can't? Google Alert filters the searches after Google returns them. So when you use the capitalization and searching options, you will get far, far fewer results than you would with the regular Google Alert.

Once you've put together your queries, you can specify what results you want to check (from the top 10 to the top 200), and how often you want the results checked (from as frequently as every day to as rarely as every month).

There are four levels of paid services available: a personal service for $4.95 a month, a premium service for $9.95 a month, a professional service for $19.95 a month, and a platinum service at $39.95 a month. But you may find that the basic free service works just fine for you.

TracerLock

TracerLock (tracerlock.com) is a hybrid tool that lets you query search engines and news sources and functions as a Web page monitor, too! It's not free, but a 30-day free trial is available, which requires you provide a credit card number.

TracerLock is actually several different monitors rolled into one: it monitors news stories, search engines, and Usenet (online discussion groups).

Once you're logged in to TracerLock, click the "Click here to edit your search terms" link. A form displays where you can list your search terms. On that same page, you also have the option of entering your own news sources that you want monitored for matches on your keyword (**Figure 4.7**). If your interest is very specialized and most news services are too general for you, this is a great option.

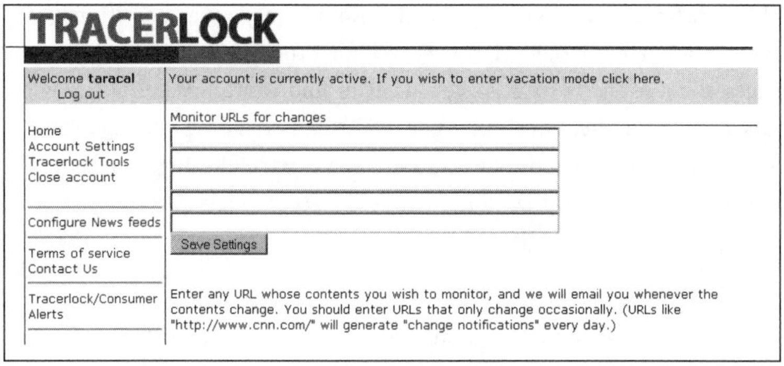

Figure 4.7

TracerLock lets you add custom URLs to its regular database of monitored news sources.

Notice on the front page that you also have the option of monitoring new additions to search engines, as well as Usenet. But you'll have to enable those. You also have the choice of getting updates for your keywords in real-time or once a day.

In addition to monitoring news, search engines, and Usenet, TracerLock can also monitor Web page changes. Why didn't I mention this with the other page monitors in the last chapter? Mostly because there's not much to it. You simply enter the URLs and it sends you updates when the page updates. (TracerLock cautions you to enter only pages that change occasionally; pages that change often, like CNN.com, will trigger alerts only once a day.) It's okay if you need a backup to the more full-featured monitors covered in the last chapter, but it doesn't offer enough features (like keyword filtering) to make it a good primary tool.

Pricing varies depending on what you want to monitor. Monitoring a single keyword will cost you $48 a year, while monitoring five terms will cost you $19.50 a month. Over the years, TracerLock has been displaced by alert services provided by the search engines themselves, but I find that it can still locate items in corners and odd places that I wouldn't have expected.

Not As Cool, But They Work

E-mail alerts may not be as glamorous as RSS feeds, or as technically nifty as directly monitoring the content of a page. But the ability to monitor what kind of data is added to huge indexes like Google's Web and Yahoo News is a tremendous advantage for the information trapper. Take advantage of it!

5

Building Queries

When I first started writing this book, I wanted to immediately jump in and tell you all about all the nifty stuff you can do with information trapping. I wanted to get right to the examples. I wanted to do the search engine equivalent of a quadruple axel and explain how easy it would be for you to do it, too.

However, it wouldn't have been particularly useful for me to show you how to do the equivalent of a fancy jump if I hadn't yet shown you how to put your skates on. Now that we've gone through the basic elements that are part of every information trapper's toolbox, you know how to use your browser as an information-trapping tool, how to find and read RSS feeds, and how to monitor pages using a page monitor.

Now it's time to learn what to trap, where to trap it, and why. This chapter presents some of the theory behind, and the practice of, setting up good queries. So go get a cool drink, sit down in front of your computer, and crack your knuckles—we're into the fun part!

In later chapters, we'll tackle what to do with the information you find, how to keep up with your feeds (even when you're on the go!), and how to republish what you gather.

For now, let's begin by thinking about the obvious question: what are you hunting?

What Do You Want to Monitor?

What are you trying to trap in the first place, and how are you going to do it? What you're trying to trap can be boiled down to two types of information: internal and external.

Internal information is information out on the Web that mentions, references, or discusses a Web site you are interested in, whether it's your own, your company's, or someone else's. Whenever I do presentations about search engines and information trapping, I often find that many people are wanting to track interest in their own Web sites. Monitoring to determine what other Web sites are linking to your own, what they are saying, or how many people are reading the RSS feed you're publishing is infinitely valuable. We'll spend Chapter 6 looking at finding and trapping internal information.

External information is everything else. As you might imagine, the concept of external information is much larger and much more inclusive than internal information. The challenge with external information lies in building the perfect query to trap information of interest because there are so many ways to describe and express a topic, idea, or even a name. For example, say you want to monitor the news for mentions of George W. Bush (which is way too general a thing to want to monitor, but more about that in a moment). Do you monitor for **"George Bush"**, **"George W. Bush"**, **"George Walker Bush"**, **"GW Bush"**, or something else entirely?

Getting the most out of the search engine

The fact that any topic can be expressed in a huge number of different ways (and therefore via a huge number of different queries) means that you've got to know a little bit about how to get the most out of a search engine. Yes, there are a huge number of queries you could use to track your topic. But only a few of them will work well. In addition, you've got to consider the size of the data pools where you'll be trapping. Google News has over 4,500 sources. Google Web had over eight billion pages at last count. Both

Manageable But What?

Manageable but complete is a great guideline. But at some point you may find yourself getting an overwhelming amount of information. You've got your queries as narrowly focused as possible, but you're not able to keep up with what you're getting. Which one should you give up—manageable or complete?

Sacrifice completeness for manageability. Getting complete coverage of your topic won't mean anything if you're drowning in feeds and alerts and can't make use of what you already have. (I'm not even sure that complete coverage is possible for all but the most obscure topics.) Drop back to alerts and notifications from whatever you consider your "core sources," whether they're news search engines, journals relevant to your topic, an RSS feed search engine like Feedster, or something else. From there you can slowly add more sources until the results are as manageable and as complete as you can handle.

Remember: you're doing this to track a topic and expand your knowledge. You're not doing this to overstress yourself and drown in information. Okay? If you can't have complete and manageable, make sure manageable comes first!

of these data pools are constantly being added to and updated. You want to make sure you get a manageable number of results that completely covers your topic. That's the goal. That's your mantra: manageable but complete, manageable but complete.

Practicing the theory of onions

Getting too many results for general searches will always be a problem when using search engines with large pools of data (which amounts to pretty much any Web search engine, news search engine, and so on).

When developing queries, I advocate practicing "the theory of onions" to narrow a search as much as possible. This involves first developing a query for your topic that is as tight and specific as you can—condensed, like the middle of an onion. Then you run that search and see what kind of results you get. Are they manageable? Probably, if your query was very specific. Are they complete? Probably not, if your query was as specific as it should have been. Next, make your query a little more general—unwrap it like you're moving out through the layers of an onion. Run the query again. Ask yourself the same two questions: is it manageable? Is it complete? Repeat this process until you're getting a good number of search results without feeling like you've been hit by the equivalent of a data firehose.

Experiment on your own a little using the theory of onions and see what happens. Most people are so used to plugging a couple words into a search engine and going to town that they don't really "get" the idea of building as specific a query as possible. If you're having problems understanding how to start with a very specific search query, here are some possible solutions that might get you unstuck.

▸ **Your language isn't unique enough.** Every topic has words of its own—its own vocabulary. A great example of this is medical terms. If you want to monitor causes of abdominal pain, a search for **"stomach ache"** will get you one level of results, while searching for **"peptic ulcer"** or **"gastrointestinal reflux disease"** will get you an entirely different, more technical level of results. If you are familiar with it, try to include the language of your topic in your search queries. It will help you immensely in narrowing down your results.

A More In-Depth Look at Building Queries

Unfortunately, this book is not a place that I can cover searching and the many types of query building in-depth—there's not enough room! This book focuses on the resources you use once you've built the perfect query. If you find you want to get down to the nitty-gritty of building solid search queries, check out one of my other books, *Web Search Garage* (Prentice-Hall). It's a couple hundred pages about how to coax information out of search engines in all kinds of different ways. You can get more information and some goodies at websearchgarage.com.

► **You're not using enough words.** The way some people put queries into search engines, you'd think they were being charged by the letter. Why not use more words? Last time I checked, Google had a query limit of 32 words. Use the limit! Throw in all the words about your topic that occur to you.

► **You're not narrowing in enough.** Get specific! Don't use **tree**, use **dogwood**. Don't use **bird**, use **cardinal**. If you have to rework your search and get more general, that's fine. That's the point. You're experimenting here. Experimenting now will pay off later in saved time.

Of course, how much you adjust your query—how much more or less specific you have to get—is going to depend a lot on the kind of resource you're using. Let's get a bird's eye view of some of the different types of resources you'll search so that you'll know what to expect.

Types of Search Engines

In general, two types of search engines index text-based data (multimedia is different; we'll look at multimedia trapping in Chapter 8). This applies to every kind of data that might be searched, from scientific journals to news stories to Web search engines.

The first kind is the full-text search engine. Google is a good example. Full-text search engines try to index every word on every page that they come across. As you might expect, this amounts to a lot of words.

The second kind is the searchable subject index. Yahoo's Directory and Open Directory Project are good examples. A searchable subject doesn't index every word of every page, or even index every available page on the Web. Instead, it tries to list sites. And it doesn't list all the words of a site, but rather just the name of the site, the URL, and some kind of brief description.

Two Types of Searches in Each Search Engine

Despite the fact that Yahoo got famous because of its Web site directory (its searchable subject index), it has in recent years implemented a full-text search engine. And despite the fact that Google has had a full-text search engine since 1998, it also offers a searchable subject index via its Google Directory. So both search engines offer full-text and subject index searching.

I mention this when people ask me "Which is better, full-text searching or searchable subject indexes?" My answer: neither is better overall. It depends on what you're looking for.

As you might imagine, there's a big difference between a narrow effective query in a full-text search engine, and a narrow effective query in a searchable subject index. The difference revolves around the "pool" of data you're searching.

Let's look, for example, at a Web site about trees that has 100 pages with 100 words on each page. Google will attempt to index that entire site. When Google finishes, that site will be represented in Google's index by 10,000 words of its content. Compare that to Yahoo's Directory or the Open Directory Project, which would index the same site with only the Web site's title and a description. In this case, the Web site about trees would be lucky to have 100 words representing its content.

Because of how much information about a site is indexed in each kind of search engine, you have to be careful about what you search for. A search for something as specific as `"southeastern knotty limbed birch tree"` would be perfect for Google but almost useless in Yahoo's Directory. Meanwhile, a simple search for `"birch trees"` could bring you useful results at the Open Directory, but a deluge of results at Google.

For the most part, you'll deal mostly with full-text search engines, so focus on generating a concentrated, narrow query.

Is there more you can do to get focused and specific in your queries besides putting in as many words as possible and using topic-specific language? Absolutely. You can take advantage of the different syntaxes the search engines offer. You can also omit keywords. We won't go over all the different syntax that search engines offer; instead I'll give you some common syntax—and then show you where to look for the more esoteric, quadruple-axel stuff.

Basic Searching Syntax

How do you search for things in search engines? You type in words. But how do you tell the search engine which words you want to search for, which ones you want to avoid, and so on? You use Boolean logic. Boolean logic simply tells a search engine that you want to search for something *and* something else, or for something *and not* something else, or for one of several different words, and so on.

For example, the search query **beans -rice** tells the search engine, "I want to search for beans *and not* rice," and that's Boolean. The minus sign in front of **rice** is a Boolean operator; it's telling the search engine that you want to make sure that word doesn't appear in any query results. If you've been using search engines for any length of time you're familiar with using minus signs to exclude words, and plus signs to include them. In fact, you may have been using Boolean logic all along and not even have known it!

The first thing you need to know about a search engine is its Boolean default. The Boolean default is the Boolean operator that the search engine will use if you enter your query with no Boolean operators (for example: **beans rice cheese lettuce tomato**). Will it search for all the words? If so, then it's using the Boolean "and." Will it search for *any* of the words? (That is, will it return as a result any Web page that has at least one of your query words in it?) If so, it's using the Boolean "or."

If you're trying to get your results as focused as possible, "and" is far better than "or," for the obvious reason that it will give you fewer and more relevant results. Unsurprisingly, most search engines nowadays default to the Boolean "and."

Experiment a little by doing the following: Begin a query by entering into a search engine a bunch of relevant words you think might narrow your search results. Don't forget that since most search engines default to "and," you don't need to add anything to the query words to make sure they're included in the query. If you want to make sure they're *not* included in the query, however, put a minus (-) sign in front of them. And to make sure that words appear only as a phrase, group them with quotes.

Take for example the following query: `"cardiac arrest" treatment prevention -"heart attack"`. This phrase would return results for `"cardiac arrest"` and include the words `treatment` and `prevention` but would exclude any pages that also had the phrase `"heart attack"`.

> **TIP**
>
> Be sure to use great caution when excluding words! The example above was designed to find medical professional-level results—in other words, Web pages whose audience of medical professionals would refer to "cardiac arrest" instead of a "heart attack." If you run this same search, you'll find that the results are from sources like professional medical journals, the American Heart Association, hospitals, and so forth. It's high-level information—just removing one phrase wiped out a whole level of results. Very powerful, but also very damaging if you use it inappropriately.

Special Searching Syntax

When you enter a plain query word in a search box, the search engine looks for that word anywhere on a page. It will look in the title of the page or in the body of the page. One way to reduce your number of results further is to use special syntax that limits where the search engine will look for a word. Search engines vary in the kinds of special syntax they offer, but in this section you'll find some almost-universal syntax you can use in your searches. In addition, look in the search engine's Help documents for information on the right way to express the syntax.

The title syntax

To use the special title syntax on Google and Yahoo, you enter `intitle:keyword`. This syntax restricts your searching to the title of a Web page. It's useful when you don't have many words by which to limit your topic. Instead, you're limiting where your word might be found. When your word is found in the title of a Web page, the page usually contains a lot of information about that keyword.

Be sure to try to get as specific as possible even when you're searching titles—a page that has your very specific query word in the title will probably get you a jackpot of information. On the other hand, you may find you need to get more general before you start getting many results. Don't use too many query words with this syntax.

The URL syntax

To conduct a special URL syntax search on Yahoo and Google, you must enter `inurl:keyword`. This syntax searches only the URLs of pages for the keyword you specify.

But be careful. We are definitely in quadruple-axel territory here. Since there's no guarantee that people will use a full word in a Web page name, it's tough to use this syntax. I tend to use it mostly when I'm searching blog entries because many blogs put the full title of their entry in their URL.

The site syntax

To conduct a site syntax search on Yahoo and Google, you must enter **site:** in the query box. This syntax restricts your search to either a top-level-domain (.org, .edu, .com, .uk, etc.) or to a single domain (like CNN.com). Why would you want to do this? Many domains tend to have their own "flavor" of information (with the exception of the .com domain).

For example, material on .edu domains, especially if you're searching for scientific/professional information, tends to be more academic (though occasionally student pages can also be found there). Information on .org domains can slant toward the nonprofit (though this is less true than it used to be). If you need to search within a single domain, check and see if that domain offers its own search or alert service before you go to the services offered by a search engine. Remember, there's no guarantee that a search engine will index every single page on a site.

WARNING

Be aware that any time you exclude the .com domain from a search, you're excluding a lot of pages. Try your search without using site syntax and then try it again using site syntax to see what information you'd be missing.

Other useful syntax

Title, URL, and site syntax are common to a lot of search engines, whether they're for news, Web searches, or RSS feeds. That's because these elements are common to all Web pages. But search engines go beyond those syntax to offer others that can help your searching. Keep an eye out for the following syntax, which you can use to narrow down your searches.

Location

Some search engines, especially news search engines, offer you a way to narrow your searches by the location of the source. Google News does this, for example. To use the location syntax, enter **location:** and the two-letter postal code of the state you want to search. For example, **location:ca** will find news from sources in California. This syntax also works with the name of a country (try **location:ireland**). General search engines sometimes allow you to narrow your search by country or region of the world, but less often by state or city.

Page size

Sometimes you can narrow down your search results to how large the page is. Using this you can try to skip the pages that contain a minimal amount of information, but this may mean you can miss useful pages.

Using the Advanced Search Form

Every time you use a search engine, without fail, look for the advanced search form. Most search engines have a basic form with a query box and maybe a couple of options. Until you visit the advanced search form (there's usually a link next to the simple search) you'll have little idea of what that search engine is capable of. For instance, compare Google's front page (**Figure 5.1**) to its advanced search page (**Figure 5.2**). The front page has a simple query box, while the advanced page has several query boxes for providing all kinds of search information, and even a few pull-down menus!

There are thousands and thousands of search engines and interfaces available, but they all have some basic guidelines in common. Look at the advanced search. Look at the help files. For each syntax you use, ask yourself: Is this going to narrow my results? Is it going to get manageable results while keeping them comprehensive? Experiment with them.

Figure 5.1

Google's front page is very simple.

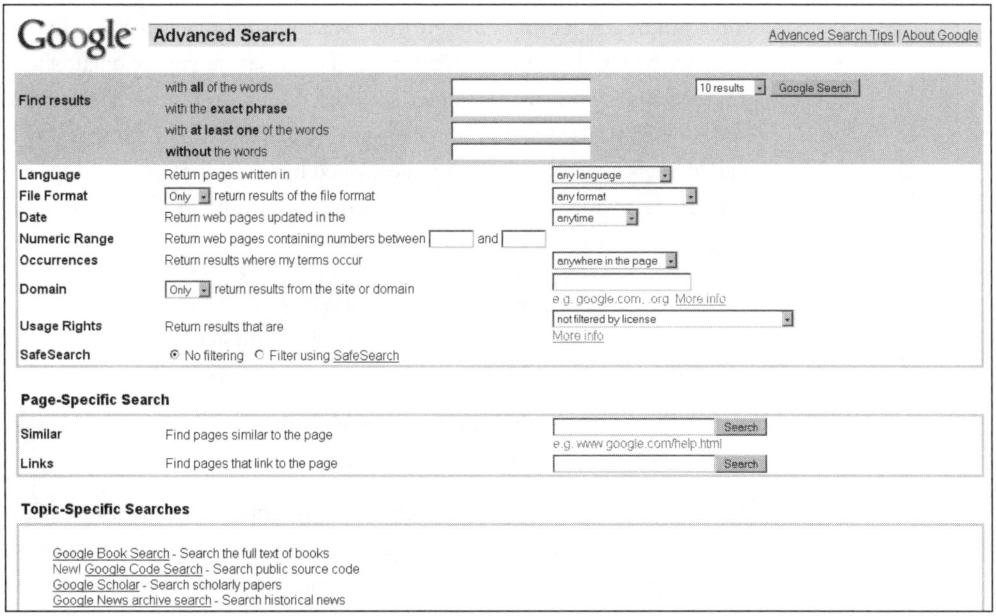

Figure 5.2 Google's advanced search page can be a bit overwhelming. See what I mean?

And my biggest recommendation for using syntax is this: combine syntax together when you can. Searching just in a title or just in one set of domains is powerful enough, but when you do both of those things together you can really zoom in on what you want to find.

The suggestions and the techniques I've gone over thus far are very useful for all kinds of data collections, be they Web pages, news search engines, article collections, sets of RSS feeds, or what have you. However, they are not useful for two other kinds of information collections—tags and conversations. For those you'll need to use a different approach.

Tags and Conversations

What are tags and conversations? Conversations, of course, are discussions that might happen on mailing lists or on public forums. You can find them via general search engines, but there are also many specialty search engines that index only conversations.

Tags you might not know about. A tag is a keyword that someone can use to describe a resource in a directory. Usually a search engine or directory that indexes tags has many people "tagging" resources at the same time. The index of words used to describe the contents of a directory built that way is called a *folksonomy*, a taxonomy developed by a group of people. Tags are not full descriptions or site titles—usually they're just a word or two.

> **TIP**
>
> You can learn a lot more about tagging and folksonomies at Wikipedia, including an overview on folksonomy at en.wikipedia. org/wiki/Folksonomy.

You will need to change your strategy when developing monitors for tags and conversations. Why? The big answer is language.

In the case of tags, you're not searching for summaries or even fully articulated concepts. Instead you're searching for a word or two words. In the case of conversations, you're looking for much more informal language, such as sentence fragments and scraps of conversations.

These kinds of data pools are very different from a structured, organized Web page. And for that reason you'll have to use different strategies for monitoring them. Later in this book, we look at where you can go to search and monitor tags and conversations, but here we're going to stick with the idea of queries and how to create them.

For now, let's take a look at searching with tags.

What about Blogs?

Whenever I talk about searching conversations versus searching the Web in general, someone invariably says, "Well, blogs are informal, aren't they? And they are kind of like conversations. So shouldn't you use the same kind of strategy as when you search for conversations?"

That's a good question. On one hand, yes, blog content tends to be less formal than that of other sites. On the other hand, the structure of a Web page makes most blogs conform to some sort of usual narrative: I did this, I read that, I had the following opinions. There are exceptions, such as stream of consciousness and fragmentary blogs, but most of them try to keep to some kind of recognized structure. With conversations, there's no existing Web page layout that must be adhered to, so conversations can become fragmented, a lot of "inside jokes" can take over, language use can become very informal, etc.

The "many-to-many" element of online conversations allows for some sloppiness and informality that the "one-to-many" characteristic of blogs makes less viable.

Searching within tags

The theory of onions is extremely important when searching huge data sets. Getting very narrow and specific is paramount. With tag searching, you have less to search. Tags are usually only a word or two. You don't have to abandon the onion completely, but try starting a little more general than you would normally. Say you had four levels for describing a bird:

1. Bird
2. Raptor
3. Hawk
4. Red-shouldered hawk

Level 1 is going to be too general no matter what you search. Level 4 would be great for Web search or a news search, but might be too specific for a tag search. When searching tags, try to stay at Level 2 or 3. Try one-word, or at most two-word, searches. Don't get too extensive or complicated.

Searching within tags can be boiled down to basically two ideas: simpler, more general. Giving instruction about searching within conversations is a little more complex.

Searching within conversations

When you think about searching within a conversation, whether it is a mailing list or an online form, try to think about how you'd talk about your topic. Create queries that reflect how you'd verbally discuss the topics.

If you're focusing on conversations that professionals are having, try to use their vocabulary. (If you're monitoring mailing lists of medical professionals, try to use medical terminology.) When you're monitoring for technical information, you can get a little geekier and use model numbers or version numbers. Read through some of the types of conversations you want to track so that you can get a sense of the kind of language that's being used. Remember the example earlier in the chapter where simply searching for the phrase **"cardiac arrest"** and removing the phrase **"heart attack"** changed the results so dramatically?

And take advantage of the advanced search forms. Tag searches don't have a lot of advanced options, but many conversations do. Use the available special syntax to narrow your results.

> **NOTE**
>
> We're just scratching the surface of tags and conversations with a few words to get you thinking about how to generate queries when approaching these resources. We'll get into some serious digging later on.

The next few chapters examine the "where" of information trapping.

6

Who's Linking to
Your Site?

It's a big wide world out there, with literally millions of topics to monitor, but we're going to start close to home—with your own Web site.

You may remember that in the last chapter I discussed the differences between external and internal information. Internal information is information out on the Web that mentions, references, or discusses a Web site you are interested in tracking. External information is everything else.

When I do presentations about search engines and information trapping, many people ask me how they can track which Web sites are linking to theirs and what they're saying about it. So wanting to trap this type of internal information seems to be a common theme. If you don't have a Web site for which you want to track interest, you may want to skip this chapter. If you do have a Web site, you probably have an audience, and this chapter is your opportunity to learn what that audience thinks of your site!

Advantages of Sleuthing Your Own Site

There are several reasons you might want to know who's linking to your site or who's reading it.

▶   **Plain ol' human curiosity.** You're putting in a great deal of time and effort into making a Web site available. Wouldn't you wonder just a little bit who's linking to it and what they're saying about it?

▶   **To help your business.** If someone's linking to you with cheers, you want to brag. If they're linking with jeers, you want to know how you can make it right.

▶   **To target your content and services.** Perhaps you run a library Web site, or an ad-driven content site. Knowing what people are saying about your site can help you focus your content for your audience ("I found a great article about x but I wish they'd cover y"). And if you know what kinds of sites are linking to yours, you can approach more of those types of sites and ask whether they'd like to link to you as well. The more incoming links, the more people can find you. And that's good!

Trapping General Site Links

Let's start our overview of internal information traps by looking at links to sites. To track this, we begin with the usual suspects: Google and Yahoo.

A Quick Query Overview

In the last chapter I noted that figuring out your search queries for internal information searching wasn't that tough. And it isn't. But let's talk about queries for just a moment. The most obvious query is your domain name, complete with the www, such as www.example.com. To monitor links to all pages on your domain, for the most part you have to monitor links to only one URL—your basic domain URL (in this case, www.example.com). That's because most search engines that find links will find any link to a given domain. For example, if I searched Technorati for www.example. com, I would find links to www.example.com. I would also find links to www.example.com/ archive/oldnews.html, or links to www.example.com/really/old/archives/news.html.

For RSS feeds it's equally simple; use the URL for your site's main RSS feed. If you have more than one RSS feed (some sites have hundreds of RSS feeds), it might be amusing to see what kind of attention the other ones are getting, but it can rapidly get out of hand. In my experience, the main feed, not a category or additional feed, is what most readers turn to. Stick with that one.

Google

To track who's linking to your site in Google, you need to use the link syntax like this:

`link:http://www.cnn.com`

Unfortunately, Google's link syntax does not work with any other keywords or any other syntax. So you can't do a query like this:

`link:http://www.cnn.com site:edu`

to find all pages from the .edu domain that link to CNN.com. (You can do that with Yahoo, as you'll see in a minute.) In addition, Google's link syntax checks the exact URL you're looking for—it doesn't find all pages within that domain that are being linked to.

Google's strengths lie in the fact that it updates its index fairly frequently, so you can pick up a lot of fresh links from its database. But you'll have a lot of links to pore through and you'll have to do a lot of the organizing yourself.

Yahoo

Because it can use other syntax and keywords in conjunction with the link syntax, Yahoo is a great way to track not only how many pages are linking to your site but also what kinds of pages are linking to your site. Yahoo offers two syntax for tracking page links:

▶ **Link syntax.** Use the link syntax when you want to find sites that are linking to one specific page of yours. You use this syntax just like you would with Google: `link:http://www.cnn.com`.

▶ **Linkdomain.** Use linkdomain when you want to find all the pages that are pointing to a particular domain, instead of just one page. The syntax looks like this: `linkdomain:www.cnn.com`. Note that you do not use `http://` with this syntax; if you do it will fail and you won't get any results.

Yahoo also makes a tool available for getting information about sites that are linking to a given URL; it's called Site Explorer.

Yahoo's Site Explorer

Instead of using query words to search, start using Site Explorer (siteexplorer.search.yahoo.com/) by typing in a simple URL, such as the URL for your Web site. When you do that, Yahoo gives you a results page with a list of the pages from that domain which Yahoo has indexed. (That's good to know; the more pages from your domain that Yahoo has indexed, the easier it will be for other people to find your site.) The full number of pages will be at the top of the results list. Beside that number is the number of pages that Yahoo has indexed that link to the URL you specified, with a hyperlink so that you can see the list (**Figure 6.1**).

Unfortunately, Yahoo only lets you see the first 1,000 results from each list, which is frustrating if you have more than a few thousand links to your site because you know you're missing most of them. Yahoo does offer the ability to export the results into a text file that can be opened in Excel, but you get the results fifty at a time (in other words, if you want to export a list of a thousand pages that link to your site, you'll have to export a list of results twenty times).

It doesn't appear that Yahoo Site Explorer lists its site links in order of date, so you can't easily monitor the results list for new additions. However, you can monitor the first results page and watch how the numbers at the top of the screen change—that is, you can keep track of the count of pages linking to your URL, and the count of pages indexed by Yahoo.com.

Figure 6.1 You'll find a variety of page links to your site using Site Explorer.

Narrowing your search

Yahoo indexes billions of pages, so take the opportunity to narrow down the kinds of results you get using Site Explorer. Remember how I told you in the last chapter that different kinds of domains (.edu, .com, .org, etc.) sometimes have different flavors? You can take advantage of that here. You can set up a search for your domain and add **site:edu** to see what .edu sites are linking to you. Or perhaps there's a particular country whose links you are most interested in; you could use that country's code in conjunction with a link search.

> **TIP**
>
> Just because a site is created and produced in another country does not mean it uses that country's code. For example, a site may be created and maintained in Japan, but its URL may end in .com. So when you use a country code to narrow down the results of your search, bear in mind you'll be excluding some sites that end in .com, .org, etc.

And of course you can do plain keyword searches, too. Maybe you'd like to find out what sites are linking to you but mentioning a competitor, or linking to you *and* linking to a competitor? (You can do two link searches in one query!) Once you begin using other syntax and keywords in conjunction with a link or linkdomain search, the possibilities are (almost) endless.

Say you're the CEO of Example.com and you want to monitor which sites are linking to you and linking to CNN.com. That's easy—your search would look like this:

```
link:http://www.example.com link:http://www.cnn.com
```

Or say you've got a blog and you want to know how many college Web pages are linking to you. In this case, you'd enter:

```
link:http://www.example.com site:edu
```

Or what if you want to know who's linking to you but mentioning the name of your competitor? You'd enter this in the query box:

```
link:http://www.example.com WidgetCo
```

Remember, you want complete but manageable!

If you can think of keywords that are at all relevant, try to use them; narrowing down your results is important. Excluding your own domain from the results helps, such as in the following example:

```
linkdomain:www.example.com -site:example.com
```

> **WARNING**
>
> Keep in mind that the link syntax and the linkdomain syntax will not work if you include *http://* in front of the URL.

Using Yahoo's RSS feeds

Yahoo offers RSS feeds of its search results, but you have to enter the URL yourself. So, for example, you'd enter the following URL and then substitute your query for the word **keyword** at the end:

```
http://api.search.yahoo.com/WebSearchService/rss/webSearch.
xml?appid=yahoosearchwebrss&query=keyword.
```

You'll find more information about Yahoo Web RSS feeds, and the encoding options for them, in the next chapter. Seeing who's linking to you across the entire Web is useful, but it does have its limitations. You might get the same results and find that the same pages are indexed over and over, or you might miss some of the more minor links to your pages.

To get a timely sense of who's linking to your site, you want to check RSS feed search engines that can sort their results by date.

Trapping Links in RSS Feeds

Trapping links from RSS feeds has one massive advantage: the feeds can be sorted by date. You know when you get a new hit that it will be fresh; it won't be something that's been wandering around a search engine index for the last few years. And because most RSS feeds are oriented toward blogs, you also know your results will be mostly commentary. That's all good.

You have two major options when you want to check for links in RSS feeds. Both Technorati and IceRocket offer link searches.

Technorati

In Technorati's (technorati.com) early days, I spent a lot of time using it to check links. Nowadays, Technorati does a decent job of searching for tags and keywords. But it's even better at checking for links to sites, which is mostly what I use it for.

You don't need to use any syntax to check for links; just enter the URL that you want to monitor in the Website URL Search form. You will get a list of all pages which link to that domain or URL, with the most recent links at the top (**Figure 6.2**).

Luckily Technorati doesn't care if you use **http://** with the URL. It displays a list of the blogs that link to that URL or a URL in that domain, with the most recent ones listed first.

You also have the option to "claim" your site. Claiming your site means that you prove to Technorati that you own your domain (this usually involves pasting a little snippet of code on your site). Once you've done that, you have the option of adding some additional information about your blog to Technorati and getting some information on your Technorati account page about the popularity and number of links to your site.

I find that sometimes Technorati delivers a false positive on a site that is on a link list, but is not part of an active Weblog discussion. On the other hand, it will sometimes find results that I didn't see on IceRocket.

Figure 6.2

Checking for links to
CNNSI.com. Note that
Technorati also shows
when the result was
found.

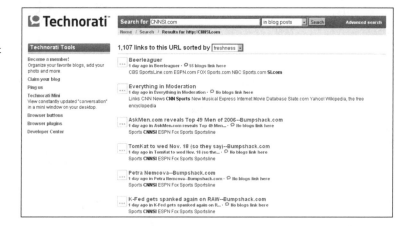

Watching Blogrolls for Your URL

Many blogs contain lists of links to other blogs; these lists of links are called *blogrolls*.

Blogrolls are great discovery tools. They exist because of two primary assumptions: if you're interested enough in someone to read their blog, you might also be interested in what they read, and if you like one type of blog, the other ones listed in a blogroll might be similar enough that you'll like them too.

If you have a blog or a site that is popular with blogs, you might find that your URL ends up on blogrolls. To track these, try using Blogrolling (blogrolling.com). Blogrolling lets you set up a blogroll and search through blogrolls for the URL of your choice. You'll be able to see how many blogs that use the Blogrolling.com service are linking to you. Run a search for your URL, and then put a page monitor on the results.

Blogrolling's search doesn't list every possible blog that links to you, of course, only those that use the Blogrolling service. But it's another interesting data point to add to your information traps.

If you don't have an account with Technorati, the easiest way to monitor its search results is with a page monitor. But I really recommend you get an account—it's free and only requires a name and e-mail address.

IceRocket

IceRocket (icerocket.com) is a relatively new search engine that offers searches for a variety of collections, from the expected (news and blogs) to the unanticipated (MySpace). IceRocket isn't as famous as Google or even Technorati, but I occasionally find results here that I don't find anywhere else (**Figure 6.3**).

When you use IceRocket to sleuth out other links to your site, you don't need to use syntax; you just enter your site's URL, including **http://**. IceRocket displays a list of results sorted by date.

The only disadvantage I've encountered with this site is that sometimes you get multiple copies of the same entry in your list of results.

IceRocket offers RSS feeds of its search results. Just click the Subscribe button at the top of the search results page and you're ready to go.

Figure 6.3 Searching for links in IceRocket doesn't require a special syntax, just a URL.

Who's Using Your Words?

Some site-based information is easy to define, such as who's linking to your URL, for example, or the number of people who read your RSS feed. More nebulous is the idea of your Web site's content, and who is using it. Because content use is an issue with anyone who has a Web site, I cover the topic in this chapter; because it is nebulous it gets its own sidebar.

Usually the idea of someone using your content is bad: another site is reprinting your materials with only an acknowledgement—or worse, no acknowledgement! And that does happen. But there is potential good to people using your content, too. Maybe someone is using your RSS feed snippets as content on their site (and thus driving people to your site!). Maybe you have an article you're trying to circulate and you want people to pick it up. Maybe you've been encouraging other sites to link to yours with a short summary of your content, and you want to see what sites are actually using the summary. Good and bad, there are many reasons to want to know if content related to your site is showing up on the Web.

There are two ways to do this. The first way is probably the way you would expect: run a Web search with a 10–15 word snippet of the content you want to monitor—the more unique, the better (**Figure 6.4**). Better yet, run two or three Web searches; Google, Yahoo, and MSN are all good choices.

Figure 6.4 Use a unique sentence from your article, and you get a very concentrated list of results.

Then use the search engine monitors we talk about in the next chapter to keep up with new matches on your content. Depending on how often you add content or how many snippets you want to monitor, you may have to update these searches often.

Monitoring for content snippets is fine in many cases, but for articles you might want to monitor the content of entire pages. Copyscape (copyscape.com) lets you enter the URL of a page and get other Web pages whose content is uncomfortably close to matching it. I find that if I do this with the front page of my site, I get a lot of people making use of my RSS feeds. However, if you have an article or information that's supposed to be accessed by subscribers only, you might want to monitor in this way to make sure that your content is not being circulated in an unauthorized way.

Copyscape provides only a limited number of results with a free account. For more results, and to get automatic e-mails when new matches of your content appear, you can sign up for a Copysentry account. Copysentry costs $4.95 a month or $19.95 a month, depending on the level of service you want.

It's too easy to be paranoid about your content on the Internet being stolen. But it's also easy to set up monitors to assure that you become aware of any instances of theft. Preparing yourself without dwelling on the possibilities is a good strategy.

Who's Reading Your RSS Feeds?

Tracking who's linking to you is something you can do to an extent via your Web site logs. But sometimes that doesn't give you the whole picture; some people have their referrers turned off in their browser (the browser doesn't tell the server from what URL they came to visit your site), and you'll completely miss pages that have links but don't send you any browsers. Using Web logs and external, Web-based resources at the same time can give you a fuller picture about what people are saying when they link to your site.

Getting an idea of how many people are visiting or reading certain parts of your site, including RSS feeds, is a different story. Web site logs are going to give you most of what you need to know, as far as sheer numbers are concerned. But Bloglines can give you counts *and* a little more information about where your information fits in the RSS/blog universe.

Bloglines (bloglines.com) indexes over 600 million articles (as of this writing) from millions of blogs and news sources. You can use Bloglines to both search for links to your site as well as see how many people are reading your RSS feed in Bloglines.

On the upper right side of the page is a query box, followed by a Search For Citations pull-down menu (**Figure 6.5**). Enter your URL there, and you get a list of sites that have linked to yours, sorted by date.

Each result includes the blog name, author name, how recently the post was made, and a small snippet. Hold your cursor over the More Info item underneath the search result to see the number of subscribers that RSS feed has in Bloglines, as well as how many other posts on Bloglines are citing that search result.

Want to know how many subscribers your own blog has in Bloglines? Easy as pie. Go back to the search box and use the pull-down menu to select Search for Feeds. Enter the name of your blog (you'll have to do a little tweaking if the name isn't unique) and you get a list of search results that include the URL of the feed, title, description, and number of subscribers (**Figure 6.6**).

Figure 6.5 Bloglines makes it easy to see who's citing your site.

Figure 6.6 Bloglines tracks how many people are reading a particular feed using its service.

FeedBurner

If you don't mind spending a little money and you want some real precise numbers about who's reading your RSS feed, sign up for FeedBurner (feedburner.com). It costs $4.99 a month (for up to three feeds) and provides a huge amount of statistical information about your feed, including how many people are subscribed to it and in what RSS feed readers, which items on your feed are getting clicked, and what user-agents and search engine 'bots are visiting your feed. For the Web wrangler who really wants to know what her visitors are looking at, FeedBurner would be cheap at twice the price!

Now, will knowing how many people read your feed using Bloglines tell you how many people overall read your feed using every possible RSS reader? No. But it can give you a good sense of whether you're popular (is *anyone* reading your RSS feed?). And it may be that you have more readers than you think.

Moving from Internal to External Information

Internal information, like URLs, numbers of readers, and content, covers a lot of the basic stuff that defines the information you provide online and reveals what your readers are like—the kind of community you are generating. If you own or manage a business, it's probably obvious to you that you need to track this. But even if you're not a business owner or manager, the knowledge of what kind of readership you have on your Web site, what they say about it, and how they link to it can be immensely valuable.

Now let's move further out from internal information to the sites and topics that interest you but don't necessarily involve you. Let's move to external information and where to find it.

7

Trapping Topic-Based Information

In the last chapter, we looked at trapping internal information—information such as who's linking to your site, or who's reading your RSS feed.

While that kind of trapping has its place, especially if you're trying to make a living from your Web site, a broader use for information trapping lies in trapping external, topic-based information. You might want to use the external information you trap to create content for your site, pursue a degree, educate yourself, and so on. The possibilities for the kinds of topic searching you can do are almost endless.

Unfortunately, so are the resources on the Internet! So now it's time to look at some large categories of information that you can monitor, from really broad, like general search engines, to more narrow, like government sites. Along the way, I'll provide some hints for searching particular kinds of sites and some things to keep in mind when you're building queries. In later chapters, we look at other trapping options, including multimedia sources.

For the most part, your largest data pools will come from general search engines, and your smallest pools will derive from very focused sites like city and state resources. Because of the different kinds of information offered at different types of sites, you have to build your traps a bit differently for each resource. But the underlying theory is the same: complete but manageable.

Monitoring General Search Engines

General search engines, the original foundation for information search on the Internet, are starting to show their age. They're large, unstructured, chaotic pools of information that can be really tough to trap. On the other hand, they are the original foundation for Internet search and therefore people who have no idea what an RSS feed is, or how to get listed in a specialty search engine, will make really sure that they're listed in a general search engine. And that, in a nutshell, is why you should consider trapping in them, even though getting the perfect query together and monitoring results can be a bit frustrating.

Google

General search engines are by definition going to have very large data pools. And Google's no exception. Google (google.com) has stopped providing a page count for its search engine, but the last time it did, Google had over

8 billion documents in its index, and I'm confident that index hasn't gotten any smaller! The advantage to that is that Google indexes astonishing amounts of material, from every possible corner of the Web.

You can monitor general search engines not only for links to your sites, as we discussed in the last chapter, but also for long queries focused on unusual, narrow topics. When applying the theory of onions to full-text search engines, make sure your topics are as narrow as possible. Google's query limit is 32 words—you want to push that limit!

Building your queries

Start building your Google queries using as many words as possible. Remember, you can always remove words later. Use as many of the special syntax options as you can think of. The title and site syntax will probably work best. Avoid **inurl**—it's difficult to guess which words might be included in the URL of a Web site.

HINTS

- Explore the Advanced Search page to see if it can help you. For example, say you're searching mostly in English and your query has a few French words. Limit your search to pages in English and see how that changes your results. You might also want to limit the country your results are coming from, if applicable, though in my experience that limits your results too much.

- If you put a tilde (~) in front of a word for which you're searching, Google will find synonyms for the word in addition to the word itself. For example, ~television would find news, TV, network, etc. You can tell which words are matching your tilded query because they're bolded in the search result snippets. Try experimenting with that. For much fun, search for a word with a tilde and then exclude the word itself, like this: ~television –television.

Trapping

For e-mail alerts of new pages added to Google's index, use the Google Alerts feature (google.com/alerts) we talked about earlier in Chapter 4. If you want your results in RSS format, use Google Alert (googlealert.com), which we also talked about in Chapter 4.

Possibilities

▶   Try medical terms using the site:edu syntax.

▶   Try academic terms with the same syntax.

▶   Try any topical keyword combined with the intitle syntax.

▶   Use quotes to group your words into phrases as much as possible.

▶   Is there any word that will help your search if you make sure that it doesn't appear in your queries? Try that by putting a minus in front of the word (**-birds**).

Are All Search Engine Indexes Created Alike?

You might think that if you set up traps on one search engine you don't need to bother with them on others. "They all index the Internet," you might say. "Isn't one just like the other?" Definitely not! Only so much overlap exists in the indexes of the various search engines. If you only monitor one, you're definitely going to miss information from the others. This might lead you to another question: "If I monitor all the major search engines, I'll be monitoring all the new pages added to the Internet, right?" Afraid not. Though you'll be covering a lot more of the Internet than you would otherwise, all the search engines put together do not index more than a part of the Internet's Web pages.

Bottom Line: monitor several search engines and you'll get all you can, but you still won't be getting everything.

Yahoo

When it comes to search engine wars, the two biggies duking it out are Yahoo and Google. Because of that, Yahoo (yahoo.com) is being very proactive in developing new syntax, updating its index of Web sites, and making its Web search easier and easier to use. Yahoo started as a search engine directory, and while the directory still exists, Yahoo is much more of a fulltext search engine now.

Building your queries

Like Google, Yahoo has a variety of syntax available and a large query limit. Maximize both as much as you can. Yahoo's also got a couple of interesting ways to narrow your results, such as searching for results only in Creative Commons (a "some rights reserved" alternative to full copyright, "all rights reserved" protection) content. There's another option for searching Yahoo's subscription-based content. You can get to Yahoo's Advanced Web Search page directly at http://search.yahoo.com/search/options.

HINTS

- Use quotes for phrases.
- Exclude words from your search results when appropriate.
- Use the special content searches with more general queries to narrow your results.
- Note that Yahoo's results show when a site has an RSS feed. This could be a useful RSS feed discovery tool for you.

Trapping

Yahoo does not offer alerts for page search results, so set Yahoo's preferences to show 100 results per page. Then run your search, and afterward monitor that page of results. That monitored page will look for changes in only the top 100 results, which is another reason why you need to make sure your query is narrow enough.

Yahoo also offers RSS feeds for search results, though you have to jump through a couple of hoops to create them—namely, you need to edit a URL. Here's how:

The base URL for getting an RSS feed of Yahoo's search results looks like this:

```
http://api.search.yahoo.com/WebSearchService/rss/webSearch.
xml?appid=yahoosearchwebrss&query=keyword
```

You need to change **keyword** to the appropriate query word. If you want to use quotes or several words, you need to make sure they're encoded properly (encoded just means writing characters in a certain way so that the browser can read them in the URL).

For instance, you want to combine words using the plus sign (+). To search for "three blind mice," use **three+blind+mice**. To remove words, use the minus sign (-). To remove "mice" from the equation, for example, use **three+blind-mice**. To establish phrases, use %22 at the beginning and at the end of your query. For example, to find the phrase "three blind mice," use **%22three+blind+mice%22**.

Possibilities

Try to see what you can pull out of Yahoo's specialty searches:

▶   Is there potential for articles related to your topic?

▶   Should you be searching Creative Commons content to see if there's material you can license and use on your site or quote from on your site?

In addition to the Web site, Yahoo has a directory, which you can also monitor. Monitoring directories, as we've discussed, is a little different than monitoring full-text search engines. Your queries have to be more general. In the case of Yahoo, it's also easier because of some of the RSS feed offerings.

Yahoo Directory

Yahoo's Directory (dir.yahoo.com) is just what it sounds like: a searchable subject index of sites and descriptions. In my experience, it is not as dynamic as Yahoo's search engine, but is still useful to monitor. And Yahoo makes it a little easier too, depending on what you're looking at.

Building your queries

For searching most directories, I don't bother to build queries. Instead I peruse the directory structure and find the subcategories that most accurately reflect what I'm interested in.

Say I'm interested in lions. I browse the directory, from Science to Animals to Mammals to Lions. The subject "lions" has its own page, but there's also a category for Ligers and Tigons (lion/tiger hybrids). As of this writing, there are only five links on this page, so it would be easy to monitor this URL using a page monitor.

In general, the deeper you go into the subcategories, the shorter the list of sites for each subcategory will be. But if you must monitor a general category, I recommend checking to see whether Yahoo Directory has an RSS feed for the latest update. The directory doesn't have feeds for every category and subcategory, but it does have an extensive number of feeds for higher-level categories. You can see it at http://dir.yahoo.com/rss/dir/index.php. For the most part, these feeds don't go more than one or two levels deep.

HINTS

- If you can't find, or immediately think of, a category that's relevant to your topic, search for a couple of topic keywords. Related directory categories will appear at the top of the search results and might give you some hitherto-unconsidered ideas of other directory pages to monitor.

- Remember that quotes in phrases work in a directory as well, as does the ability to exclude keywords.

Trapping

If you want to monitor for new sites in one of the more general categories, check to see if Yahoo has an RSS feed for that category. In the case of the sub-sub-subcategories, they usually have a sufficiently small number of links in which you can use a page monitor to check them for changes (**Figure 7.1**).

Figure 7.1 This page is small enough that you can monitor it for changes.

Possibilities

▶   A directory is your chance to use more general keywords than you would with a full-text search engine. So experiment with all those two-and-three-word queries that were getting you too many results in the Google searches. What directory categories are they matching up to? Are they categories that would be worth monitoring?

▶   What happens when you search for as general a topic as you can? Are you coming up with useful directories? Would it be worth it to dig down into some subdirectories and see what you find?

Ask

Several years ago, Ask Jeeves (the company has retired the butler and changed its name to Ask) was the serious also-ran of the search engine world—a definite third-tier search engine. Now, more and more, Ask (ask.com) is a definite player (**Figure 7.2**).

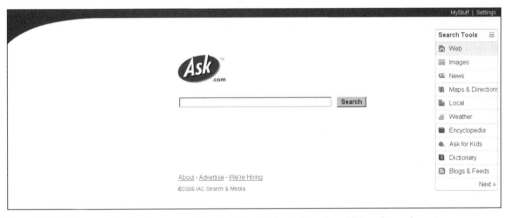

Figure 7.2 Ask has a very basic home page. Tools on the right point you to additional search options.

Ask used to be known as a "natural language search engine," that is, you could enter your search as a question and Ask would interpret your search and (hopefully) find what you were looking for, either on the Web or in its own index of questions. Now it's more of a full-text engine, having integrated technology from Teoma, a search engine company that Ask purchased a few years ago.

Building your queries

Ask has a pretty spartan home page. There is an advanced search available at ask.com/webadvanced, however. Options on the Advanced page include the ability to narrow searches by the last time pages were updated or by their geographic location. You can also specify what words must or must not appear in a search, as well as words that should appear in a search. The "should search" makes your search a little fuzzier—it weighs results which have "should words" higher in the results, but doesn't completely eliminate those results which don't have the "should words." If you want to use words that could really focus your topic but also have the potential to torch relevant results, take advantage of Ask's "should search."

HINTS

- Take a look at the options to narrow your search on the right side of the results page. They vary a lot in how useful they are. Some of them are actually interesting and potentially useful, while others are downright ridiculous. Ditto for the related names search in the same place. Use these additional results as a spur for inspiration, but don't expect them to be useful all of the time.

- Notice that each of Ask's results has a little pair of binoculars next to it. Hold your mouse over that pair of binoculars and a little pop-up window displays, showing you what that page looks like (**Figure 7.3**). This can come in handy when you're trying to get a quick idea of a site but don't want to visit or check for page load.

Figure 7.3

Hold your mouse over the binoculars and you can quickly get an idea of whether a page is useful or not.

Trapping

Ask doesn't offer RSS feeds or e-mail alerts. As a workaround, visit the Preferences page (ask.com/webprefs) and change your result number to 100. Then do the searches you want and save the results in a page monitor. To narrow your search further, you can also use the Advanced Search page to restrict your results to more recently updated pages.

I am less excited by Ask's current status (though it's good) than by its future possibilities. In the past couple of years, the company has made huge strides in the online search engine world, mostly by doing things a little bit differently than the established search engines. Watch Ask for tools that will be useful to you, the information trapper.

Possibilities

Take advantage of Ask's search suggestions and quick preview tools:

▶   Can Ask's search suggestions help you refine your queries at all?

▶   Ask's Preview tool is the place to quickly review large numbers of sites, so that you don't have to visit each one. Take advantage of the binoculars feature.

Microsoft Live Search

Yahoo and Google are the major search engines right now. But of course things can change very quickly. And when a five-ton gorilla like Microsoft enters the scene, you can almost count on things changing. Microsoft entered the search engine arena with MSN Search, but it has rebranded its site as Microsoft Live Search (live.com/?searchonly=true). This new search engine should be on your list of resources to trap, partially because Microsoft is working incredibly hard to become a major player, and partially because it's put together a few interesting innovations (**Figure 7.4**).

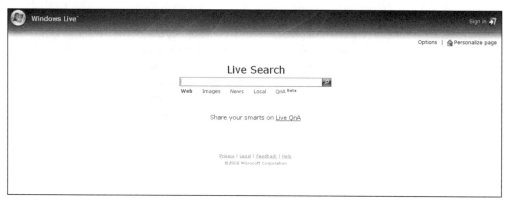

Figure 7.4 Microsoft Live Search.

Building your queries

You might think at first glance that Live Search doesn't have any special syntax. Microsoft certainly doesn't go out of its way to highlight them on the front page. There are some available, though. Try the following syntax:

▶ **Contains.** Looks for pages containing the file types you specify. For example, `contains:mp3` would find pages that link to MP3 files. This is different from Google's filetype operator, which would find the MP3 files themselves.

▶ **Intitle.** Looks for words in the title.

▶ **Inbody.** Looks only for words in the page body, not in the page title. Useful when you're looking for words common to an HTML infrastructure, such as "title."

▶ **Link.** Finds pages that link to the specified URL.

▶ **Linkfromdomain.** This is an unusual syntax! Linkfromdomain finds those links that are coming *from* a specified domain. Wondering who your competitors are linking to? Use this syntax to find out.

▶ **Prefer.** Sort of a midway point between "or" and "and." Add `prefer:` to a query keyword if you would like to have it in your results, but it isn't absolutely necessary. (Got any query words you're not absolutely certain about? This is the syntax for you.)

> Live Search does have that single query box on the front page that searches several sets of data, including news and images. But Live Search doesn't have an advanced search page. Instead it offers advanced search options on the search result pages. One of the options is a set of sliders that lets you change some of your search options without having to specify syntax or query words.

Trapping

Unlike Google and Yahoo, Live Search offers its search engine results in RSS format. To get an RSS feed for your search results, just add **&format=rss** to the end of any URL in your Live Search search results, like this:

```
http://search.live.com/results.aspx?q=woodworking&format=rss
```

Possibilities

Because Live Search offers RSS feeds, you can monitor a lot of searches without worrying about using page monitors or getting false positives. Take advantage of this feature and stock up with queries.

Open Directory Project

The Open Directory Project (dmoz.org) is one of the reasons my hair is rapidly turning gray. It offers so much and yet is so frustrating at the same time. On the one hand, Open Directory Project comprises a group of editors working together to build a searchable subject index, and I agree that the world needs more searchable subject indexes. On the other hand, it's sometimes a bear to search, and you never know when the categories are going to be updated. Despite the drawbacks, in some ways I feel it's the best directory out there, better even than Yahoo Directory.

> __TIP__
>
> Open Directory Project is the directory on which the Google Directory is based. But in my experience, the data in the Open Directory Project is updated much more often than the data in the Google Directory.

Building your queries

You *can* browse the Open Directory Project (ODP) just like you browse Yahoo's Directory. However, it may not be as fruitful. Earlier in the chapter, we used an example of browsing for "lions" in Yahoo's Directory, where we browsed from Science to Animals to Mammals to Lions. Using Open Directory Project, the pathway looks like this:

Top: Science: Biology: Flora and Fauna: Animalia: Chordata: Mammalia: Carnivora: Felidae: Panthera: Lion

I could get as far as Animalia if I were browsing, but after that I'd be lost. I thought a "chordata" was something you play on a guitar. I recommend browsing through the categories until you're stumped. Then use the search engine at the top of the page to search only within that category. From there you're directed to the right places. Browsing and then searching is worth it: as of this writing, the Open Directory Project has more lion pages than the Yahoo Directory does.

HINT

Let your queries get a little more general, but drill down as much as you can into the directory structure before you start using the search box. It will save you a lot of time.

Trapping

The ODP doesn't offer RSS, nor does it offer e-mail alerts. You have to choose the categories you want and then feed them to page monitors.

Possibilities

The ODP is a little different from the Yahoo Directory. In addition to indexing Web sites, it also indexes RSS feeds relevant to a category, as well as articles relevant to a category. So when you're monitoring here, you'll not only be able to keep an eye out for relevant and often very credible content, but you'll also learn about RSS feeds that contain content relevant to the category. For these reasons, and because of the fact that I find this directory in some instances to be better populated than the Yahoo Directory, I recommend trying a few extra categories here. The extra monitoring time will be worth it.

We've covered five different directories and search engines here. But are those all the possible ones? Heavens no; there are hundreds out there! To cover them all would take up far too much space, but here are a couple more that I think you should at least consider when you're preparing to trap the general Web. I don't go as in-depth with these as I did with the first-tier search engines, but there's enough information here that you should be able to do some experimentation on your own.

Try a Cluster for Your Search

Perhaps you're having problems developing the perfect query—the exact words you want are eluding you. In these cases, it's a good idea to veer off the track of regular search engines for a moment and try something else: clustering search engines.

A clustering search engine "clusters" results into groups. The groups are built around a certain topic. Say you do a search for **chips**. A clustering search engine might cluster your result into groups like potato chips, poker chips, wood chips, and chocolate chips. Instead of having to review all the search results at once, you could then choose a group that was most relevant to your search.

Clustering search engines can help you figure out query words that are relevant to search. Let's look at the chip example again. If you're trying to do a query on poker chips, you could peruse the cluster that groups results about poker chips and see what words appear over and over again. Ask yourself what caused the clustering engine to put all those results together. Perhaps those words are ones you could use to refine your query.

There are many clustering search engines available. Here are a few for you to try:

- **Clusty** (clusty.com) is a service of Vivisimo, one of the first clustering search engines available. Conducting a search for "chips" on Clusty not only produced a variety of clusters, including "tortilla" and "health programs" (sometimes the reasons for a cluster aren't immediately obvious!), but it also produced lists of possible matches for chips within search results (in this case, from Wikipedia pages).

- **Mooter** (mooter.com) displays lists of search results using a visual layout of the clusters it finds to match your query (**Figure 7.5**). Once you choose a cluster you want to explore further, it then provides a more traditional layout, with clusters on the left and search results on the right.

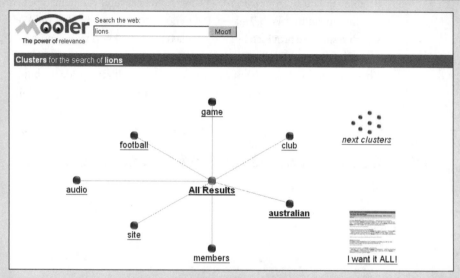

Figure 7.5 Mooter provides results in a cluster of ideas instead of a list of Web pages.

- **iBoogie** (iboogie.com) clusters several different kinds of Web pages, including news, images, and medical information. You can try the clustering on the other searches if you like, but I find iBoogie still works best for Web pages. It actually slices clusters pretty thin—for example, it makes a distinction between poker chips and casino chips!

Clustering search engines aren't the best option for every day search result monitoring. In my experience, they have smaller databases than the major search engines. But when you need some help generating words for your query or understanding what vocabulary is used around a particular topic, they help a lot.

A9

Brought to you by Amazon, A9 (a9.com) offers several different types of searches, including Web, Images, Reference, Movies, and Books. The Web search results are provided by Google, massaged a bit by Amazon and Alexa (a service that provides traffic and popularity information about Web sites). Check out the book search with narrow queries. You'll get "inside the book" results featuring book passages containing your search query (**Figure 7.6**).

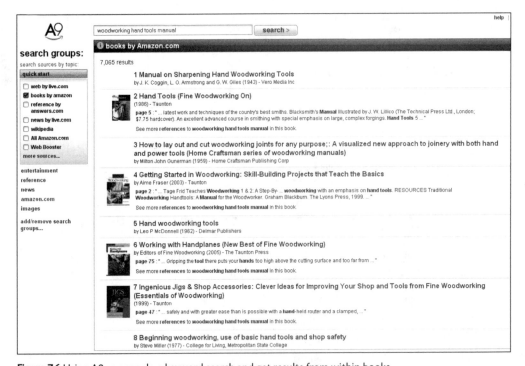

Figure 7.6 Using A9 you can do a keyword search and get results from within books.

No RSS feeds or e-mail alerts, unfortunately, so you have to monitor result pages.

Once thing you'll notice when you visit A9 is a series of checkboxes that lets you apply other resources to the search results—resources like reference, news, yellow pages, and more (**Figure 7.7**).

Figure 7.7 A9 offers the ability to search a huge number of resources.

You can get a giant overview of these extra searchable resources—over 450 of them—at opensearch.a9.com/searches.jsp.

There are so many resources here that there's another search engine available just to find them. If you're a registered user of A9, you can add these resources to A9 as extra columns on your search. If you're not an A9 user, you can add these sources to your search temporarily. It's easy to get overwhelmed here. On the other hand, it's a simple way to dip your toe in the wealth of available specialty search engines.

Gigablast

Gigablast (gigablast.com) is a small company compared to Yahoo or Google, and contains a Web index that is a bit smaller as well. I'm including it here because there's constant work going on to update it and add more features.

Gigablast is a full-text search engine that offers a number of search options, including for blogs, travel information, and government information. Search results provide related phrases and query words, and sometimes even related sites (**Figure 7.8**).

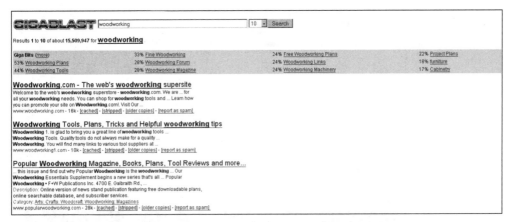

Figure 7.8 Gigablast shows related phrases at the top of its search results.

Note that the Advanced Search page has an option to search within a list of sites you specify, which is handy if you want to search and monitor the results from a group of sites instead of just one. Gigablast includes "Giga Bits" in its search results, which may help give a few ideas for additional query words.

Monitoring News Search Engines

General search engines have the advantage of trying to index large quantities of the Web. They have the disadvantage of dealing with huge sets of information, of dealing with unstructured Web pages, and with indexing Web pages that haven't been updated in months or years.

News search engines counterbalance these disadvantages. The sets of information they index are much smaller, they are pretty much all news, and most of the news search engines don't keep their index for more than 30 days. If the topic you want to trap is in any way related to current events, news search engines are the way to go. Even if they aren't—you're into those old woodworking tools, for example—it's worth it to set some traps at news search engines. You never know when a newspaper's Lifestyle or Hobby section is going to interview some woodworker with the world's largest old tools collection.

As you might imagine, several of the search engines offer their own news searches, but there are independent ones as well. We look at both in this section.

Yahoo News

Yahoo News (news.yahoo.com) looks somewhat overwhelming when you first get to the front page. There's lots of news links, multiple tabs to various types of news, and even pointers to several other sites on Yahoo. Don't worry about any of that. What you want to do is search, and searching will cut through all this extraneous stuff. The Advanced Search page is located at search.news.yahoo.com/usns/ynsearch/categories/advanced/index.html.

Building your queries

When you're using the Advanced Search page, set the results to sort by date instead of by relevance (**Figure 7.9**).

The rest is up to you. Note that Yahoo divides the news into categories, which is one way to narrow your searches without having to figure out query words, and might be useful to those of you doing tricky searches. Say you're trying to track news about certain pharmaceutical businesses. Using Yahoo News' advanced search, you can search for the word **pharmaceutical** in the business category and get a start on a good query. From there you'd probably want to add the names of drugs, companies, and so on that you were trying to track. But the business category would ensure that you were getting more business-oriented results, and not science or medical results.

> **HINTS**
>
> - Take advantage of the category offerings of Yahoo News.
> - Use the location syntax. If the topic in which you're interested has a geographical area, the location syntax can be a blessing. The Advanced Search page notes that you can search by state and by country, but in many cases you can also search by city as well. Try entering a search term and enter Austin in the location box. Notice that your search results are restricted to media in Austin, including television stations and newspapers. Nifty, huh? This is great for localized information trapping.

Figure 7.9

The Advanced Search form has many options. Make sure you're using the one to sort by date.

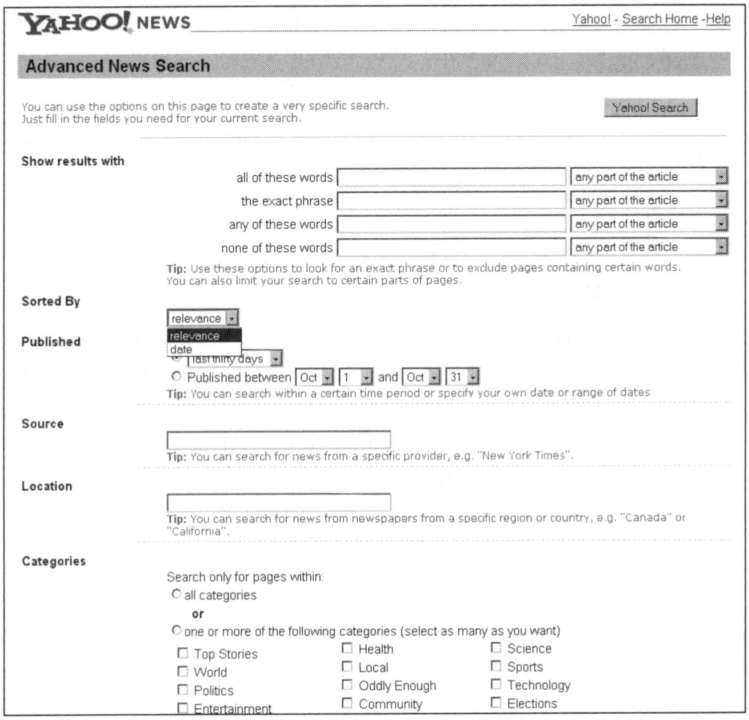

Trapping

For some reason news search engines have better trap mechanisms overall than Web search engines. Yahoo offers news alerts via the Yahoo Alerts system, which we talked about earlier, or via RSS feeds. RSS feeds are available on the right side of the front news page. Yahoo News also has topical RSS feeds, which you may find useful depending on how general your topic is. You can get a full list of those feeds at news.yahoo.com/rss.

Possibilities

▶   Yahoo News' search indexes a lot of general news searches but puts them into categories. If possible, try developing a query that relies on the categories to do the heavy work and lets you search using more general keywords.

> ▶ Sometimes the location search lets you search for media sources in a single city. See if it's possible to work that into your search.

> ▶ Don't forget to take advantage of Yahoo News' wonderful RSS feeds.

Google News

For a long time Google News (news.google.com) was my favorite news search engine. And while other competitors have entered the scene, it still has a lot to offer, with over 4,500 sources and both e-mail alerts and RSS feeds available.

Building your queries

Google News has an excellent advanced search available at news.google. com/advanced_news_search. Here you can narrow your search by location (sources available in a particular country, or state in the United States). You also can narrow your query word search to the headline of the story (great if you've got a keyword that just can't be narrowed down).

> **HINT**
>
> Google News, as you've seen, has some great options for advanced searching. Take advantage of them. The title search is immeasurably useful when you're having trouble narrowing down your query. In addition, I find the ability to narrow my search to sources in a particular state or country also useful. Later in the chapter we're going to look at monitoring the news and issues of a country. Google News' location syntax (as well as Yahoo News' advanced search) is a big part of that.

Trapping

Google News offers e-mail updates via its Google Alerts product, as well as RSS and Atom feeds. At the end of every results page, check out the left side of the page. There, under the page navigation, are text links to RSS and Atom versions of your search.

Possibilities

Google claims to have 4,500 news sources in its index, and has claimed this for years. My guess would be that it uses a lot more. Try some of your more obscure queries on the wide range of content indexed here.

MSNBC

Unfortunately, the MSN news search (newsbot.msnbc.msn.com) does not offer an advanced search form or even much searching help. However, it does offer quick searching, RSS feeds, and a source list at newsbot.msnbc.msn.com/s/publishers.aspx so that you can determine what you're actually searching through.

Building your queries

You're not going to have a lot of choices with MSNBC and there's not a lot of guidance for special syntax. So just use as many words as you can to narrow your query.

> **HINT**
>
> It's challenging to really narrow your query without special syntax, but try. Go over the list of sources to make sure this is an engine you want to search.

Trapping

Despite the fact that the home page for MSN News Search is on MSNBC, the results page is on Live Search. As with Live Search, just add **&format=rss** to the end of your search results URL to get an RSS feed.

Possibilities

News search engines are quickly becoming an expected feature of Web search engines, but there are other specific engines too—ones that have indexes that go back further than 30 days and ones that index things that might be tough to find on the Web.

FindArticles

FindArticles (findarticles.com) is affiliated with the LookSmart search engine. But as a search engine, LookSmart isn't all that popular nowadays, whereas FindArticles is. It indexes over 10 million articles, many of which FindArticles claims can't be found on the regular Web. Some of the articles require payment, but FindArticles also has extensive free information as well.

Building your queries

Use the Advanced Search form. There are a couple of unusual options here. The most useful one for you is the ability to browse the publications list and select which publications you're going to search, from 1UP to the St. James Encyclopedia of Pop Culture. You can search one periodical at a time or many (**Figure 7.10**).

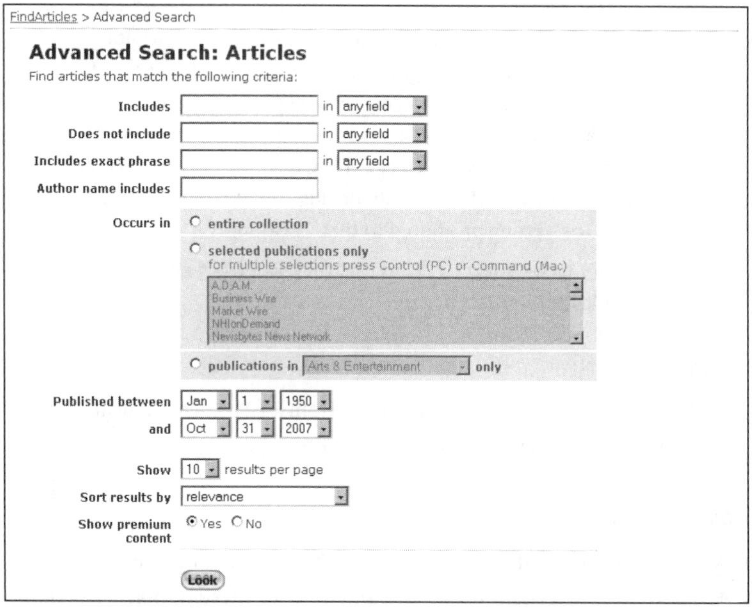

Figure 7.10

This compact Advanced Search form lets you list a huge number of periodicals in your search.

Another useful feature is the Show Premium Content option at the bottom of the page. Premium content is content that will cost money to look at. I usually turn that off, although for academic, legal, and medical searches, you might want to consider leaving it on.

- It will take some time to scroll through all the available publications and pick out which ones you want, but this time investment is worth being able to search a very specific set of publications. If you don't have the patience or can't get enough information from the publication names to know if they are appropriate for your topic, see if you can use the category listings below the publication listing.

- You can restrict your results by how many pages the article has. If you're trapping a topic area that might get you a lot of false positives—say, if you're searching for some aspect of business and you keep finding announcements about promotions and business moves and such—you might want to set this to get results of over one page. That way you can avoid all the roundup articles of Joe Smith moving to this company and Jane Doe getting promoted to that CEO job.

- Be sure to set your results so that they sort from newest to oldest!

Trapping

FindArticles offers RSS feeds. At the bottom of the search results is the ubiquitous orange button and a link to an RSS feed.

Possibilities

▶ FindArticles makes it very easy to search at a detailed level by source and even by article size. Make the most of these options. Try doing general searches among a particular set of sources.

▶ Occasionally try searching for premium (paid) content and see what kind of information you find.

▶ Try a few very specific searches—FindArticles indexes lots of vertical-market publications.

HighBeam Library

HighBeam Library (highbeam.com/library/) is a paid service. You can search for free—and I recommend you do—so that you get a good sense of whether HighBeam is useful to you or not. If you want to access full articles, it is going to cost you. But there is enough here, it is inexpensive enough, and the trapping options are sufficiently broad that I think it's worth it.

Building your queries

Again, go straight to the Advanced Search page. Like FindArticles, you can pick publications to search. Unfortunately, you can include or exclude only five publications at a time. Note that you can also include or exclude certain types of information, such as newspapers, images, books, transcripts, maps, and so on, rather than choosing from categories of information, such as health, business, sports, and the like (**Figure 7.11**).

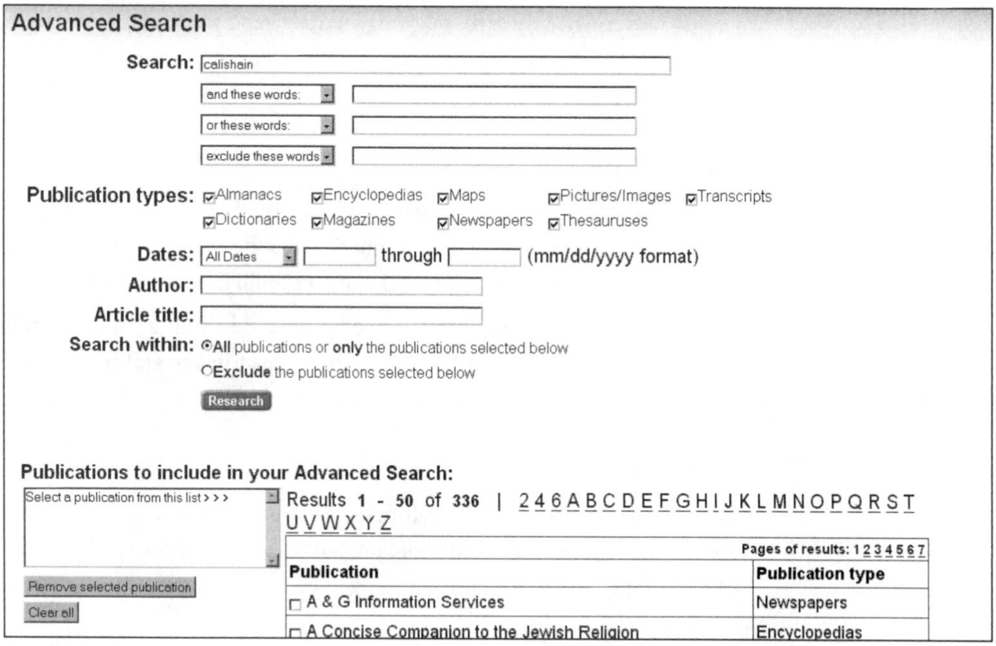

Figure 7.11 HighBeam lets you search not only by specific articles, but also by publication type.

Unless you're researching a very unusual topic, you can safely leave out the maps. The almanacs and dictionaries are questionable as well.

HINT

Check out the Web search. HighBeam offers a Research Group option, which lets you set up a specific set of resources that you want to search. At first glance, the available resources don't look like a lot, until you realize that you have the opportunity to choose aggregate sources like Google News, and very large sources like PR Newswire. Check the sources here and see if they'd be useful to you.

Trapping

HighBeam offers several opportunities for trapping searches. You can set up an RSS feed based on keyword searching (and actually you can set up RSS feeds for publications, which will cover new articles released in the publications you specify). You may also set up e-mail alerts based on keyword searches. And you can save your searches for later use and review them if you've got something that isn't quite worth an alert, but you want to save it for later.

All this convenience isn't free (although a free trial is available). If you wish to subscribe to HighBeam, it will cost you $19.95 for a monthly subscription or $99.95 a year.

Possibilities

▶   HighBeam's advanced search is a wonderful thing. Take advantage, if you can, of extremely narrow queries like the author search: is there a noted journalist in your field that you could be monitoring?

▶   Restricting your searches by media type; running a more general search and restricting the results to, say, just image and transcripts, could yield some very interesting results.

Hoovers

Hoovers (hoovers.com) has a well-deserved reputation as a premium service that provides business information, but what's less known is that it has both a nice news search engine and a business search engine—and it offers e-mail alerts!

Hoovers is not cheap. Subscriptions start at $599 a year and go up to over $10,000 a year (discounts are offered to nonprofits, and periodically special offers are available). However, if you're a business searcher you'll find a lot to love about Hoovers.

Hoovers actually gives you the opportunity to do three types of information trapping: Saved Searches, Watch Lists, and e-mail alerts. Let's take these one at a time. This information-trapping tool gives you the opportunity to get general news alerts and specific company information at the same time.

Saved Searches

The Saved Search page lets you build several different types of saved searches, including company searches, such as companies within a certain radius of a certain place with a certain number of employees, and so on (**Figure 7.12**).

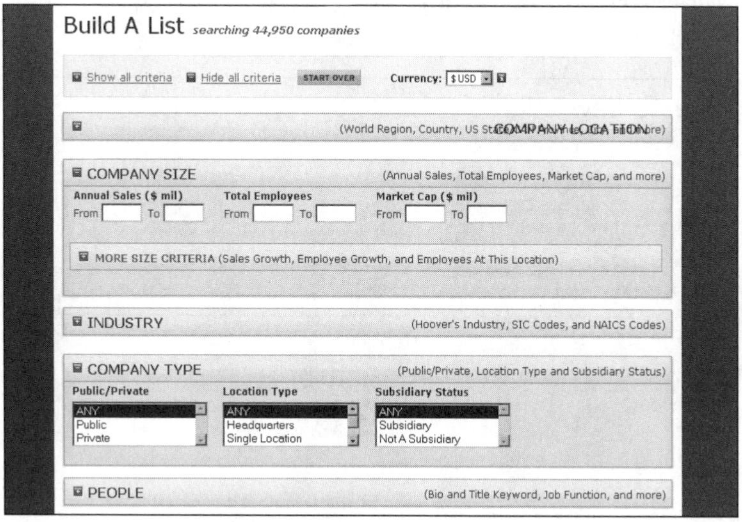

Figure 7.12

Want to do business monitoring within a specified area? The Saved Search is a "must try."

The nuts and bolts of all the different types of Saved Searches is a little outside the scope of this book, so I encourage you to investigate Hoover's offerings. Meanwhile let's take a look at the more prosaic trapping features.

Hoovers' Saved Searches can build a custom news search that lets you search both by keyword and company stock ticker. You won't have the option to choose between publications, but you can choose whether you want to search for news stories, press releases, or both.

You can also search for companies that will or are in the process of filing for an IPO. You can search underwriters, location (state or metro area), and industry. And the stock screener lets you specify a series of data points about publicly traded companies and receive listings of stocks that match those data points (again, this is a little outside the scope of this book, but worth investigating because this type of information isn't easy to find on the Web).

Watch Lists

Hoovers' Watch List feature is much simpler than Saved Searches. Enter a company name or a stock ticker, and you get the option to sign up for significant developments (major news concerning the company, provided daily), news alerts, and press releases (either delivered daily or as they're available) (**Figure 7.13**).

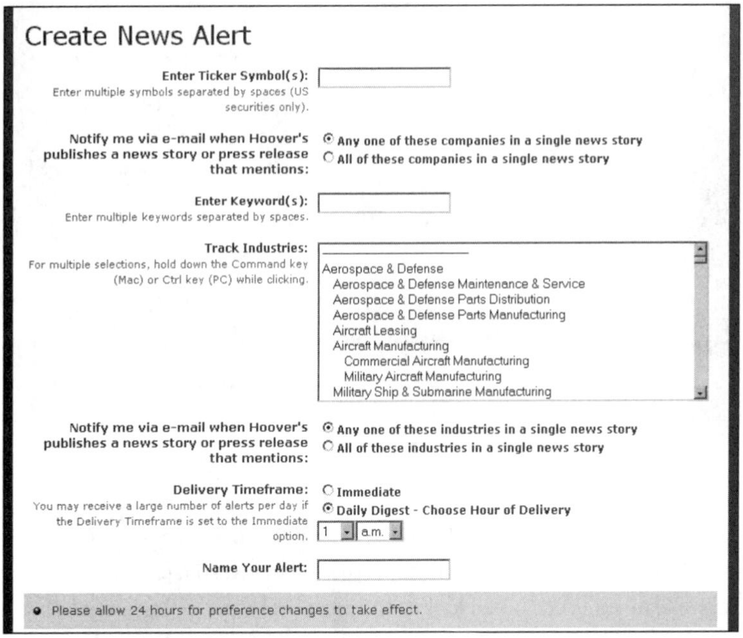

Figure 7.13

Hoovers lets you combine stock symbols with keywords for e-mail alerts.

In addition, there's also the option to add a keyword to the watch list. Be sure to take advantage of this if your interest in a company is specific—for example, if you want to monitor Coke to see when it starts using Splenda in its diet drinks, enter **Splenda** in the keyword box.

E-mail alerts

The Watch Lists and Saved Searches have e-mail components, but they're also saved to a My Hoovers page that aggregates all that information. On the other hand, e-mail alerts are just what they sound like: major e-mail. The e-mail alerts screen lets you choose e-mail alerts for stock ticker symbols (or even multiple symbols within the same story) or specified keywords. You can have news alerts delivered to you as they occur or in a daily digest (you specify the hour). As you might expect, the available news search slants toward the business and the general, but it's fairly extensive.

WARNING!

If you get Hoovers e-mail alerts sent to you "as they occur," you could get a lot of e-mail!

Building your queries

Hoovers does not offer much in the line of fancy syntax, so stick with general keywords and phrases.

HINTS

- Hoovers gives you an opportunity to do monitoring for stock tickers combined with keywords. Take advantage of this feature.
- If you're interested in business, try some of Hoovers' more abstract searching using the IPO targeting and company builder features.

Trapping

Hoovers does offer a lot of e-mail alerts, but some of its searches are relegated to the My Hoovers page. I would make as much use of the e-mail alerts as possible and remind myself to periodically visit the My Hoovers page.

Possibilities

Hoovers costs a lot of money, so if you don't take advantage of as many features as possible, you're wasting some serious cash. If you do any kind of business monitoring, you've got to make the most of this site. How could you best monitor using a combination of stock symbols and keywords? Are there any ways you could make really unusual searches, such as the ability to find a company within a specified radius, applicable to your search?

Northern Light

Northern Light (nlresearch.com) used to be both a Web search engine and a news search engine that offered free news alerts. The site has undergone a couple of incarnations since that time and has now become a paid service, but it's worth the $9.95 a month, especially if you're looking for news in periodicals that cater to a particular industry. There is a 30-day trial period available, and searching the available libraries is free. Accessing full-text articles will cost you, however.

Building your queries

Visit Northern Light's Search Help page at nlresearch.com/help.php. Northern Light offers a wide variety of advanced searching, including the ability to use *stemming* in your searches. Stemming involves searching for a string of letters with a special character at the end—usually an asterisk. A search engine that allows stemming will find all versions of that string of letters. For example, searching for moon* would find moon, moons, moonlight, moonbeam, and so on.

HINTS

- Take advantage of Northern Light's ability to narrow the searches by industry (see the trapping notes that follow).
- If you're interested in monitoring a particular industry or business within an industry but you're having a hard time generating the perfect query, Northern Light's search alerts menu is a blessing.

Trapping

Once you're registered and logged in to Northern Light, you'll see several tabs. Click My Alerts, and a page displays that has a section labeled My Search Alerts. From there, you'll see a Create New Alert button. When you click that button, a form displays for creating a narrowly focused alert (**Figure 7.14**).

You can limit your search by business function (sales and marketing, human resource management, and so on). You can also limit your search by Websites, News, and News Archives, but I recommend keeping the search focused on Publications, which finds everything. Use the Preview Results button to check and make sure you're getting a good number of results—not too many, and not zero. (Use the radio button on the query page to ensure that you're getting results sorted by date and not relevance, so you can easily see how many results for your search have been generated in the last few months.)

Figure 7.14 A lot to fill out, but you can really narrow your queries.

When you've adjusted the query and the publications so you're getting a useful number of results, click the Save Alert button. You'll be kicked back to the original Search Alerts page, only this time there is a saved alert available. You can review any results since you last looked at the alert, as well as edit the alert (change the search parameters) or delete it.

One caveat: when Northern Light sends you e-mail alerts, they give you only a link back to the content, not a summary of the content in the articles found. Furthermore, the information is sent in an HTML e-mail. If you use an e-mail account that is not HTML-capable, then you won't be able to link back to Northern Light's alerts.

Possibilities

We've looked at search engines that break out searches by publication, and another engine that breaks out searches by kind of content. Northern Light breaks down its sources by kind of research. See if you can use specific types of research when building your research queries.

News searching is the cornerstone of information trapping. When you're trapping at news search engines, you're referring to a constantly updating pool of information that is, on the whole, far more credible than the entire Web. But the downside is that you're missing things like personal commentary and information and commentary on topics that have not attracted the notice of the media. For these types of searches, you need to be monitoring blogs.

Searching Blogs

Blogs don't have the credibility of established media, but as a resource for commentary, discussion, unusual perspectives on current events, and coverage of topics that might not have hit the radar of the media, they are invaluable. True, you will have to turn your—ahem—bullpuckey detector way up. On the other hand, you'll find resources and perspectives that you won't find in major media in a month of Sundays.

Feedster

We looked at Feedster (feedster.com) earlier in the book. It's great for finding RSS feeds, and blog commentary as well!

Building your queries

Feedster indexes only RSS feeds, which means that its advanced search should be hideously complicated and let you do all kinds of strange and very detailed searching. But it doesn't. It's a very basic keyword search with the option to find links, entries from a particular feed, etc.

That's not to say that there isn't a couple of special syntax available. You can search for words in a title using a title syntax like this: **title:keyword**. You can search for one word or another using **or**. Remember that you're searching blog commentary, so you might want to use more casual language or even try introducing a few misspellings into your queries if your search would seem to warrant it. For example, if you're doing searches for layman commentary on medical issues, you might use less formal terms.

HINTS

- Don't be afraid to do a lot of different queries. Searching commentary isn't like searching news stories.
- Try using slang and other informal language when doing your search.

Trapping

Feedster offers two ways to keep up with new search results. The first one is via RSS feed, which is the one I use. You're also supposed to be able to get new results via e-mail alerts, but I've never had good luck with that. I set up the alerts, but I've never actually received any e-mails. I recommend sticking to the RSS feeds.

Possibilities

Unfortunately, Feedster and other search engines tend to get overwhelmed with results from *splogs*, or spam blogs. To avoid this, be sure to make your queries as specific as possible.

IceRocket blogs

IceRocket (icerocket.com) offers a variety of different searches that I encourage you to experiment with. However, we'll focus on blog searching.

Building your queries

IceRocket doesn't offer a bunch of special syntax, so focus on keywords. Take a look at the Advanced Search page to see if you can take advantage of searching by post title or tag (which I talk about in future chapters).

> **HINT**
>
> When you're running some experimental queries, pay attention to IceRocket's Search Results page. It shows you what "tags" are used in the posts that you're finding, and those tags may in turn help you build better and more detailed searches.

Trapping

Check out the right side of the page for RSS feeds of your search.

Possibilities

Alhough IceRocket's search offerings are rather thin, I like what it offers after the search results. Click the Trend It button at the top of the search results to see how popular your query term has been in blog posts (**Figure 7.15**).

This is a great way to find more popular query words that you can use with your topic. You may end up using this more than IceRocket's blog search itself!

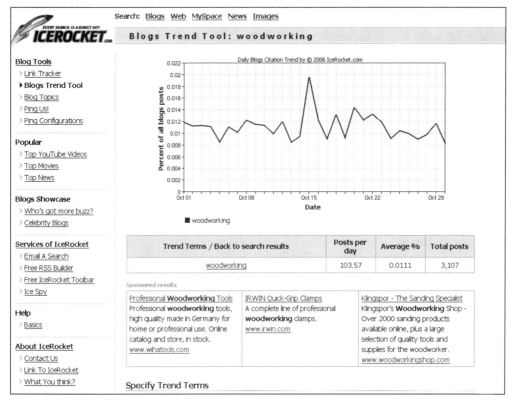

Figure 7.15 IceRocket lets you view the popularity of your query term.

Blogdigger

Blogdigger (blogdigger.com) isn't the best-known blog search engine in the world, but it's got a solid pool of blogs that it searches and offers a couple of interesting features.

Building your queries

Like IceRocket, Blogdigger doesn't offer much in the way of special syntax. Focus on keyword searches.

HINTS

- In addition to a general blog search, Blogdigger offers Blogdigger Local, which allows you to narrow your search to a city and state. I find this works better when you search for a brand name or a proper name instead of a general search (if searching Colorado, using "Denver Post" works better than using "newspaper"). If you're running a local business, this is a terrific way to get blogging feedback on your industry in your area.

- Blogdigger also offers Blogdigger Groups, which allows you to combine several blogs together (as long as they have RSS feeds). This is a handy way to review several blogs at once via an RSS feed. My only recommendation is that you make sure the blogs are not overly active, or you'll have a hard time keeping up with them.

Trapping

Like IceRocket, the RSS feed for keyword searches is on the right side of the Search Results page. There's a link for an Atom feed there, too.

Possibilities

▶ Blogdigger has low volumes of results, but also very low volumes of blog spam.

▶ Feel free to use more general queries here.

▶ Is there any way that your searching could take advantage of the Blogdigger Local feature?

Google Blog Search

With blogs being so hot, it's no surprise that Google has picked up on the interest and made available its own blog search (google.com/blogsearch). And though in some respects it has a ways to go before it catches up with established blog search engines like Technorati, it's still a useful addition to your monitoring toolkit.

Building your queries

You can build your queries using Google's advanced blog search at google.com/blogsearch/advanced_blog_search. If you're a frequent user of Google, this should look rather familiar; a lot of Google's Web search technology transfers to the blog search. However, this doesn't mean that you should use the blog search the same way you use a Web search. URL searches, for example, aren't going to be very useful. Instead, try narrowing your query by limiting words to a blog post's title, or by the language of the blog.

HINTS

- Google's blog search, for some reason, defaults to providing results in order of relevance. Use the link on the right side of the page to get the results by date.
- Use the "References" link with each search result to see other blog posts that link to the one in the search result.

Trapping

Google's blog search makes trapping easy. At the bottom of each search result page are four links. Two are for getting the results as an Atom feed (10 or 100 results) and two of them are for getting the results as an RSS feed (again, 10 or 100 results). I recommend you stick with the ten results. If you've generated a search that provides 100 results at a time, your query is probably not narrow enough!

Possibilities

If you've used Google for any length of time, the syntax of Google's blog search will be very familiar to you. Take advantage of that and go for building more complex queries.

Sphere

Sphere (sphere.com) is a newer blog search that's got a very nice set of search results.

Building your queries

At first blush, Sphere doesn't seem to have much in the line of special syntax, but if you check out the Hint page at sphere.com/tips, you'll see a variety of available syntax, including page title, blog names, and domain name (**Figure 7.16**).

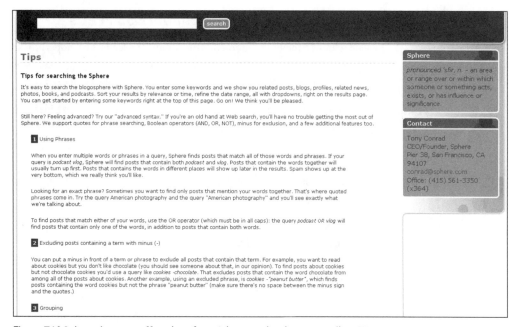

Figure 7.16 Sphere does not offer a lot of special syntax, but has an excellent Tips page.

> **HINT**
>
> If you're hunting more for blogs than for individual entries, try the Featured Blogs offering, which suggests blogs based on your keyword search. Sphere also offers blog profiles, which provide information about the activity level and content of each blog in the search result.

Trapping

Look for the orange RSS button at the top of the search results page.

Possibilities

▶ If you're having a hard time finding blogs that match your topic, use Featured Blogs in conjunction with a couple of general keyword searches.

▶ If you are thinking about tracking a single blog and don't know if it's worthwhile, use the Blog Profiles feature to see how active the blog is and how much data you could potentially get from it.

Managing Keyword-Searchable RSS Feeds

I spend a lot of time in this book talking about RSS feeds, and hopefully at this point you're as enthusiastic about them as I am. Okay, that may be a little too much to ask. But hopefully you find them as interesting as I do.

RSS feeds are one thing. But the next level beyond that—the next idea—is keyword-based feeds. Keyword-based feeds, as you might remember, are feeds based on searches on the query words that you specify. So instead of very general feeds—all the national news from CNN, for example—you can get feeds for just the town or the mayor of the town, or even the mayor's favorite hobby.

Having RSS feeds that are very specifically focused on just the topics in which you're interested will, as you might imagine, save you a lot of time when you're checking your information traps. On the other hand, when you decide that you want to generate and use many keyword-based RSS feeds, you run into another problem: how to *efficiently* generate keyword-based RSS feeds. The problem is that you end up having to do so many of them.

Take Google News, for example. You might go to Google News and decide that you want to get three of its general RSS feeds: one for technology, one for business, and one for science. Compare that to getting keyword-based RSS feeds. You might decide that there are fifteen keyword-based RSS feeds that would be relevant and useful to your topic. So you'd have to run each of those fifteen searches and save them as an RSS feed. Now multiply those fifteen searches by every resource that offers keyword-based RSS feeds, and you'd spend an astonishing amount of time just setting up the feeds. I have attempted to solve that problem with a tool called Kebberfegg.

Using Kebberfegg

Kebberfegg, which you can find at kebberfegg.com, is a free service that attempts to make it very easy to set up keyword-based RSS feeds across many resources—over 3 dozen as of this writing (**Figure 7.17**). You can view your generated feeds as a plain HTML list, or you may get them as an OPML file that you can import into an RSS feed reader. (Think of an OPML file as a bookmark file for RSS feed readers.)

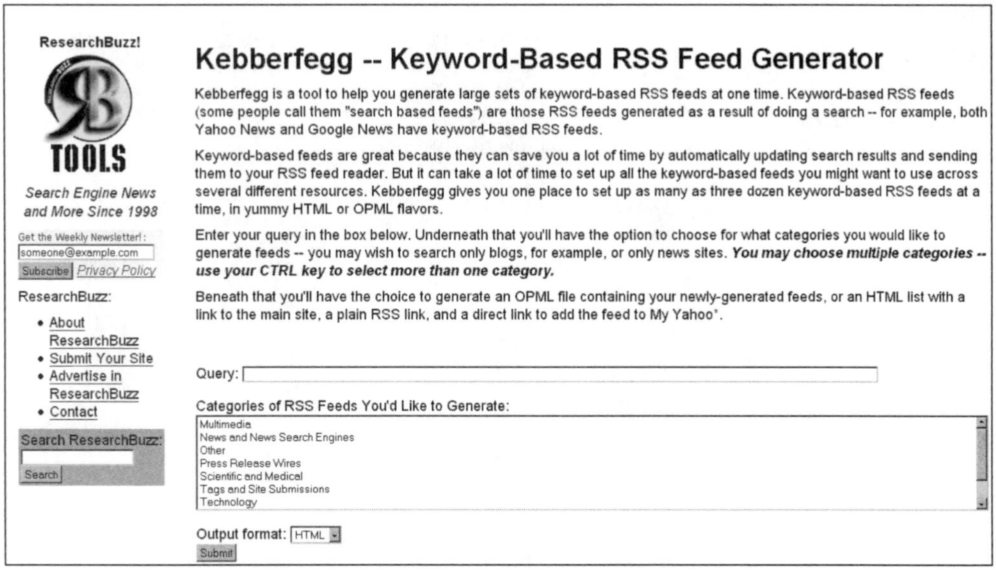

ResearchBuzz!

TOOLS

Search Engine News and More Since 1998

Get the Weekly Newsletter! :

someone@example.com

Subscribe | *Privacy Policy*

ResearchBuzz:

- About ResearchBuzz
- Submit Your Site
- Advertise in ResearchBuzz
- Contact

Search ResearchBuzz:

Search

Kebberfegg -- Keyword-Based RSS Feed Generator

Kebberfegg is a tool to help you generate large sets of keyword-based RSS feeds at one time. Keyword-based RSS feeds (some people call them "search based feeds") are those RSS feeds generated as a result of doing a search -- for example, both Yahoo News and Google News have keyword-based RSS feeds.

Keyword-based feeds are great because they can save you a lot of time by automatically updating search results and sending them to your RSS feed reader. But it can take a lot of time to set up all the keyword-based feeds you might want to use across several different resources. Kebberfegg gives you one place to set up as many as three dozen keyword-based RSS feeds at a time, in yummy HTML or OPML flavors.

Enter your query in the box below. Underneath that you'll have the option to choose for what categories you would like to generate feeds -- you may wish to search only blogs, for example, or only news sites. *You may choose multiple categories -- use your CTRL key to select more than one category.*

Beneath that you'll have the choice to generate an OPML file containing your newly-generated feeds, or an HTML list with a link to the main site, a plain RSS link, and a direct link to add the feed to My Yahoo'.

Query: [   ]

Categories of RSS Feeds You'd Like to Generate:

Multimedia
News and News Search Engines
Other
Press Release Wires
Scientific and Medical
Tags and Site Submissions
Technology

Output format: [HTML ▾]

Submit

Figure 7.17 Kebberfegg can quickly generate lots and lots of RSS feeds.

Let's take a look at how it works. It's really easy:

1. Enter in the query box the words you want to search. Then notice that beneath the query box is the category list.

2. Generate a keyword feed list for one category, or select multiple categories by pressing the Ctrl key. (You could also select all categories by pressing Ctrl + A, but I don't recommend it—I'll tell you why in a minute.)

3. Notice beneath the category selection the keyword feed sources from each category are displayed. You also have the option to receive the results in HTML or OPML. Choose HTML for now.

   When the query is finished, you get a result that looks like **Figure 7.18**.

4. For each result, you can add the feed to My Yahoo, forward it to your e-mail via RSSFwd, or a couple of other options. You can even just look at the plain RSS feed!

Figure 7.18

Kebberfegg gives you a list of keyword-based feeds in several different formats.

Using Kebberfegg generates *a lot* of RSS feeds. You may decide you don't want as many, or you may decide that one RSS feed provides better results than the other ones you've generated. Because of that I recommend you not just dump the feeds into your RSS feed reader and prune them later. Instead, use the Add to My Yahoo button on each feed to get a preview of what the feed will look like. (You don't have to have a Yahoo account to do this.) This will give you a page with the feeds' last five headlines. A quick glance at those is often enough to let you know whether you want to monitor that feed or not.

> **TIP**
>
> Sometimes the My Yahoo preview doesn't work, especially when there are no results for your keyword search. In that case, I would set the ones aside that look interesting but don't work in Yahoo, and preview them one-by-one in an RSS-capable browser like Firefox.

Using OPML results

Instead of generating HTML files, advanced users may want to check out the OPML results, which generate a set of RSS feeds that you can import into an RSS feed reader. Getting your results this way will generate a list that you can save to your computer and then import into your feed reader. But the same warning applies: import these but look them over quickly before you integrate them into your monitoring routine. You'll save yourself a lot of time in the long run by taking a few minutes now.

Breaking up your searches

Kebberfegg makes it really easy to generate keyword-based feeds: if you run three searches generating feeds from all categories, you've generated 100 feeds! Because of the very different sources from which you're generating RSS feeds, you may want to break up your searches. For the tag site searches, you may want to get more general, since you're searching only keywords. In fact, you may want to generate your keyword-based RSS feeds for tag sites separately from the other available keyword-based feeds, since you won't feel the need to compromise between the narrow feeds made for news search engines, general search engines, and blog search, and the general feeds for tags and other few-keyword searches.

Kebberfegg can generate a lot of feeds for you, and save you a lot of time, but you've got to remember the rules: generate queries that are as narrow as possible considering what you're searching, and make sure you review the feeds before you dump them all into your feed reader.

A Few More Sources?

So far we've looked at trapping on general search engines, news search engines, and blog search engines, and we've taken a look at a tool that allows you to generate several keyword-based feeds at one time. It's good to have Web search engines in reserve to filter for and find the minutiae on your topics of interest. News search engines will keep you updated on recent happenings, and the blog search engines will point you toward commentary and that under-the-media-radar material.

Yet you've barely scratched the surface. If you use these three types of searches as the foundation of your trapping, you'll be off to a good start. But if you use them to the exclusion of anything else, you'll have a problem. There are many more types of search engines that could be monitored, but in this chapter we look at two more: commercial and governmental. We then look at finding other search engines that match your interests.

> **TIP**
>
> Because the rules for searching them are so different, we look at two other kinds of trapping—conversations and tags—in Chapter 9. In Chapter 8, I discuss the idea of trapping multimedia.

Trapping Commercial Information

Why would you want to find commercial information? Maybe there's something you want to buy. Maybe you want to monitor Amazon for a certain book. Maybe you want to see how well your industry's items sell on eBay. Maybe you want to know when prices are going up or down. I know some researchers disdain monitoring retail and commercial sites for information, saying, "Those sites are only about prices." But thanks to supply and demand and capitalism, prices can give you an idea of how popular something is (or isn't), and if demand for things is trending up or down. And besides, don't you really want to know when the next Terry Pratchett book is coming out?

Amazon

It might seem weird to start with Amazon (amazon.com) since it's an actual store, not a price aggregation or comparison site. But Amazon is huge, it sells practically everything, and it's popular enough that customers can in some ways reflect the tastes of the Internet as a whole—at least the Internet in that country which Amazon is selling to (Amazon has several versions for several different countries).

Searching Amazon

Amazon has the usual single query box at the top of its pages, but that isn't all Amazon offers by a long shot. Many of its categories of information have their own advanced search engines. Let's look at books, since that's what Amazon is known for. Take a look at the Advanced Search page (the direct URL is amazon.com/exec/obidos/ats-query-page/) and you can see that you can search for a huge variety of features, including ISBN, keyword, format, reader age, and so on. Other categories offer feature searches more relevant to their formats. The advanced search for DVDs is amazing (**Figure 7.19**)!

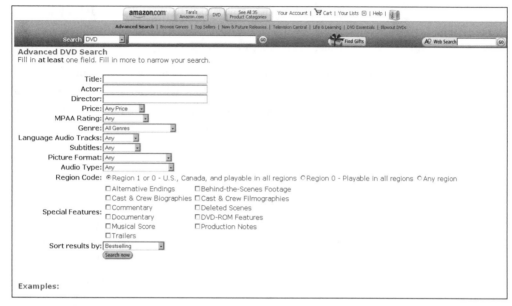

Figure 7.19 Amazon's Advanced DVD Search offers a huge number of options.

You won't get these kinds of search options when you're actually building your searches, but I recommend you use them when you're making your test queries, if any of them are at all relevant to your search. They'll bring to light books (or DVDs or electronics or CDs or whatever) that you might not have thought of, and might help you generate more query words. Asking you to use the wonderful advanced search options that Amazon gives and then telling you to go back and use the more limited alert services sounds counterintuitive, I know. But I want you to at least see what the possibilities are for your topic in the category you're searching before you have to limit yourself with the trapping tools.

Third-party Amazon RSS

YayWasTaken.com offers a generator for Amazon keyword-based feeds at yaywastaken.com/amazon/. Because the feeds are keyword-based, they're more extensive than the ones offered by Amazon. It also offers images, descriptions, and more information than Amazon's feeds. Using the service is simple. Start by entering this URL:

```
yaywastaken.com/amazon/amazon-rss.asp?keywords=keyword
```

Replace **keyword** at the end of the URL with whatever keywords you're interested in. Aside from that, the usual rules apply: get really specific and run some test queries (on Amazon) first.

If you don't want to hack URLs but instead want to fill out a form and get a feed, try Paul Bausch's Amazon RSS feed generator at onfocus.com/amafeed/. Specify the keyword and department in which you're interested, and how you want to sort, and the generator will create a feed for you. You can also generate a feed based on Amazon's power search syntax, if you're familiar with it.

Page monitoring at Amazon

Maybe you're really interested in a keyword-based search, or maybe you're interested in monitoring an entire category. I feel for you! You have one more option, though it may not work that well for you. You have to use a page monitor. You can also use a page monitor if you don't want to use RSS feeds. It's just a bit tricky.

Run the keyword search of your choice. Your keyword should, on its list of results, generate a list of categories on its left that shows you which categories have results that match your search. Pick the category of your choice.

Say, for example, I want to monitor for software related to woodworking. I run a keyword search and pick "software." There are only a few results and they all fit on one page, so I can just put this URL into a page monitor and I'll be set (**Figure 7.20**).

But say I wanted to monitor Home and Garden, which has well over 100 results. The first thing I would do is take a quick look-see at the results and see if there's any keyword I can use to remove results en masse. I notice that there are several parts available from Woodstock International, and they're really not what I'm looking for.

I change my search to **woodworking -woodstock**. That instantly reduces my search results to a manageable one page. Beyond that if I chose I could narrow my results more by choosing a subcategory (kitchen, home and decor), eliminating more query words, etc.

So use a combination of narrow query words and eliminating brand names and words that describe what you don't want and try to get your results

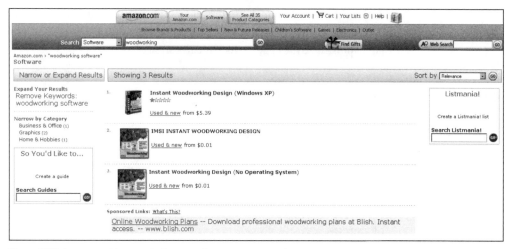

Figure 7.20 An unusual keyword plus a smaller category equals easier monitoring.

down to one page. Then put that page in a page monitor. It isn't perfect, but it's a possibility. Use Amazon's alert offerings whenever you can, or carefully put together an RSS feed via a third-party offering.

eBay

I know I said that Amazon offers everything, but it's nothing like eBay. eBay, an online auction site, not only offers many commercially available items, but items you may not have been aware were for sale, like advertising space on someone's forehead, ghosts, religious icons found in slices of toast, and more. There are several ways to monitor eBay, from services that the site itself offers to third-party services. To use the services that eBay offers, it's best that you have an account.

Searching eBay

Just like Amazon, you start with eBay's advanced search. There are two major differences, however: eBay's advanced search covers its entire site, and you can use the advanced search to build your traps.

I love eBay's advanced search. It's very different from any advanced search I've ever seen. You have some amazing search options here, including searching for items within a certain distance from a specified zip code or major city, searching for maximum and minimum prices, and searching for items that are listed with specific currencies (**Figure 7.21**). There are also more prosaic ways to search, like by category.

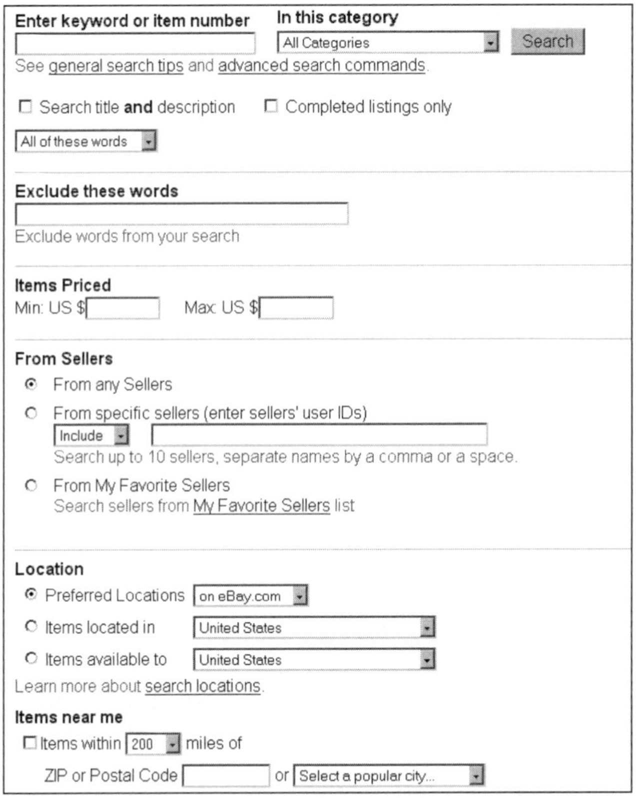

Figure 7.21

eBay's advanced search even offers the ability to search by location.

How you should use this search depends on what your goals are. First go through and narrow the search as much as you can. Start with the categories, then move to where the item is located. If it's suitable, use the feature that lets you narrow your search to a specified radius. It can narrow your results tremendously. Run a few test queries and see what kind of results you're getting.

Then you have a decision to make. Are you monitoring these items with the intention of possibly purchasing something in the future? Do you just want to get an idea of what's ending up being listed online? Then you're all set.

TIP

If you're a retailer looking for wholesale lots on eBay, you may have noticed that sometimes the wholesale bidding gets very fast and very furious. I find that setting a trap for lots that have a "Buy it Now" price can give me a good heads-up on sets of items that can be bought immediately instead of having to go through a bidding war.

Maybe you're a seller instead. Maybe you're not interested in when items get listed, but instead want to know how much items are being sold for. That way you know what to price your items for, or maybe you want to get a sense of what a fair bid price would be since you're planning to buy something expensive.

In that case, go to the top of the Advanced Search form and tick the Completed Listings Only box, which is right under the query box. You only receive an alert when a completed listing for your keywords shows up on your search results. Then you know whether an item sold or not, what it sold for, how many bids, etc.

Once you've generated a query, review the results. If they look good (useful to your topic, not too many of them) choose Add to Favorite Searches at the top of the page. You're asked to name your new search. When you've chosen all that, you're set. eBay will e-mail you whenever a new auction (or a completed auction, depending on your settings) matches your specified queries, for as long as you have indicated.

I love eBay's ability to turn the advanced search into an e-mail alert. But there are other ways to track eBay as well. If you're interested in RSS feeds, you'll be pleased to know there's a third-party service that generates eBay RSS feeds for you, in addition to eBay's RSS feed offerings.

eBay RSS feed offerings

For a while, eBay has offered RSS feeds of general information about its site—announcements and so forth. But now it's offering RSS feeds of its search results. Do a query, and then search at the bottom of the page for a line that's marked Tools. You'll see a little orange RSS feed icon on that line. That's it! You're all set.

Coupons and Best Deals

All work and no play makes Jack a dull trapper. So let me take a few minutes out of the chapters and tell you about some personal trapping that can save you some money—coupon and best deal blogs.

Coupon and best deal blogs are just like what they sound like. They're blogs that aggregate information on specials and pass it on to you as quickly as they can. What's in it for them? A lot of times they use affiliate links, so that when you go to a company's site from their sites and buy something, they get a little cut of the deal. Occasionally the blog is actually a company that sells the product itself.

What's the catch? The catch is that these are specials, and they expire, so you've got to keep on top of the sites if you want to find the best deals. Consider it fun practice for trapping. I don't want to get you or your credit card in trouble, but here are a few best deal sites you may want to know about:

- **Woot** (woot.com/Blog/Default.aspx) might be bad for your wallet—you've been warned! Woot is actually a company that sells things. Every day it offers a super deal on one item. The offer lasts until the end of the day or until Woot runs out of the item. That's it. The items tend to be electronics and the write-ups describing them are a blast to read.

- **Slickdeals** (slickdeals.net) doesn't go for the extensive descriptions and fun writings. Instead it offers single-line descriptions of three or four deals a day from a variety of online stores. Expired deals get a little red "expired" tag next to them. RSS feeds are available.

- **Dealhack** (dealhack.com) strikes a happy medium between Woot and Slickdeals with a little bit of commentary and several offers. At this writing, deals on the front page include everything from a cookware set and a large LCD TV to a refurbished Roomba and DVD sets. Don't miss the rebate, coupons, and clearance sections either.

Looking at these pages is a little different from visiting regular shopping sites, but give them a try.

eBay third-party services

RSS Auction, at www.rssauction.com, actually offers two levels of RSS feed generation. The first one looks an awful lot like eBay's advanced search page! Fill that one out and specify how long you want the feed to be active (from 1 to 12 months) and RSS Auction will generate a feed for you. The second one will generate a feed of items being offered by one particular seller. With both searches you have the chance to mail the RSS feed to you (though I don't know why you'd do that; eBay's e-mail alerts are just fine). RSS Auction also sends out alerts for searches of Buy.com and Half.com.

Shopping and price researching can be fun, but let's shift gears. Let's shift gears a lot. Let's go from things you might want to pay for to things you've already paid for via your taxes: government services. While government sites are not as advanced as some sections of the Internet in offering monitoring services and RSS feeds, they're getting better all the time.

Trapping Government Information

One thing I like about tracking government information is that it's so practical; by setting a few information traps you can become a more informed citizen and learn things that help you take advantage of government services in your community. Let's start with the smallest common unit of government sites, the city site, and then expand to state sites. We'll then look at national services and do a quick overview of international government sites.

City sites

Maybe you know the Web site for your city. In case you don't, let me teach you a couple of tricks. Take the name of your city and plug it into a full-text search engine as part of the phrase `"city of"`. Every time I try this trick it pops the official city site up to the top of the results. If you're not sure your results represent the official site, look for one of three things: a URL ending in .us, a URL ending in .gov, or a description along the lines of "official site of the city of." If you're getting official sites, but not in the state for which you're searching, add the state name as a keyword (`"city of Springfield" Missouri`).

> **TIP**
>
> Sometimes you'll be interested in a city that's fairly small. It may be so small it really doesn't have a Web site, or there's nothing much there. In this case, you may want to visit the state's Web site. Often states have sections that contain information on their various municipalities.

What are you looking for?

Offerings at various city Web sites vary a lot. Generally the larger the city is, the greater the offerings are, but any city site that's active at all generally has something. It's important to be very specific about what you're looking for.

Depending on your topic, you might look for events calendars, press releases, city council meeting notes, adverse weather announcements, warnings of scams and other crimes, or announcements of changes to city services. That's not to say there isn't much, much more at the average city site, such as online services to provide permits and such, searchable databases of city codes, budgets, contact lists, and so on.

Trapping the information

How deeply you want to trap on a city site depends on what you want to use it for. Want to be a better-informed, more active citizen? Then look for the What's New page and put a page monitor on it if there's no option for e-mail alerts or RSS feeds. Want to keep close tabs on what the city council is doing and the business of the city? Watch the press release pages and monitor the page that has the city council meeting notes.

City sites vary on how many built-in trapping mechanisms they offer. Sometimes they offer a newsletter that covers the entire site. Sometimes they offer e-mail alerts of press releases and alert type information (weather issues, etc). It's rarer that RSS feeds are offered, but more and more feeds are being added to city sites all the time. For the most part, though, I suspect you'll have to rely on your own page monitors. State Web sites have far more information, and from what I can tell are better prepared with alert services.

State sites

Finding a state Web site is simple. Just enter the URL **state.xx.us** in your browser, in which **xx** is the postal code of a state (NY, PA, SC, FL, and so on). Note that this does not work for DC (the address for the District of Columbia is www.dc.gov), or Puerto Rico. Sometimes this URL will redirect to a new one (if you start at **state.hi.us**, you're taken to Hawaii.gov) but this URL will point you to the right place. As you would imagine the state sites offer a whole lot more in the line of services than city sites. They've got lots of services, lots of database lookups, and lots of communications from election officials.

Let's use as an example the state of Wisconsin. It's located at wisconsin.gov.

> ### TIP
>
> If you're getting stuck finding state information, try govengine. com. This site divides out state government data into easy-to-parse lists of information. There are also some countrywide, but state-focused, resources here as well.

As you might imagine, a state's Web site can be overwhelming. Not only does it have to encompass a state's government, but also tourism issues, business considerations, and non-governmental services and opportunities for citizens (like job banks). Because of this, it's easy to go to a government Web site and have your brain lock up!

Instead, let your eye wander over the front page. Some government sites have their information broken out by audience—businesses, visitors, residents, and so on. Others delineate their site by services. And still others go for recent news and pointers to featured offerings.

In the case of the state of Wisconsin, it's a mix. The front page has news and updates in the middle, services and information divided into several broad categories on the left, and quick links to presumably popular products and services on the right. For you, the trapper, there are a couple of specific things to look for.

> ### TIP
>
> Sometimes it's easier to find these things in a text-only site instead of a page that is heavy with graphics. Because of the laws regarding access for the disabled, most government sites have text-only versions. Look for a prominent "text only" link toward the top of the page.

The first thing to look for is some kind of press release page. Many time press releases for all state agencies and offerings are jammed together. Generally less useful is a What's New page, which in my experience focuses more on the state's Web site instead of offline services. Sometimes—more and more frequently—state sites will offer RSS feeds for their Web sites (some even offer e-mail alerts—try to take advantage of that).

The second thing to look for is some kind of membership offering. Some government Web sites offer free registration so that you can create your own My State page, which allows you to specify what you're interested in and get everything on a customized page. Sometimes that's it—no e-mail alerts or RSS feeds—but a customized page is easier to monitor and provides more information.

In a few cases, depending on what state you're looking at and what you're looking for, you may find that nothing really meets your needs for monitoring. In that case, you can either monitor the agency home page that most closely matches your interests or you can monitor the home page of the site itself. Neither is ideal, but either one is better than not looking at the site at all. You can also try searching the state Web site for your query words, and monitoring the query results, but search engine quality across state Web sites varies a lot. Be careful.

Federal sites

As you can see, the state Web sites are a leap in complexity compared to the city Web sites. So you might imagine that the national sites are another leap of complexity. And that is the case, but I think there's been a longer, more consistent effort on the part of the U.S. government to develop its Web presence than there has been for the states as a whole.

There are many places from which you can monitor U.S. government information, but there's one place in particular where I like to start looking.

FirstGov

FirstGov (firstgov.gov/) is an effort by the U.S. government to create a portal of easily accessible government information. And it's done a pretty good job! Of course, it's a tough task. There are tons of government agencies and what seems like infinite programs and departments in which you might be interested. Don't despair! Start with the RSS Feed page, move to the A-Z Agency List and then try the search engine. Note that the search engine is not searching every agency Web page. It's just searching an overview list of the types of agencies available. So keep your queries more general.

The RSS Feed page. Yes, the federal government does offer RSS feeds! And as you might expect it offers a lot of RSS feeds! This aggregation feed (firstgov. gov/Topics/Reference_Shelf/Libraries/Podcast_RSS.shtml) points you to the RSS feed pages of various agencies. If you don't have very detailed, esoteric needs, you might be able to stop here, get a couple of government agency feeds, and be all set. But if that's not the case, well, proceed to the agency list.

The A-Z Agency List (firstgov.gov/Agencies/Federal/All_Agencies/index. shtml). This page includes a comprehensive list of government agencies, from the 9/11 Commission to the Animal and Plant Health Inspection Service, and from the Office of Thrift Supervision to the Wyoming state, county, and city Web sites. It does include pointers to state resources, so this is another place to look if the state homepage is confusing you. If you know the name of the agency, you can go straight to it, but otherwise you can do a little browsing. Sometimes there won't be an agency that covers exactly that you're looking for. In this case, head to the full-text search engine for a little general searching.

FirstGov's full-text search engine is available from a query box on the upper-right part of each page (**Figure 7.22**).

Figure 7.22

The A-Z Agency List with FirstGov's ever-present search box on the upper right.

After spending several chapters encouraging you to get more detailed in your searches, I'm going to back up and ask you to get more general.

Describe in a word or two what you want. If you're looking for census data, type **census**. If you're looking for information on Alaskans, type **Alaskans**. If you're looking for information from a particular state, include the state name.

I've found that the underlying descriptions of the agencies are adequate, so just doing a general search usually locates the information I want. Even though FirstGov offers a huge amount of data, it's still a very small data pool compared to the entire Web. You may have to do a little experimenting to find what you want, but I don't think finding the agency or department relevant to your interests will take long.

Trapping department-level information

As you move between different department homepages, you'll discover two things: the departments do not have a common design and they vary a lot in their trap-worthiness. Let's look at the Department of Agriculture, for example (**Figure 7.23**).

Figure 7.23

The USDA Web site. Notice the news is located in the middle of the page.

Trapping Government-Generated Medical and Scientific Information

Credibility is a very real issue when it comes to researching scientific and medical information online. These are two areas in which, perhaps more than other topic areas, you don't want to find yourself searching among noncredible or undocumented information.

For that reason, you really need to know about PubMed and Science.gov, two governmental Web sites that provide access to scientific and medical research. These are major, busy, well-known sites, and as such have spawned several third-party tools that you may find useful.

- **Science.gov** offers both a searchable subject index of science-related government sites and the full-text information of over 45 million Web pages. Be sure to check out its Advanced Search page. You can narrow your search both by science topic and by date range. Science.gov also offers alerts. Once registered (it requires only an e-mail address, user name, and password), you can run searches and then save the searches as alerts. Alas, search results are only sent out once a week, on Wednesdays.

- **PubMed** (ncbi.nlm.nih.gov/entrez/query.fcgi) is a service of the U.S. National Library of Medicine and provides access to over 50 million citations for life science journals going back to the 1950s. You can do searches from this site, and PubMed does offer the ability to save searches, but in my experience PubMed can be pretty overwhelming for someone with little medical background.

- When I need to search PubMed, I find **ClusterMed**, at clustermed.info/, very useful. It takes your search results and "clusters" them (remember the sidebar on clustering earlier in the chapter?) into topics more easily understood by the non-medical professional. A search for "autism," for example, is clustered into topics including face processing, autism and Asperger's syndrome, and children with autism spectrum disorders. ClusterMed does have a subscription component, but you can also use a free version that's limited to 100 results at a time. Make those queries specific!

- If you want to use PubMed for RSS feeds, I encourage you to try **Hubmed**, at hubmed.org/. Hubmed is an alternative (friendlier) interface to PubMed that also lets you easily generate RSS feeds. It makes PubMed a lot easier to use, especially if you're not a medical professional who might miss some of PubMed's power functions.

Visiting this front page you see no indication of RSS feeds or newsletters to which you may subscribe. What fresh information do you see? You see a pointer to current food recalls. This is a page you could monitor (or get the available alerts by e-mail). Returning to the front page, notice that there's an Announcements and Events box on the front page, which would also benefit from a page monitor. Notice too that there's a Newsroom link that provides you with updates on department events—another candidate for a page monitor.

On the other hand, the U.S. Maritime Administration site puts headlines, announcements, and program listings all on one page—the front page—which makes it a very rich source for a page monitor.

In general, you want to keep an eye out for virtual "press rooms," events announcements, calendars, and anything that begins with the phrase "see our latest." Some places also offer newsletters—those are generally for consumer-level information. If you're looking for something higher-level or more esoteric, you're going to be doing a lot of page monitoring. You will not be able to rely on the newsletters.

The next level of trapping government information is international sites. Most countries have Web sites, but the quality and scope vary even more than they do among city, state, and federal sites.

You have a secret weapon, though. I'll show you what it is in a minute.

Monitoring International Sites

Alas, you can't go to Google and search for **"the country of X"** and get the official country site. Often you get gunk. So you have to rely on a third-party site that aggregates official country sites. Try the CIA Factbook, at cia.gov/cia/publications/factbook/index.html. It provides extensive information about each of the countries of the world, including a map, demographic information, and governmental information (**Figure 7.24**).

But the important thing it provides is the "official" name of the country, which you can then use on a search engine.

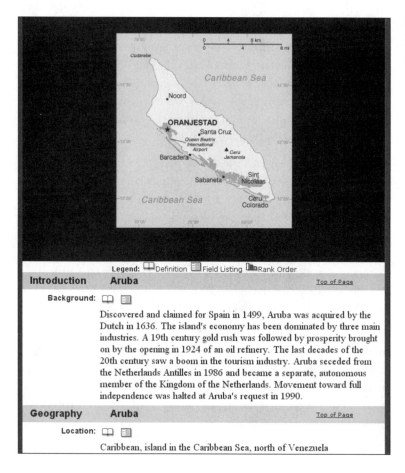

Figure 7.24

The CIA Factbook looks at Aruba.

For example, the conventional long name for Argentina is Argentine Republic. If you do a search for **Argentina** on Google, you will get over 519 million results. However, if you do a search for **"Argentine Republic"**, you will get only 305,000, and the first result at this writing is a page about Argentina from Embassy.org (a very good resource for US embassy information) that points to an official Argentina embassy site, and from there you can continue to the country.

Keep it simple

You might remember earlier in this chapter my observation that city Web sites can be fairly complex, state Web sites can be more complex, and U.S. government Web sites often are even more complex. So you may be assuming that foreign government sites will be the most confusing of all due to your possible nonfamiliarity with that country's government or language. That assumption is partly true and partly false.

Any official government Web site has the potential to be mind-bogglingly complex. But because your interests are probably not going to be in minutiae that might be buried on such a site, it may not be that difficult to find what you're looking for. Except in extremely unusual situations, you will probably not be interested in the day-to-day issues of a country (and if you are, you most likely are familiar with the government or language of your country of interest). Your interest more likely will be broader—a country's environmental record (but not how it handles recycling in one province), or its industries (but not the activities of one bakery in one town).

If you do have such focused interest, then I would presume that you're familiar enough with the country to be able to navigate the offerings of its Web site without too much difficulty. If you aren't, then try to get the information you need from news search engines. Confine your queries to the media of that country, and try to do keyword searches. Sometimes you can get information from keyword searches of the news that it's tough to get from a country's Web site.

Type of content

What will you find on the average country's Web site? It varies a lot. For some countries, you'll barely find a Web presence. For other countries, you'll find very complex offerings that span tens of millions of pages of content.

Let's take for example the Republic of Iceland, which has a Web site at government.is/. Information on the front page includes pointers to various ministries, a link page, and even a pointer to Iceland's constitution. The middle of the front page is kind of a What's New for Iceland (**Figure 7.25**).

Figure 7.25

The Republic of Iceland Web site has all the news located on the center of the front page.

This is a well-designed, extensive Web site, especially for a country of less than 300,000 people. On the other hand, a country's site may be not much more than a page of information about embassies and general demographics about the country, with pointers to third-party links. It will vary a lot.

Where to look and what to monitor

What you end up monitoring on a country's Web site depends on what interests you. Often you can narrow your interest down to a certain ministry or easily described topic (agriculture, business, demographics, for instance). If that's the case, try to find the ministry or department in that country's governmental structure that addresses that topic. For example, I'm interested in digital information collections provided by countries, so I tend to monitor the pages for a country's national library. RSS feeds tend to be scarce in my experience, so you need to use page monitors.

If you have more of a general interest in a country, you're going to have quite a task. If the front page has the latest news on the country's workings, like Iceland, monitor that. If it doesn't, try to find the What's New page (in my experience there's usually some permutation of a What's New page). But don't rely just on the country's site. Find the major media for that country and monitor its headlines—the front page of that media's Web site or RSS feeds. You might also want to find that country's embassy in your country and monitor it too, but really, a general interest in a country is a huge thing to try to encompass. If there's any way at all to do it, narrow it down.

When You Want What Isn't There

My space is limited in this book—there are only so many trees in the world. And you may find that the specific topic for which you want to do information trapping is not presented in this chapter. In this case, you can start your own hunt for search engines and other large-index resources to monitor. I can suggest two techniques for doing that: the easy, incomplete way, or the much more difficult, but more thorough way.

The easy, incomplete way

The easy, incomplete way is to visit some general searchable subject indexes like Yahoo Directory or Dmoz, and browse through the directory to the more general categories for your topic. From there, look for a subtopic called Web Directories, or Directories, or Search Engines (**Figure 7.26**).

This list of Web directories will introduce you to deep sources of information about your topic that will include What's New pages to monitor, pointers to news sources and search engines, and other data-rich places at which you can trap information. The one downside is that searchable subject indexes usually do not include everything, and you may miss some things.

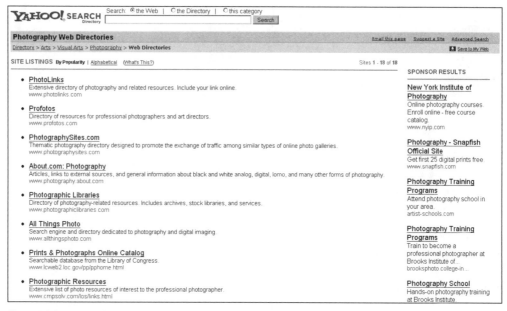

Figure 7.26 Getting photography pointers to information collections from the Yahoo Directory.

The more difficult, but thorough way

With the more difficult way you may find more sites, but it will be, well, more difficult. Start with a full-text search engine and run a query about your topic, but use modifier keywords to slant your results toward search engines and information collections. What kind of modifier keywords? Terms like **search**, or **what's new**, or **category Advanced Search** are good query phrases to use when you want results that are geared toward finding search engines.

What you're trying to add to your topic words are words that would normally appear on a search engine or directory's home page, or on a search engine or directory's search page.

When you're narrowing a query by using a lot of additional words, try to use more general words. The combination of tightly focused topic phrases and more general additional phrases should yield results that contain directories of interest, sometimes blogs, sometimes link lists, and sometimes even pages from various Yahoo properties. **Figure 7.27** shows an example of this search run in Google.

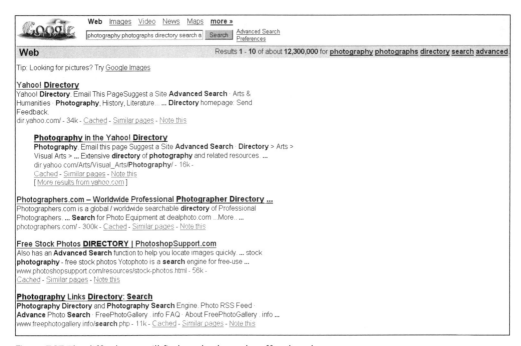

Figure 7.27 The difficult way will find you both good stuff and gunk.

You will find many resources this way, but at the same time you'll find a lot of gunk not relevant to your search. You may also find that you have to rerun the searches again and again to catch various resources. You may end up finding much more material than if you searched only in a directory, but it will take you more time, and it will be more difficult.

Moving Beyond Text-Based Information

So far in this chapter we've looked at various categories of specific information that you might want to monitor, and explored a few ways that you can find even more specific search engines than the ones we've looked at thus far.

But up to this point it's all been text-based. As I'm sure you've noticed, there's far more than text posted online nowadays. There are images, audio, and even video. Thankfully, even as all these different types of information are being added, more search engines and resources are becoming available to trap them. In the next chapter we're going to look at something loud, colorful, and fast-moving: multimedia trapping.

8

Multimedia Trapping

Despite the huge strides in Internet-based multimedia, it's easiest for search engines to index text-based information, so that's what's easiest to find. However, several companies have made huge strides in the development and deployment of multimedia search engines, especially in the past year.

There are several reasons to want to keep up with the latest cool podcasts or the newest audio or the latest video. Many blogs have turned to providing an audio or video format (especially corporate and marketing blogs), and video online has exploded in the last year. For example, sites like YouTube and Yahoo Video have been indexing thousands of hours of content.

You can track multimedia with traps, but you have to do it in a roundabout way, specifically by starting your multimedia search using general, text-based search engines! After that, you can go for specific multimedia sites in a variety of categories, from audio, to photos, to video.

Searching Audio

Why would you want to trap audio? The variety of audio content that's indexed and available online is almost as varied as the kind of text content. There's music, of course, but there are also podcasts (like talk shows, with a huge variety of topics), instructional audio, conference calls, interviews, and more. Even if you're not sure if your topic would be served by trapping for audio, at least try a few queries at the resources we cover here, and see what you find. You might change your mind! We'll start by using Google's regular search engine to find audio, specifically MP3s.

Using general search engines

Though it's unlikely that you'll find actual ready-to-play multimedia in Google's Web search results (except for one resource which we look at a little later in the chapter), you can find pointers to multimedia. It just takes a little search tweaking and a special syntax we haven't looked at yet.

I'm referring to the filetype syntax. Filetype finds pages that have a specified string at the end. Searching for **filetype:mp3** yields MP3 files that have been indexed by Google. To narrow your results, you must use very broad keywords (such as **reggae**, **rock**, **metal**, **"Dance Dance Revolution"**, etc.). Using this syntax shows you that Google does index those files, but unfortunately not their contents. In other words, Google can tell you that there's an MP3 file in a certain place, but not what words are in it, how long it is, etc.

TIP

In talking about music online, we can't avoid the fact that there are legal and non-legal sources of music available. Your searches will find you both. When deciding what you're going to download, take the high road and go for the legal music. That way, you won't have to worry about the Recording Industry Association of America (RIAA) sending you a subpoena or about downloading something you don't want—like a virus coming from illegal or shady sites.

The MP3 file search is, depending on what you're looking for, either useful in a very narrow way (it certainly gets you few enough results that you should be able to monitor them easily using a Google Alert) or a silly party trick. If you're doing genealogy searches, for instance, a general Google search for MP3 files might not be helpful. If in your case this type of search falls into the "silly party trick" category, then you can move away from Google and try either some other search engines that are audio oriented or some massive audio archives. In those you might find narratives and interviews with people who lived in the area where your family lived a hundred years ago.

TIP

Try a news search engine if you're looking for MP3 music downloads. Sometimes you're able to find pointers to new band sites or MP3 aggregation sites. Try a keyword for the kind of music or audio content you like plus the words `"mp3 download"`. So you could search for `reggae mp3 download` or `mashups mp3 download`. You may not get a lot of results, but you will often bump into things you might not have found otherwise.

Using audio-only search engines

Audio search engines are all over the map in what they offer and what kind of search limitations you can use. One thing most of them have in common is that they're not very easy to trap. With that in mind you really need to narrow your searches. Thankfully the first tool we're looking at, Singing-fish, makes narrowing searches really easy.

Singingfish

Note that Singingfish (singingfish.com) searches both audio and video one at a time. That's the first and most important way to narrow your search results. There are more options on the left side of the page (**Figure 8.1**).

Figure 8.1

Singingfish lets you narrow without using keywords.

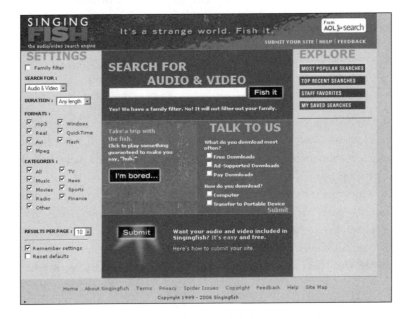

You can narrow your results by format, category, and duration, which is a big one if you're searching for music. That's because if you limit your results to files more than one minute long or (even better) three minutes long, you eliminate partial songs and song samples which otherwise will clutter up your results.

You can only display up to 20 results at a time, and Singingfish does not offer RSS feeds or e-mail alerts, so narrow your query and what you're searching as much as you can so that the page monitor can do its job. On the positive side, you have many opportunities to limit your results, and I find that Singingfish brings in results from all over the Internet.

TIP

Having trouble narrowing your results? Band and artist names can work wonders, but when even that doesn't work, try adding the keywords *live*, *interview*, *new*, *mix*, or *preview*.

Ithaki

Ithaki (ithaki.net/multimedia/) is a meta-search engine that offers several different types of searches, including MP3 and MIDI files. You don't get any search options for its MP3 search beyond keywords, but I find that Ithaki finds a limited and ultimately monitorable set of results. If you want to trap for a more general keyword, like a musical genre, start here. Again, you have to use a page monitor; no RSS feeds or e-mail alerts are available.

Google's Song Search

Remember how I noted earlier in the chapter that there was one way to directly search for audio content on Google without noodling around with special syntax? This is it—sort of. If your audio interest is in music, you might find this search useful.

There isn't a direct URL for using this feature. Instead, you start your search on Google. Search for a musician name, band name, or song name. If Google matches it (and in my experience it sometimes misses; Google doesn't have music results for all musicians), a band name and more information displays at the top of the page. From there, you can drill down into more music results for musicians, album names, and even song names.

This service is of limited usefulness for an information trapper. If you want to monitor a musician for new releases, Amazon's a much better way to go. But if you wanted to do something really offbeat like watch for songs with a certain keyword in the title, you could do it using Google's Song Search and a page monitor.

AltaVista Audio Search

If you're an old-school Internet searcher, you might be raising an eyebrow—who in the world uses AltaVista nowadays? Everybody still uses it for Babelfish, and I recommend also using it for the audio search (altavista.com/audio/default). As you can see from the front page, you can specify several different types of audio, from MP3, to Real, to AIFF. You can also filter your searches by audio lasting more or less than a minute. I recommend you search for more than a minute to avoid song clips. Search results aren't available in RSS feeds, darn it, but at least you can get 50 results to a page and monitor that. To get 50 results at a time, visit AltaVista's Web search at AltaVista.com and change the settings to 50 results per page (**Figure 8.2**).

Figure 8.2

Tweaking AltaVista's
Web search settings
makes audio search
easier.

AltaVista doesn't say that impacts the audio search, but it does.

Searching the Internet and even multimedia-specific engines for audio is a hit-or-miss proposition. Fortunately you've got an option besides search engines: several different archives contain music, podcasts, and general audio files.

Let's start with a real hot topic: podcasts.

Searching and monitoring podcasts

Podcast, podcast, podcast! Just like RSS a few years ago, podcast is now officially the buzziest buzzword to fly around the Internet. Everyone's getting a podcast. Some people are even getting vidcasts. But what the heck is a podcast to start with, and how can it help you with your information trapping? Let's begin with the basics.

What is a podcast?

A podcast is an audio file—usually an MP3—that's distributed automatically to audio-playing devices like iPods, or audio-playing software on a computer. It's distributed via a special kind of RSS file. (Remember what we talked about earlier in this book? RSS is just a kind of XML, and XML is just a text file that uses a certain kind of markup language.) You subscribe to podcasts in the same way you subscribe to RSS feeds.

Podcasts are audio files, but you may also start hearing about vidcasts—which is the same concept only using a video file instead of an audio file. Vidcasts are in early development and the concept is very much the same, so we'll stick with audio podcasts for the purpose of this section.

What do you need to listen to a podcast?

There are lots of different software packages out there for listening to podcasts. A free program that might do the trick for you is iTunes, from Apple. You may download iTunes for either Windows or Mac at apple.com/itunes/download/. If you have an Apple-brand music player, like an iPod, you can use that to play podcasts. If you don't, you can play podcasts from your computer.

Why should you listen to a podcast?

Podcasts are like blogs. They're not quite as numerous (yet) but they're every bit as varied. I suspect that no matter what your interest, you'll find a podcast that fits. And podcasts are more portable. If you trap an interesting text news story, you'll probably end up reading it at your computer desk. On the other hand, if you find a podcast series that's worth listening to every episode, you can load it on an iPod or a different music player, and take it with you. You can listen to it in your car. You can listen to it while you're working out. You don't have to sit in front of the computer.

You may have noticed that there are podcast series and podcast episodes. These equate to blogs and blog entries. A single podcast would be a blog entry. All of the podcast episodes would be the blog. For the most part, you might find podcasts for which all episodes are appropriate to your trapping. On the other hand, you might have an interest that's esoteric enough that only individual podcast episodes suit your needs. As you'll see in the next two sections, you have the option to find both podcasts to which you can subscribe and keyword-based RSS feeds of interesting podcast episodes.

Finding podcasts

Let's start with finding podcasts in general. As you might imagine, finding podcasts is a lot like finding blogs—you can look in search engines and directories.

Podspider (podspider.com) offers both a searchable subject index of pod-casts and the ability to search podcasts by keyword (podcasts in several different languages are offered). Podcast listings include descriptions and pointers to the last couple of episodes. Beware! Like blogs, podcasts can be started and abandoned. What's the point in subscribing to a podcast when the last episode is more than a year old?

Yahoo Podcasts (podcasts.yahoo.com/) lets you search for podcasts or browse a searchable subject index. In addition to searching for podcasts, you can search just for podcast episodes (**Figure 8.3**). Unfortunately the podcast episodes aren't listed by date, but you could still try to watch a set of search results via a page monitor. Yahoo Podcasts also lists podcasts that are popular, as well as podcasts that are highly rated by listeners.

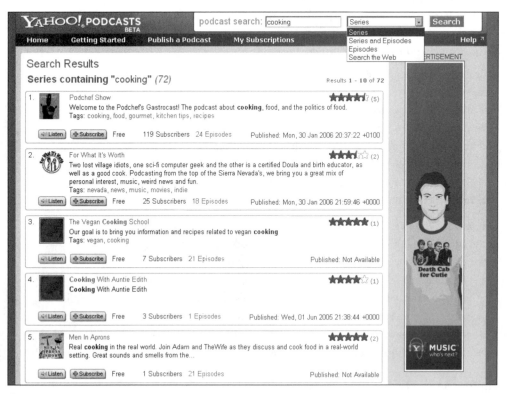

Figure 8.3 Browse and find both podcasts and podcast episodes.

Podcast Directory (podcast.net/) has many different ways you can browse available podcasts. You can search them by location. You can browse them by tag, or by popularity. You can even browse through a video podcast directory. If you have a general interest in podcasts, you might want to subscribe to any of the several RSS feeds that list popular podcasts. And don't miss the sections that provide extensive lists of hardware and software for listening to podcasts.

Get a Podcast (getapodcast.com/) is basically a podcast search engine. The front page lists a variety of stats, including the latest searches, new podcasts, popular podcasts, and recently viewed podcasts. Podcast listings include a list of recent episodes available for that podcast, a description and number of page views, and extensive episode descriptions when available (**Figure 8.4**).

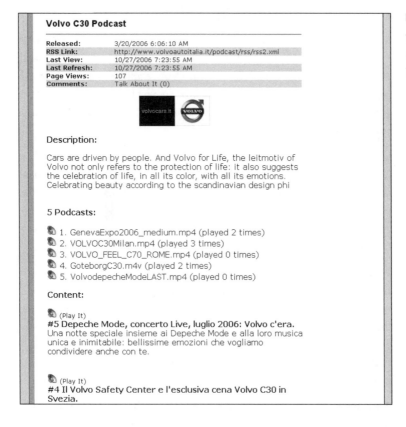

Figure 8.4

Want easy-to-review details about podcasts? This is the place to look.

This is a great place to get an overview of what a podcast offers in its episodes.

The resources we've just examined are great for showing you what podcasts are available, but you might not want to subscribe to entire podcasts. Instead, you might just want to hunt for episodes that are relevant to your topic of interest. You can do that with keyword-based RSS feeds for podcasts. There's even one search engine that lets you search the audio of podcasts!

For the resources that follow, all you have to do is run a keyword search and save the RSS feed for that search. You then add the RSS feed to iTunes as a podcast. Bingo. As new podcast episodes match your keyword, those episodes will be automatically downloaded to iTunes. That's all there is to it! You can catch up with your information trapping by listening to podcasts as you work out at the gym.

Monitoring podcasts by keyword

del.icio.us may sound familiar to you—wait a minute—isn't del.icio.us a tagging site? Yes! And guess what, you can search for the tag **podcast**, along with any other keyword in which you're interested (**del.icio.us/ tag/podcast**). So the URL would work if you're just looking for podcasts in general, or you could add a keyword to it, like this: **http://del.icio.us/tag/ podcast+reggae**.

Monitoring Del for tagged podcast episodes doesn't work quite as well in iTunes as the two other resources we look at in this section (there's no guarantee that a Del user is going to link to an actual podcast as opposed to the podcast's Web site). But this trap does turn up some very unique finds. Try it for some of the more general keywords that are getting you too many results in other search engines.

Blogdigger Media (blogdigger.com/media/) is a blog search engine, but it also offers a lot of unique searches as well, like this media search. It doesn't search just podcasts; it can also search video and images too (make sure those options are unchecked if you want to focus only on podcasts). Blogdigger doesn't seem to have as large a database as some of the larger search engines like Technorati and Feedster, but it offers a number of multimedia searching options.

PodZinger (podzinger.com) is very cool. Up to this point all the search engines we've looked at let you search for keywords within a description of a podcast or an episode of a podcast. But PodZinger lets you actually search within the transcribed audio of a podcast! How nifty is that? If you're trying to run very specific searches, or you keep coming up with keywords that don't ever seem to make it into episode descriptions, try PodZinger. Bear in mind that automatic auto-to-text transcription isn't always perfect, and you may have to do some experimenting to get a query that gets you a useful number of results.

Podcasts only sound like they're really esoteric. Actually they're based on two longstanding technologies (RSS and MP3) that work very well together. Use them as an opportunity to continue your information trapping while getting unchained from your desk.

> ### TIP
>
> There are dozens of paid music services online. If you subscribe to any of them (iTunes is probably the best known,) be sure to check and see if they offer any kind of new music roundup. iTunes (apple.com/itunes), for example, has "New Music Tuesdays" and updates on the front page of its service to keep you posted as to what music has been added to the site. You can also monitor Amazon for new CD content, as we talked about earlier—often Amazon has samples of music content available.

Audio archives

Audio archives are often easier to monitor than search engines. An archive is one collection of information, and often resides on one server, so you know it's being completely indexed. There are probably thousands of music collections online, so I will hit only the highlights here, which include a fantastic old-timer, an unexpected resource, and an amazing archive.

IUMA

IUMA (iuma.com), short for Internet Underground Music Archive, has been around since 1993, offering music in a dazzling array of genres from a dazzling array of artists. Music is available in Real format and in full MP3 songs. Do some sample searching here before you decide what you're looking for—IUMA offers an amazing number of genres. You may not have heard of any of the artists here but you will find something that interests you, I promise. And bless its little heart, IUMA makes it easy to get updates on the latest additions.

On the front page, look for the New Arrivals section. You can browse recent listings by genre, state, and how recently new material was added to the site (from the last seven to the last 30 days). There are no RSS feeds for this page, but it's a perfect candidate for a page monitor. Just look out for pop-up ads—IUMA has a lot of them.

MP3

MP3 (mp3.com/) started out as a rather small site, then it broke out to be one of the darlings of the Internet era, and then it self-imploded like so many other companies, and then it died, and then CNET brought it back. Like IUMA, MP3.com contains information and songs from thousands of artists in dozens of genres. Unlike IUMA, some of these artists are very high profile. Videos are available at the site as well. MP3.com does not have an easy way to check on new additions like IUMA does, but you can go to the Listening Room, which offers new music streams as they're added to the site. MP3.com also offers charts of the most popular music in each genre; those are also candidates for page-monitoring software.

MP3.com has current popular artists as well as other music; IUMA has lesser known, but still current artists. But, as you might expect, there are lots of other kinds of music out there, like music that is more than a few years old. While it's an utter fallacy that everything that's ever been recorded is already on the Internet (though that would be nice), there really is already an astonishing amount of old music digitized. You can find a lot of it at the Internet Archive.

Internet Archive

Audio is only one part of the Internet Archive (archive.org). It also contains cached Web pages, video, and text. However, the audio part of the Internet Archive is a collection in and of itself. You'll find recordings of live concerts, open sourced recording labels, presidential recordings, and a lot more. And wonder of wonders, there are RSS feeds available for the most recent additions to the archive!

A lot of what you'll find at the Internet Archive is esoteric to say the least; if you're interested in only the latest and most popular stuff you don't want to monitor the Internet Archive for new music. But if you are looking for new music of a lot of different types, or especially live music archives, monitor this site.

Audio blogs

A lot of us have very emotional connections to music. We have very strong ideas about what we like and don't like and could talk for hours about what we want to listen to and what we can't stand. So knowing that, you wouldn't be surprised to discover that music has its own genre of blog called an *MP3 blog*. From here you can get all the new music RSS feeds you can stand, but you'll probably have to do a little digging to find what you like.

Before you can trap you have to find the MP3 blogs that have the music you want. Start by visiting Feedster (feedster.com) or Technorati (technorati.com) and do a search for **"MP3 Blog"**. The number of results you get will be limited enough that you can narrow it just a little further by adding a few keywords for the kind of music you're searching for (try searching for genres of music or artist names, but don't get really detailed) and perhaps an artist name or two. The results you get will include blogs that just review music, and blogs that post music, often with the artists' permission (it's a great way to get exposure for a lesser-known band).

I have yet to monitor MP3 blogs in a professional capacity, but I personally find them invaluable. I'm interested in all kinds of music, and just by reading the RSS feeds of half-a-dozen MP3 blogs, I learn about music that I can't imagine I'd have heard about otherwise. If you have some time and you're at all interested in music, look around for some MP3 blogs and put their RSS feeds in your reader. You'll get some nice surprises out of it.

Of course audio is not the only multimedia on the Internet. It wasn't even the first multimedia on the Internet, really. That honor belongs to images. And from images the Internet has exploded into more images—mainly photography—and even recently into video. Keeping up with all these images—and avoiding the ever-present concern of naughty images—is tricky, but it can be done. The next section shows you how.

Monitoring Images

When I refer to images, I'm referring to a wide territory—photographs, cartoons, drawings, maps, illustrations, and so on. Photographs tend to have their own search engines, but the other types of images are often lumped together in image search engines. If you use the special syntax that the image engines offer, you can often remove or avoid certain types of images in your results.

Let's start with Flickr, since it's familiar to you from earlier discussions in the book and it consists mostly of photographs.

Flickr

Do you remember Flickr (flickr.com)? It's an online photo site owned by Yahoo. It's searchable by tag, and search results are provided in an RSS feed so that you can monitor new images as they're uploaded to the site. As I mentioned earlier, this is a great place to try out those general search terms that would provide impossible numbers of results on a general search engine, but might give you surprising results on photograph search engines, like screenshots or pictures of events.

> **TIP**
>
> Flickr has enjoyed amazing success. Perhaps because of that, there are now many photo-sharing services to choose from. To check out another photo service that offers RSS feeds of search results, try SmugMug (smugmug.com).

Google Images

Google used to crow about the extent of its image search (images.google.com), noting how many images it had indexed and so on. It doesn't do that now; instead it just primly notes that it has "the most comprehensive image search on the Web."

I don't know about that—there's really no way to compare it to other image searches without an index count—but I do know a lot is indexed by Google, in a lot of different formats. Google Images does not offer an RSS feed of its search results, so you have to narrow your search enough to get it in the scope of a single page, and that means taking advantage of Google Images' Advanced Search.

Google Images Advanced Search

The Google Images Advanced Search is available at images.google.com/advanced_image_search. You can limit your search by color (you can search for black and white, grayscale, or full color). You can also limit your search by filetype—GIF, JPEG, or PNG. Photography is usually saved in

JPEG format. So if you limit your search to only GIF or PNG files, you'll tend to have few photographs in your search results. On the other hand, if you limit your search to JPEG format images, then your search results will tend toward photography, although not exclusively.

Google's Advanced Search also offers the ability to limit your search by image size, which I find handy when I'm searching for large photographs or trying to limit my search to "bugs," or icons that people use on Web pages. Experiment with the advanced search to narrow your results as much as possible, and then watch them using a page monitor.

Ask Images

Ask is a relative newcomer to image search, but it's got a lot to offer (ask. com/?tool=img). Unfortunately, one of the things it doesn't offer is an Advanced Search page. On the other hand, Ask does offer related images searches that might help you narrow your searches. Run a search and take a look at the results page (**Figure 8.5**).

Figure 8.5 Review search results and get suggestions for other searches.

On the right side of the page is a list of suggestions for narrowing your search. Try these to see if you can get a manageable list of results. You may find that the related searches aren't particularly useful, and you probably don't want to expand your search, but the suggestions can come in handy. No RSS feeds are available, so you need to use a page monitor.

Yahoo Images

Yahoo Images (images.search.yahoo.com) also offers an Advanced Search page, which you can view at images.search.yahoo.com/search/images/advanced?ei=UTF-8. Note that you can limit your searches to image size and color, but not filetype. In addition, while the color options are more limited (black and white, or color), the image size options are more extensive (a wallpaper option has been added).

Yahoo Images also offers the ability in the advanced search to narrow searches by the domain in which the images appear. You can also do this in Google Images (just add the site syntax to your search), but unless you're doing a medical search (narrowing your results to .edu) or perhaps an archival search (narrowing your results to .gov or a country code like .uk or .ca), I wouldn't limit my search to a particular domain. Again, no RSS feeds, so stick with a page monitor.

Avoiding the naughty stuff

One thing that always comes up when you're running multimedia searches is the possibility of accidentally running into Naughty Stuff. You know— pictures and video that have less than nothing to do with your searches.

If your searches are narrow enough, you should be able to avoid naughty pictures and content. However, don't count on that. Instead, use the advanced searches and set the filter to remove adult content from your search results. Filters like this aren't perfect, but between that and very specific searches you should avoid content that you don't prefer to see.

But what if the unthinkable happens and you end up getting some stuff in your search results that makes you go ick? Report it; look for a link on the search results page. Some resources we're mentioning in this chapter (like Flickr) don't want to have any adult content. And other resources, like Google Image Search, will want to know if a filtered search is letting through inappropriate materials.

Monitoring Videos

Videos online have been sputtering along for the last several years, but it hasn't been until more people had broadband Internet access that online video content really took off. Nowadays, you can do everything from watch a news broadcast to watch kids play the Dance Dance Revolution (DDR) video game. It all depends on where you look and what you want to monitor.

Google Video

Google Video (video.google.com) is a little odd in that it's a combination of a video store and a repository for things people upload, as well as a place where institutions partnering with Google can park their videos. Materials might range from a lecture on physics to a cat beating up a hammer (no kidding!). Start with general searches and try to use more academic language. If you do a search for glaucoma, for example, you get stock footage, news stories, interviews, and even advertisements in Russian. While it's a variety of results, at this writing it returned only 29—which you may feel is enough to comfortably monitor.

Try using Google Video's advanced search options, which include the ability to find only short, medium, or long videos, and to find only videos that are free. Don't forget to sort your results by date! That option is also available from the Advanced Video Search page (**Figure 8.6**).

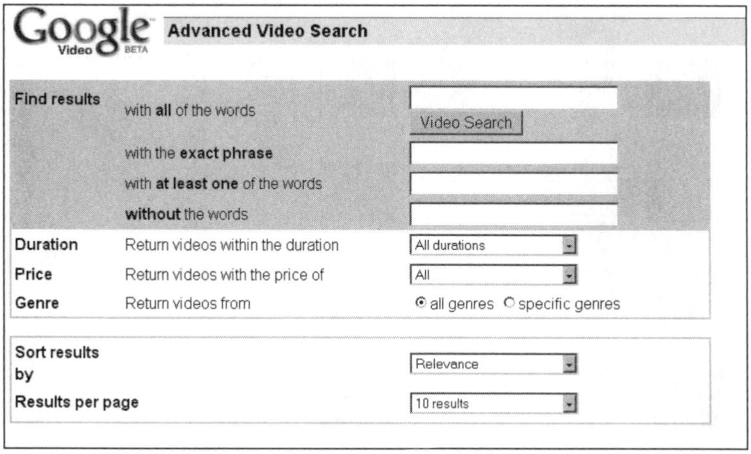

Figure 8.6

Google Video's Advanced Video Search page lets you sort results by date.

While Google Video does offer some feeds (including for its most popular and for comedy videos), RSS feeds do not appear to be available for search results. You need to use a page monitor to trap these.

Searchforvideo

Searchforvideo's front page includes a huge index of categories, as well as a listing of popular videos and featured publishers (searchforvideo.com/). There are also pointers to podcasts that have videos as well. Just glancing at the front page leaves the impression that Searchforvideo reflects a more "pop culture" attitude than Google Video, and searching for glaucoma bears this out: It yields news stories, music videos, and even a few videos from MySpace.

Searchforvideo's default configuration for its search result is a grid, which shows only the source of the video and a thumbnail. Be sure when experimenting with queries to use the detail button at the top of the search results page so that you get snippets and a little more context about the video (**Figure 8.7**). Notice you can also sort your results by date.

Figure 8.7

Be sure to use the detail button to get a results page that's much easier to quickly review.

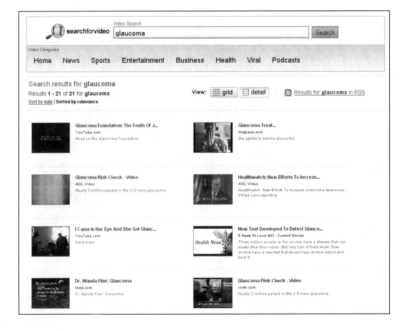

Searchforvideo doesn't offer advanced search, so you need to rely on keywords to narrow your search down. On the other hand, you can get RSS feeds for your search results, so you won't have to rely on a page monitor.

Yahoo Video

Yahoo Video has a monster number of videos indexed, so general searches get you in trouble here (video.search.yahoo.com). On the other hand, it's also got a great Advanced Search page, so you have several options besides keywords for narrowing your search. On the front page are featured videos, with tabs available for Popular Videos, Videos by Category, and Tag.

A search for glaucoma delivers 299 results as of this writing, which is far more than Google Video or Searchforvideo. Fortunately, the Search Results page brings you an excellent level of detail, providing information such as the file type of the video, length of the video, and source (**Figure 8.8**). At a glance you can tell if a video is ten seconds long (probably not very useful) or an hour (an hour long video devoted to your topic could prove very useful).

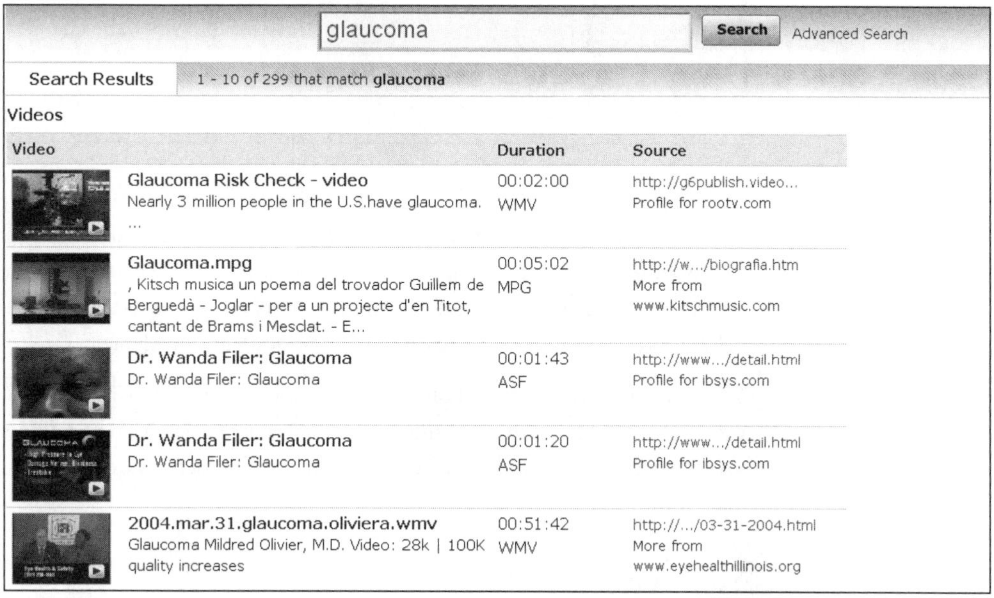
glaucoma
Search
Advanced Search
Search Results
1 - 10 of 299 that match glaucoma
Videos
Video
Duration
Source
Glaucoma Risk Check - video
Nearly 3 million people in the U.S.have glaucoma. ...
00:02:00
WMV
http://g6publish.video...
Profile for rootv.com
Glaucoma.mpg
, Kitsch musica un poema del trovador Guillem de Berguedà - Joglar - per a un projecte d'en Titot, cantant de Brams i Mesclat. - E...
00:05:02
MPG
http://w.../biografia.htm
More from
www.kitschmusic.com
Dr. Wanda Filer: Glaucoma
Dr. Wanda Filer: Glaucoma
00:01:43
ASF
http://www.../detail.html
Profile for ibsys.com
Dr. Wanda Filer: Glaucoma
Dr. Wanda Filer: Glaucoma
00:01:20
ASF
http://www.../detail.html
Profile for ibsys.com
2004.mar.31.glaucoma.oliviera.wmv
Glaucoma Mildred Olivier, M.D. Video: 28k | 100K quality increases
00:51:42
WMV
http://.../03-31-2004.html
More from
www.eyehealthillinois.org

Figure 8.8 Yahoo Video will bring you a lot of search results, fortunately via an excellent results page.

Since you are getting so many results, be sure to take advantage of Yahoo Video's Advanced Search. Here you can narrow your search results by the length of the video (try limiting your results to videos that are over a minute long), by the size of the video's play screen, by the file type of the video, and by the domain of the video (**Figure 8.9**).

Figure 8.9

Yahoo Video's Advanced Search page. Try limiting your video searches by domain.

I can't imagine how anyone could use the file type to specifically narrow search results (other than just getting fewer of them), but experiment with the domain restrictions. Searching in .org domains only, or .edu domains only, tends to deliver fewer results, which themselves are more academically slanted.

Yahoo Video Search does not offer RSS feeds; you have to use a page monitor. You might find with the number of results you get that it's better to do several searches for your keywords—one restricted to each major domain—and monitor each of the results pages.

YouTube

I don't know if YouTube was the first online video site out there, but it's certainly the most popular video site and has helped spur the explosion in popularity of online video sites (youtube.com). YouTube hosts the videos that you're searching, so you see immediately that the level of detail in search results is very useful, though you might not get as many results as you would on other video search engines.

Let's go back to the example we've been using for this entire section, glaucoma. If you run a search for glaucoma on YouTube, you get fewer results than other engines (15 as of this writing), but you also get information like tags, user ratings, duration, and context (**Figure 8.10**). So there's more detail here than there is even in the Yahoo Video search results.

Figure 8.10 YouTube has limited results with lots of detail.

When you click on the name of a video you go to that video's page. Here you can see how many times a video's been viewed, what it's rating is (YouTube users can rate a video up to 5 stars; not all videos are rated) and see comments on the video (**Figure 8.11**). (Often comments point to other similar videos.) Detail pages for videos also have pointers to related videos, which might give you ideas for tags or ideas to search.

Figure 8.11

Detail pages point you to other videos and review current ones.

You can get RSS feeds from YouTube, but it's a little awkward. You have to edit a URL. YouTube offers RSS feeds for tag searching. The RSS feed for a tag search looks like this:

youtube.com/rss/tag/keyword.rss

Simply replace **keyword** with the word you want to track. For instance, you'd use the following URL if you were doing a search on glaucoma:

youtube.com/rss/tag/glaucoma.rss

If you want to use multiple keywords, you'd simply use a plus sign (+) between the keywords:

youtube.com/rss/tag/glaucoma+surgery.rss

In the cases where you're finding that tag search is not working, or you want to do very extensive, keyword-dense searches, try using a page monitor on your search results.

The Future Is Now

If you're a long-time user of the Internet, you might find it challenging to adjust to the idea of trapping multimedia. Hasn't text always been king? However, with broadband becoming the de facto standard for accessing the Internet, the constant rise of personal expression online, and even the popularity of cameras in cell phones, it's clear that multimedia isn't going away. In fact, it's going to get more and more popular.

You may find you have to do more query experimentation with these resources, as well as develop different strategies for reviewing what you find. But I think you'll find that it pays off. Multimedia can provide information in a much richer context than regular text.

9

Trapping Tags and Conversations

In the past few chapters, we've spent a lot of time looking at various types of resources you can trap, such as news, government, multimedia, and more. And one thing I've repeated constantly is that if you want to generate queries that are as narrow as possible, you must avoid being general; get specific by describing the topics you want to track as minutely as possible.

For one chapter—and only one chapter—I'm going to ask you to put that advice aside.

Why? Because this chapter looks at how to monitor and trap tags and conversations. Tags are extremely general, and conversations have their own idiom of searching. For each of these two types of searches, you have to take a different perspective for your searching.

But it's worth it! Conversations are great for finding technical support, news, and rumors about your topic of interest, and discussions of fitness of one item over another. Like blogs, conversations are also useful for quickly finding discussions on current events. Tags are part of group-developed "folksonomies" and can be an easy way to find manageable numbers of resources about general topics. I do tag searches for things I'd never dare to use Google or even Feedster for.

This chapter looks at where to find tags and conversations, and how to trap them. It also provides some query-building advice so that you can get out of the "narrow, narrow, narrow, specific, specific, specific" groove for just this one chapter.

The Tao of Tags

Tags are a relatively recent phenomenon on the Web. Of course, describing a resource using keywords has been happening almost since Day One. But having keywords used by a group of people gathered into a single *folksonomy* and then using that folksonomy as a browsing tool for the entire site is relatively new.

A Folksonowhatnow?

A folksonomy, as we've already discussed, is like a taxonomy, a structure of organization imposed upon a collection, whether that collection is books, animals, minerals, or something else. A taxonomy is generally developed by a specific group with an idea in mind of what's going to be classified. Everyone who works on organizing the collection works within the taxonomy. For example, the way the Library of Congress organizes its collection is a huge taxonomy designed to encompass millions of subjects. It's created and regulated by a specific group. As a result, I can't approach the Library of Congress and tell them I've created 500 subject headings about Kool and the Gang that I want added to their taxonomy. Well, I could, but it wouldn't happen.

However, a folksonomy is much more organic than the efforts of the Library of Congress. Like the Library of Congress, it's developed by a specific group, but it's the group that's using the collection and usually anybody can join that group. Unlike the Library of Congress, it isn't developed and then imposed upon a collection, but grows as more items are added to a collection. Tags can have formal language, informal language, or words that aren't in any dictionary you can find.

This level of flexibility might drive a reference librarian crazy, but it's ideal for the Internet. After all, the Web is not a library. Pages and data are being added constantly, there's no card catalog that covers all the content, and there's no governing body that approves each page as it's added to the Internet and makes sure it's plunked into its proper classification slot. If groups of users who add to a collection can be involved in creating some kind of structure for it, so much the better for the users and for you, the trapper.

> **TIP**
>
> What kind of resources are organized with tags? It seems to have started with online bookmarks, but now tags can be used to search a variety of resources, from photos to blog entries. There's even a meta-search engine for tagged items, as you'll discover a little later on in this chapter.

The advantages of tags. . .

Tags have several advantages:

▶ They're created by people who are contributing to a collection of resources. Because of this, they tend to be more relevant.

▶ They use mostly general words to describe the contents of the collection. For instance, a page about bookmarks of Google resources might be tagged `Google Tools Bookmarks`. So for once you can use general searches to find the topics you're looking for. If you're trying to monitor a very general topic, like Yahoo or Google, you'll find sites that use tags invaluable.

▶ Resources using tags generally have visual displays of the tags being used and how popular they are, which can help you in deciding which words to use for their queries.

But while these are definite advantages, there are also some disadvantages to using tags as well.

...and the drawbacks

I suspect when tag sites become really popular, we'll have to watch out for spammers trying to make sure their resources are listed with every conceivable relevant keyword (and maybe even a few not so relevant). Because you don't trap tags by date and multiple people can bookmark the same resource, you sometimes see "waves" of a resource—several people bookmarking it over a multiple week period. So it can show up in your traps over and over and over again. (Sometimes I use this as a benchmark of how popular a resource is.)

In addition, because tags are geared toward very general searching, the mechanisms for searching with them can sometimes seem woefully limited. For example, you can only search for one tag, and you can't exclude or add tags to your search. So sometimes you'll find that you're doing general searches whether you want to or not.

> **TIP**
>
> Not every trapper is going to find tags useful. If you're a medical student looking to keep up with professional/academic news about a particular disease, photos in Flickr are not going to help you much. And if you're a legal analyst, you might not feel that searching blogs with tags is going to offer you a lot. But at least take a look at what your topic keywords are finding at these sites. At worst, you will have spent a few minutes seeing how other people use your preferred vocabulary. At best, you will have found a couple new traps and gotten ideas for taking your search in a different direction.

Resources That Use Tags

There's more being tagged than just Web sites—there are photographs, blog entries, and even life goals! We discuss these later in the chapter, but for right now let's start with the sites that tag general links.

Tagging seems to have started with *social bookmarking*, which involves a group of people on the same site tagging their bookmarks and then describing them with a few words. Users could then explore who was using the same tags, which bookmarks in the group were most popular, and so on. Get a critical mass of people doing that, and voilà, you have a large set of resources and a folksonomy. The grandpa of this kind of site is del.icio.us.

General tag sites
del.icio.us

If you're a longtime search-engine user, del.icio.us (del.icio.us) will drive you a little crazy at first, but I promise you'll get used to it. And it's worth it. Instead of snippets and lots of information about search results, you often get just a resource name, relevant tags, and the time and date it was added. Sometimes you get an additional line of description. You'll see what I mean when you visit the front page of the site.

The reason it looks that way is because del.icio.us (which I call *Del*, for short) is basically a huge bookmarks depository. When people add something to their Del bookmarks, it's so they can find it later, and less so they can learn about cool new sites. However, I find that the resource titles are generally enough to give me an idea of what they're all about. I also find that I can get a heads-up on resources here that I don't normally find anywhere else.

On Del's front page (**Figure 9.1**), the most recent resources are added. On the right side is a list of the most popular tags.

What you will not see is a search box to find tags. That's okay. To find items tagged with the words you're interested in, use the following URL and replace `keyword` with the tag you're interested in:

`http://del.icio.us/tag/keyword`

You have to get a little creative. First put aside all the really narrow queries and do those general searches you've been dying to do. For example, tagging services like Del are the only places where I trap for the extremely general tags `"Google"` and `"Yahoo"`, and they work very well!

Figure 9.1 Popular and recent additions to del.icio.us.

If you find that your searches aren't returning many results, get more creative. Since tags are often used one at a time, someone might create a tag by putting two words together.

For example, **"GoogleAPI"** is a legitimate tag in the Del system, as is **"weight-loss"**. If what you'd like to search for is usually expressed as a phrase, search for it as one tag. And as you can see from the Google example, you can also take a common word and experiment to see if it has any derivatives.

You can also do multiple tag searching as well. Just put both tags in the URL separated by a plus sign (+). So entering the following URL locates resources that have been tagged with both Yahoo and Google:

`http://del.icio.us/tag/yahoo+google`

If you're having trouble deciding what to look for, do a couple of searches for tags that generally describe your topic. Notice on the right of the results page a list of related tags that may help prod your brain.

Del tag searches are simplicity to trap. Notice at the bottom of each page of search results a familiar orange logo. That's a link to the RSS feed for this tag search. There are two things you have to watch out for when trapping with del.icio.us. Because Del searches are so easy to monitor, and it's so easy to do the general searches that are difficult to do elsewhere, you might find yourself tempted to generate and gather lots and lots of RSS feeds. Before you do that, take a close look at the results pages for your searches. Each item includes the date and time it was added, and the results are listed newest first, with ten to a page.

So it's easy to look at the tenth item of the page and see how active the feed is. Was the tenth item added a week ago? Great—this is an active but slow feed. Was the tenth item added a year ago? You can still add the RSS feed, but you might not see updates very often, which is okay. Was the tenth item added half-an-hour ago? Not so good—you can still monitor this search term, but you'll have to keep up with a very busy RSS feed.

The second thing you have to worry about is resource repeats. When I'm monitoring the Google tag, I might see the same resource two or three times in a week, especially if it gets mentioned by a popular blog or directory. I don't worry about this—the repeats are few enough that they don't hinder the flow of information, and they're usually described well enough that I don't waste my time visiting a site I've already visited.

With del.icio.us being so popular, it's easy to realize that there would be lots and lots of other similar bookmarking services. One of them, Spurl, has taken its bookmark service and turned its data into a search engine called Zniff. I like it as a complement to Del.

del.icio.us Tool Fest

del.icio.us has become a bookmark tool of choice for several thousand people and has its own API. The application programming interface is a way for programmers to use the features and data of Del in their own programs, and has spawned a huge number of tools, some of which you might find useful. Here are some fun ones:

- **Bookmarklets** (quickonlinetips.com/archives/2005/02/absolutely-delicious-complete-tools-collection). Several tools that let you perform specific Del search tasks, such as searching by user name instead of keyword tags (if you wanted to find everything I've bookmarked, for example), searching your own bookmarks, and more.

- **del.icio.us Filtered** (deliciousfiltered.stuhlmueller.info/). Get Del feeds without entries.

- **Trendalicious** (glozer.net/trendalicious.html). Get a sense of what the popular bookmarks are in Del at the moment.

Zniff

At first glance, Zniff (zniff.com) looks like a regular search engine. But it's indexing the bookmarks generated by people who use Spurl, a bookmark service like del.icio.us. Zniff also searches a collection of eight million Web pages from Iceland!

Notice that the dates on the results you get are not recent. I suspect there's some kind of lag between users entering items into Spurl and the items making it into Zniff. Because you can't get a sense of how "busy" a tag is, you have to do some experimenting. And hey, while you're at, it, check out Zniff's help file. Unlike many tag searches, it lets you search for phrases, do "or" searches, or even do stemming searches. (A *stemming search* is when you search for part of a word and add a wildcard character to find the rest of a word—so searching for moon* would find moonlight, moonlight, moons, moonpie, and so on.) While it helps to be as specific as possible in your searches, you can take advantage of this advanced syntax to try to coax out a little additional information from your traps.

Zniff and Del aren't the only general tag search resources. Heck, they're hardly even the start. If you want to do some more searching through general tag sites, try these sites:

▶ **BlinkList** (blinklist.com). A newer resource, BlinkList offers both RSS feeds of search results and suggestions of tags you might want to search for as you are typing in your searches. There aren't as many results as you'll find on Del, but it's newer.

▶ **RawSugar** (rawsugar.com). RawSugar is another new tagging resource, but it offers suggested links and related links, as well as a list of the users which have used the tag for which you're searching and what other tags you're using. As you might imagine, using RawSugar could turn into a huge time sink, but on the other hand, it points you to other tags you might never have thought about.

Access to RawSugar's Showcase section is free, but to do more searching you have to register. Registration is free. Make sure that you're searching the full directory of sites, instead of just RawSugar's Web 2.0 Blogs search.

Tags for specific kinds of searching

The aforementioned tools generate very general sets of data. Of course they do, they're bookmarking tools—by design they're repositories for general information. But tags are used in other settings as well. One of my favorites is Flickr, which tags photographs, but there are other ones too.

Flickr

Before we get into Flickr (flickr.com), I am warning you: keep in mind that you're trying to do research here. Do not get distracted by the pretty pictures. Flickr can turn ten minutes into two hours. If this chapter just kind of trails off in the middle, send out a search party.

I'm sure my intrepid editor won't let that happen. Flickr is a photo-sharing site that also lets users tag their photographs. When searching for photographs, it's my favorite place. It's updated very frequently, the quality of the materials on the site is good overall and non-spammish, and it provides an amazingly quick reference to pictures of current events. Name an event, and it seems like someone's there snapping pictures, ready to put them on Flickr.

The front page of Flickr shows you recent photos and news, but the Tag Search page, at flickr.com/photos/tags/ is where you want to be **(Figure 9.2)**.

Figure 9.2

Popular tags at Flickr.

You can use the Advanced Search page to search for multiple tags, or for keywords in the tag and in the picture description. However, most of the time I find that searching tags works fine.

You might think that, as an information trapper, you won't find anything really useful on a photo site like Flickr—you may be thinking it's only about birthday parties, bunnies, flowers, and such. But do some experimenting with your searches; I think you'll be surprised. While most of what's on Flickr is indeed photographs, other graphics are included too.

For example, if you enter a search for **Google**, which you might think is a weird search for a photo site, look at the kind of results you get (**Figure 9.3**).

Figure 9.3

Getting Google-tagged pictures at Flickr.

You get pictures of Googlers and Google-related activities, but you also get screenshots of Google resources, explanatory graphics, and even conceptions of services being offered by Google. And while many of these might be posted on blogs and elsewhere on the Web, they would be extremely difficult to find—what keywords would you use? Flickr's a nice shortcut.

When choosing tags for searching Flickr, again go for common words. As you can see, Google and Yahoo work well. Try turning phrases into single tags like I suggested doing with Del. Remember the searches we did with Del—**googleapi** and **weightloss**? Try those here. Notice that **weightloss** works, while **API** doesn't. Experiment, experiment, experiment!

Flickr is terrific for current events, as I've said before. Try searching for **minnesota state fair**. As of this writing, I got over 700 results!

In late August and early September 2005, Hurricane Katrina devastated the Gulf Coast. As of this writing, over 19,000 photos are tagged with **hurricanekatrina**, from pictures of candles and prayers, to radar pictures of the hurricane itself, to pictures of people living in shelters.

After chapters and chapters of trying to narrow your search, you may be getting a little frustrated at trying to come up with tags that match your topic. If this is the case, try the Explore section of Flickr (flickr.com/explore/). Here you can explore photos, but you can also use a Flickr feature called *clustering*, which groups photos and finds other tags relevant to what you're searching for. Start with the URL **flickr.com/photos/tags/keyword/clusters/**, and replace **keyword** with the tags you want to search. Try entering **Google** again. You get a page that looks like **Figure 9.4**.

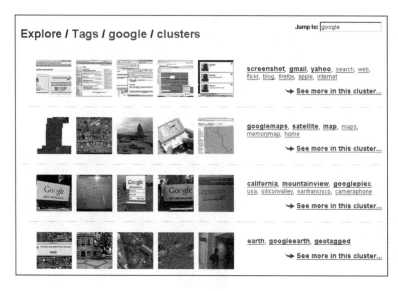

Figure 9.4

Clusters of Flickr tags related to Google.

Notice that the search results are divided into several different sets of tags, some of which you might have anticipated (**GMail**, **Googlemap**) and some which you probably didn't (**memorymap**, **geotagged**, **mountainview**). If you're having a difficult time finding tags that focus on what you're looking for, use the cluster feature for some extra ideas. (In addition, you'll find a list of related tags at the bottom of regular search results, which may help you too.)

Trapping Flickr streams is easy, as RSS feeds are offered for searches. (Look for "Feeds for photos tagged with keyword. Available as RSS 2.0 and Atom" at the bottom of a page of results.)

Would you rather get your alerts by e-mail? Notifyr (notifyr.com/) will send you an e-mail whenever a Flickr page in which you're interested is updated—this can be any kind of Flickr page—a Flickr user's page, an individual picture's page (in case you're watching for new comments), or a page of Flickr search results. You don't need to register to use Notifyr; all you need is an e-mail address.

Have you been seduced by Flickr yet? Spent hours and hours looking at sunsets, lightning, and cute kitten pictures? I know. Time to go look at something else. Blogs, for example, have such an extensive presence on the Internet as a whole that it shouldn't surprise you that there are tag searches for them as well.

Searching blogs with tags

You've already seen that blogs in general have plenty of search engines. But in addition to doing regular searches for blogs, you can also do tag searches. They're like the Flickr searches: sometimes blog tag searches give you a shortcut to resources you would not have found otherwise. Technorati and IceRocket are two major search sources.

Technorati Tag Search

Technorati's Tag Search page (technorati.com/tag/) starts with a list of "hot tags" and the hundred most popular tags, but if none of those interest you there's a search form. This is the place to try all those blog searches you wanted to do in Feedster but which got you too many or too many irrelevant results. You'll see when you get the results back that you're actually getting results from many different sources.

At the top of the results list are tags related to the one for which you just searched. Keep those in mind for later. (Also note at the top of the Search Results page that there's a tab for searching photos!) You can get your trap down at the top of the search results where there's an orange button linking to an RSS feed. Play and experiment with general blog searches here, and then take your experiments to IceRocket.

IceRocket Tag Search

IceRocket is possibly not as well known as Technorati, but it's got a good blog search (blogs.icerocket.com/tag/). As you can see in **Figure 9.5**, there's a special syntax that lets you search for tags.

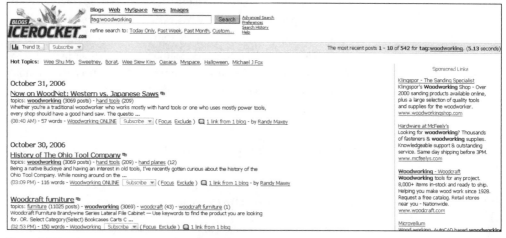

Figure 9.5 Use the tag syntax or simply pick a tag.

The results are divided by date, giving you clear information at a glance as to how busy a tag is. From the results, you can also exclude individual blogs (for example, if there's one that doesn't really meet your topic requirements but is heavily represented in the results). On the other hand, if you find a blog that's great and you want to see more of it, you can also focus on it and see its entries exclusively. On the right are several links for RSS feeds. IceRocket doesn't seem to be indexing quite as much as Technorati, but what it does index I think is well worth trapping.

Are bookmarks, photos, and blog search the only things out there that are being tagged? Good heavens no. There is a huge variety of tagged resources available with more being added every day. Here's a taste of a few more.

43 Things

43 Things (43things.com) is a site that collects life goals for people and where they're located. Users can track their progress with their goals and support each other. Goals are searchable by tags. Goals include losing weight,

paying taxes, watching less television, reading 100 books in a year, and so on. If you're doing any kind of cultural or current event searching, you should have a ball—and set a few traps—rummaging around in this site.

Connotea

For academics, this site (connotea.org) allows users to tag reference resources and papers. While not as active as del.icio.us, the resources added here are as a whole from more credible sources and are much more academically oriented. Medical trappers definitely need to visit here. It does require registration. If you find useful resources at Connotea try the similar academically slanted service, CiteULike (citeulike.org/).

Shadows

Shadows (shadows.com) is combination of bookmarking application and community. Tagged resources can be sent to groups, and the resources there can be commented upon by users. Nice to see tagged resources and feedback at the same time! Like Connotea, Shadows requires registration.

The general searches which would be just about guaranteed to drive you crazy in searching the general Web and other large data pools are just right when searching tag engines. Even if some of these resources don't, at first glance, seem like ones that would be appropriate for your topic, at least take a moment or two and try a couple of searches with them. I think you'll be surprised.

And I think you'll be equally surprised about monitoring conversations. When I'm trying to keep tabs on certain technical issues for a computer, or opinions on current events, or experiences with medical problems, conversations will sometimes point me toward issues that don't bubble up in news search engines until much later. There are some things you have to be cautious about when monitoring conversations, but it can be well worth it.

The Zen of Conversation Trapping

Before the Web was all that, the Internet was all about e-mail. And despite the fact that the Web gets much attention, e-mail is still in some ways the killer app of the Internet. Millions of conversations are started, ended, and continued every second of the day on public mailing lists. They cover everything from aardvarks to zephyrs. Some of the conversations are desultory and not particularly useful to you, the trapper, but on the other hand the amount of free technical support, spirited discussion, problem solving, and other data flow can be very helpful. But as I noted earlier, conversation trapping is not without its problems.

The bummer of conversation trapping

The first stumbling block of conversation trapping is credibility. When you're searching with news search engines you can start out with a baseline of credibility to which you can assign a story. You might, for example, consider the Washington Post a high-credibility source, and give other sources varying levels of credibility depending on how well you know them, what they're reporting on, and so on.

With conversations, that baseline should be zero, since you can't assign any credibility to what you're reading until it's corroborated or you have some other reason to trust it. That's not to say a lot of good information can't be found in online conversations. But you don't know in some cases who's posting, what the agenda is, where they got their information, and so on.

Another stumbling block is language. I've mentioned earlier in this book that in conversations people tend to be a little sloppier than when they're writing for a Web page.

Yet another glitch is the fact that information gets old. It's usually not much of a problem with news stories—when a situation changes, the news story is updated to reflect the new information. Sometimes, however, the updating doesn't happen, and the same old, outdated information bounces around and around. For an Internet-wide example of this, consider the case of Craig Shergold. Craig had cancer and wanted to receive greeting cards—in 1989. Over ten years later, long after Craig was cancer-free and long after he appeared on TV, letting the world know that the cards could stop, this appeal for cards was still circulating around the Internet and only now seems to be slowed down.

Keep all this in mind as you trap. You may discover over time that there are some mailing lists you trust more than other ones. In reading through the resources presented in this section, you'll learn there are ways you can concentrate your trapping on one list if that works best for you. There are many places online where you can watch conversations.

Trapping conversations

Generally speaking there are three types of conversations you can track:

▶   **Usenet.** Usenet is a collection of thousands of newsgroups set up in a hierarchy that's been available for over twenty years now. While not as popular as it used to be, it still generates a lot of traffic.

▶   **Mailing Lists.** Discussion groups that are distributed to their members mainly through e-mail. As more closed conversations are less subject to the ravages of spamming and trolling, mailing lists have become more popular over the last few years. And many of them have publicly available archives that you can search without being on the list, or without requiring more than a basic free registration.

▶   **Discussion Boards.** Discussion boards are areas on Web sites that contain discussions, usually on very specific topics or groups of topics.

When it comes to monitoring Usenet, Google Groups is your best bet. But for the other types of conversation trapping you have lots of options.

Google Groups

Google Groups (groups.google.com) is actually a combination of a mailing list host and a Usenet search service, but the mailing lists have not caught up with the still prodigious Usenet traffic! So we concentrate on that option.

Your first task when preparing to trap Usenet is to figure out where you're going to trap. Most topics you want to monitor will be well served by limiting the search to a newsgroup or a set of newsgroups.

Usenet's newsgroups are arranged in a hierarchy—major categories like comp (computers), sci (science), rec (recreation), and so on. (There are a bunch of little categories as well.) Underneath the major categories there are subcategories, sub-subcategories (sometimes even more sub than that), and newsgroups. You can search by single newsgroups but I find it's easier to search by category.

If you don't find any major category that really covers what you're looking for, then you've got a couple of options. You can do a full Usenet search (if your search is specific enough this shouldn't be a big deal) or you can try to find individual groups that cover what you're looking for. Searching for individual groups also shows you mailing lists that Google Groups is hosting.

The searchable listing of groups is at groups.google.com/groups/dir. Use moderately to fairly general words to do your searching, such as sports, baseball, money, woodworking, autism, or medicine. When you get search results they look like **Figure 9.6**.

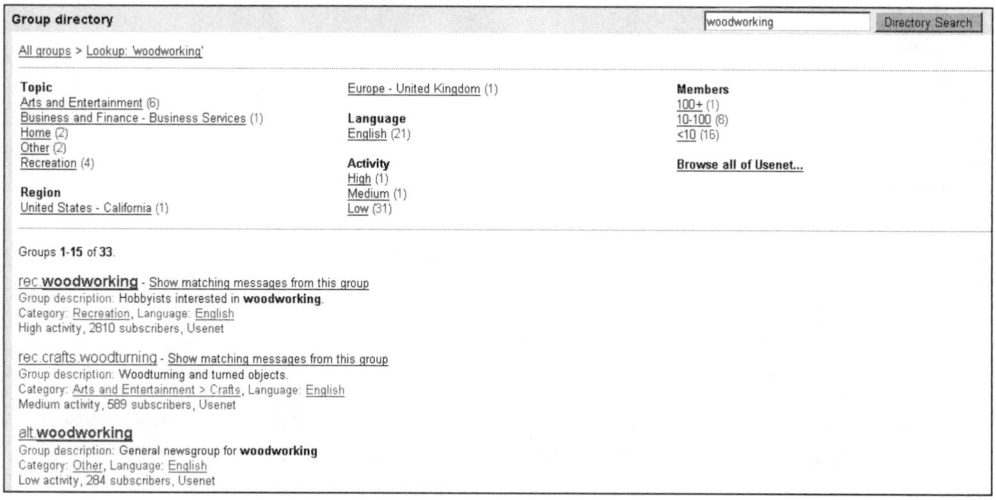

Group directory | woodworking | Directory Search

All groups > Lookup: 'woodworking'

Topic
Arts and Entertainment (6)
Business and Finance - Business Services (1)
Home (2)
Other (2)
Recreation (4)

Region
United States - California (1)

Europe - United Kingdom (1)

Language
English (21)

Activity
High (1)
Medium (1)
Low (31)

Members
100+ (1)
10-100 (6)
<10 (16)

Browse all of Usenet...

Groups **1-15** of **33**.

rec.**woodworking** - Show matching messages from this group
Group description: Hobbyists interested in **woodworking**.
Category: Recreation, Language: English
High activity, 2810 subscribers, Usenet

rec.crafts.woodturning - Show matching messages from this group
Group description: Woodturning and turned objects.
Category: Arts and Entertainment > Crafts, Language: English
Medium activity, 589 subscribers, Usenet

alt.**woodworking**
Group description: General newsgroup for **woodworking**
Category: Other, Language: English
Low activity, 284 subscribers, Usenet

Figure 9.6 Group listings from Google Groups.

Groups will be divided up at the top by category, region, language, activity, and number of users. Then the list of groups will appear below. Group listings include group name, description, and if the group is one of Google's mailing lists, the number of members.

But let's start with the categorical searching. Let's go back to the antique woodworking example. I want to monitor groups for mentions of antique woodworking, and after some browsing I've decided that the recreation hierarchy of newsgroups is my best bet. So I search for:

```
"antique woodworking" group:rec*
```

The group special syntax lets me restrict my searches to a single group or a category of groups. The rec* searches every group in the recreation category. (You can also search under subcategories—group:rec.sports* will search only those groups in the sports subcategory.)

So what kind of results can you get for this? I got less than 125 results as of this writing, but you won't be able to tell how recent the newest results are until you go to the switch on the right and choose to sort by date instead of by relevance (**Figure 9.7**).

Figure 9.7 One page of search results for this Google Groups query goes back several months.

Once you've done that, you can view the date of each posts—each post has a date and time—and see how recently the newest post is, and how old the oldest is. In this case you can see that **"antique woodworking"** isn't a particularly busy search term and would make a good trap. Down at the very bottom of the page is a signup form for e-mailed search alerts for Google Groups.

In addition to the group syntax, Google Groups offers other special syntax that you can use to narrow your search. Being familiar with Google searching, you should be familiar with intitle, which is used to find keywords in the title. It works the same in Google Groups. Between that and the group syntax, you should be able to narrow your searches quite a lot.

For most of your trapping needs, monitoring the entire Usenet or groups of newsgroups should be sufficient. But there will be times when you find a single group that has so much great information in it that you want to read it exclusively. In these cases, you need to have a Google Groups account.

How Do You Build These Searches?

So how do you build effective searches for conversations, if just getting as narrow as possible won't do it?

If you make good use of the intitle syntax, or any other resource syntax that allows you to limit your searches to the subject line (which in this case is considered the title) of a post, you can get by with general searches. Since titles of Usenet and mailing list posts are generally designed to get attention and to continue a conversation, they're usually good for searching.

If your searches on titles aren't getting you anywhere, try slightly more specific searches within the body of the list posting or newsgroup posting itself. I find that newsgroup searches work very well in technical arenas when you include direct quotes of error messages or specific model numbers for technical items. Usually when people are requesting technical help they are as specific as possible and provide an extensive level of detail.

So where you might on a Web search be forced to search for **"collapsing drive from WidgetCo"**, a newsgroup search might allow you really narrow in on **"collapsing Widget2400ZBQ from WidgetCo"**.

Try using model numbers, complete error messages, drug names, the full names of medical conditions, and other precise nouns that people might use in describing a problem and asking for help. That's a lot of what takes place in online conversations. Try searching for the most specific query words—the model numbers, medical condition names, error messages—in the title.

If that fails, think of the topic you want to monitor, and try to articulate it as a question. How would you describe it? What would you ask? (**"What are the latest treatments for muscular dystrophy?"** **"What's happening with the Arizona Cardinals?"** **"What are the latest antique woodworking collectibles?"**) Take the questions you generate and pull out the keywords, then search for them (**treatments "muscular dystrophy"**, **happening Arizona Cardinals**, **antique woodworking collectibles**). Leave out the time-related words, such as new or latest. The fact that you're only getting the most recent messages will take care of your information timeliness. If those questions don't find you specific enough information, ask a different question, extract the relevant words, and start over.

What you're doing when you create your queries this way is thinking about how an information-rich conversation might start—by creating a question. The theory is that a query based on a question that will bring you information-rich answers will hopefully also point you towards good query results.

You may already have a Google Groups account and not know it! If you've signed up for GMail then you have a Google Groups account. Just use the same user name and password that you'd use to sign on there. If you don't you can register. Registration is free.

I don't think you necessarily need a Google Groups account unless you're following individual newsgroups. But it may turn out that you do want to follow individual newsgroups—a group may cover your topic perfectly and may not be worth filtering by keyword. There may be several groups that fit your topics this way.

When you first log on to Google Groups your page will look like **Figure 9.8**.

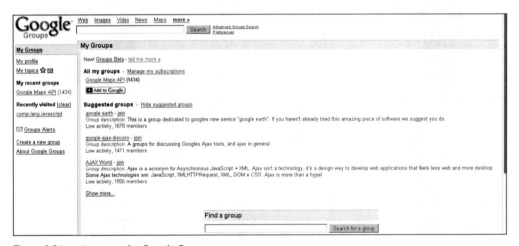

Figure 9.8 Logging on to the Google Groups account.

There is a Groups Lookup at the bottom of the page where you can search for newsgroups and mailing lists of interest.

So say you find a few newsgroups to which you want to subscribe. When you join them you're given several subscription options as you can see in **Figure 9.9**.

I always choose to read the newsgroups to which I subscribe on the Web— what's the use of having a Web-based interface if you don't use it?—but you may wish to receive regular e-mail or digests.

Once you've subscribed to a few newsgroups, reading them via your Google Groups page will look like **Figure 9.10**.

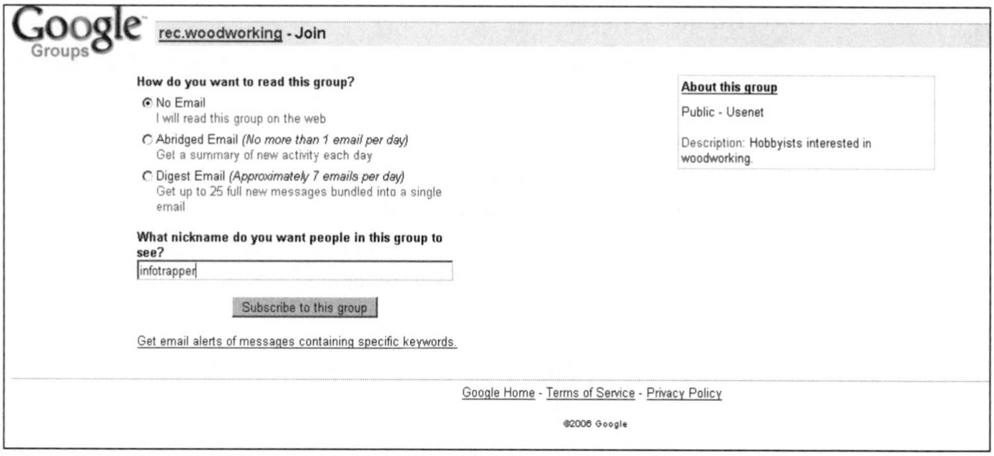

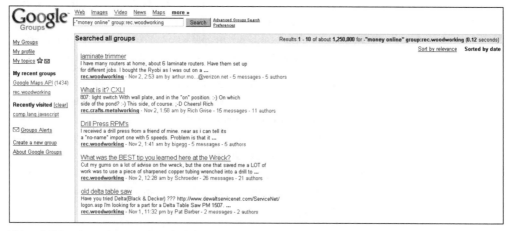

Figure 9.9 Signing up for newsgroups.

Figure 9.10 Reading a group in Google Groups.

From there you can read your messages, "star" topics you find interesting (useful when there are long, long discussion threads you want to follow because it gathers them all into one place), and read your messages. And how do you trap the new messages? But subscribing to them, of course!

Google News is a mix of Usenet newsgroups and mailing lists—but really for the most part it's newsgroups. Yahoo Groups, on the other hand, is an ancient and extremely active set of mailing lists, and a gold mine for information trappers.

Yahoo Groups

You don't, strictly speaking, need a Yahoo account to read Yahoo Groups (groups.yahoo.com), but I recommend it. Many of the groups don't let you read the archives unless you're a member, and by signing into Yahoo you'll easily be able to sign up for groups. Some groups don't offer public access to their archives at all. You have to be given permission to join the list, after which you can read the archives. I find there are few enough of those that they don't hinder my information trapping.

Yahoo's mailing lists are set up under a sort of hierarchy. Yahoo has set them up into a searchable subject index that's very Yahooesque. But you may find keyword searching to be your best bet.

The rules for keyword searching for mailing lists here should be much like what you used with Google Groups: moderate to very general words. Because Yahoo Groups offers only mailing lists, it can provide you with a little more information in its search results, including extended descriptions, a count of the number of people who are subscribed to a mailing list, and whether the mailing list archives are accessible to members or not.

When you decide to subscribe to a mailing list and click on the name of the list from the search results, you get a little more information about the group—like how many new members it's gained and how many links, photos, and messages it's added in the past week. Pay attention to this! The activity of the list is going to determine your strategy to keep up with it, and how much use you might get out of it. A group with hundreds of new messages a week should be approached with more specific and narrower queries than a group with only a few dozen messages a week.

And that's how we get to talking about trapping. As you may have already guessed, your strategy with Yahoo Groups is going to be different than your strategy with Google Groups. For one thing, you can't search the entire body of messages at once—you're going to have to first identify useful groups, then search them individually. How you go about that depends on the group itself.

Public groups—groups which have no restrictions on membership or post-reading—will offer RSS feeds of the latest posts. The RSS buttons are in the same area as the latest posts (**Figure 9.11**).

Figure 9.11 Publicly readable groups have RSS feeds available at Yahoo Groups.

These are full feeds of all the posts. I recommend using these feeds in conjunction with something like FeedDigest or FeedShake to extract just the words in which you're interested. We talked about those tools way back in the early chapters.

When groups are not public and are for members only, then you have to do something else. I recommend using a page monitor. It's not as streamlined as using an RSS feed, but you won't have a lot of options here. You can either monitor the front page, which shows you the latest posts (this is okay if you're monitoring a not-particularly-busy group), or you can monitor a page of search results for that particular group (necessary if you're monitoring a very busy group). If you want to monitor a page of the latest posts of a group that requires registration before you can read the archives, check your page monitor to make sure you can specify a login name and password when monitoring that page. Most page monitors offer this option.

Though your methods of finding and monitoring information on Yahoo Groups will be different than what you use with Google Groups, the kinds of things you'll be monitoring should be the same, as we talked about earlier in the chapter. Product names, condition names, model numbers, error messages. Continue the tactic of creating questions relating to your topic, extracting the relevant words, and then plugging them into the search. You may find some mailing lists to be so information-rich you want to completely monitor them instead of just looking at search results. You have ways to monitor both.

Google Groups and Yahoo Groups are without question the largest Usenet and mailing list resources out there. But there are other repositories of mailing lists as well. And though you may not find that you want to monitor every last one of these, they're worth looking at.

> **TIP**
>
> Some of the following resources just show you what mailing lists are available. They do not allow you to search archives. You may find lists here you want to monitor, but you'll only be able to monitor them by subscribing to them. In the next chapter we look at managing information flow via e-mail accounts.

Topica

There are actually two kinds of searches you can do on Topica (lists.topica.com): you can search for lists and you can search for messages.

On the front page is a directory of mailing lists you can browse or a search box. That search box will find you mailing lists. However, once you run the search you get more options (**Figure 9.12**).

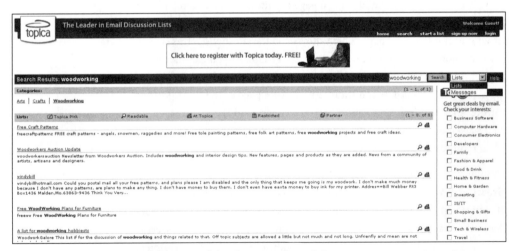

Figure 9.12 Once you do an initial search, you can do a second search for groups or messages containing your keyword.

Yes, you do get a list of relevant groups, but on the right you get another search box with the option to search for more lists or—and this is the important bit for you—search messages!

But let's look at the groups first. The search results for groups don't give you as much information as, say, the search results for Yahoo Groups, but if you click on the name of the group in the results you get an additional information page that includes the number of subscribers and the approximate list activity, as well as a link to read the archives if they're readable by anybody. Use this information to determine list activity and how you want to monitor it.

Back to the message results. Your search results will initially list posts in order of relevance, I believe. Click the date header to resort them by date, as you see in **Figure 9.13**.

List Name	Subject	Author	Date
PRIVATE RETREAT FOR FIBROMITES	Re Re Re Cat	Squirrely	01/02/02
PRIVATE RETREAT FOR FIBROMITES	Re Re Re Re Cat/Jo	vividana	01/02/02
Elements of Change	FW [TheGreenWitchesSpell] THE GREEN ...	Athena	02/02/02
C&C Owners	RE exterior woodwork	Risberg, Jerry D	03/26/02
C&C Owners	Re exterior woodwork	Bryden MacDougall	03/26/02
C&C Owners	RE exterior woodwork	Lawrence Aqui	03/26/02
C&C Owners	RE exterior woodwork	r-@ns.sympatico.ca	03/26/02
C&C Owners	Re exterior woodwork	Allen B. Miles Jr.	03/28/02
Woodworkers Auction Update	WOODWORKERS AUCTION UPDATE - 4-19-02	David K. Eller	04/19/02
InventorEd-L	Re WondeRip fence's web site online	Larry Loo, M.D.	06/03/02
InventorEd-L	RE WondeRip fence's web site online	Mike Turco	06/04/02
InventorEd-L	Re WondeRip fence's web site online	Larry Loo, M.D.	06/04/02
National Community Forestry Center, N...	Shoptalk A Community Bulletin Board	Jesse McLean	06/19/02

Figure 9.13 Sorting by date in Topica gives you the oldest results first.

When you normally resort items by date, what do you get? You get a list with the newest items first. In this case you get the oldest items first, so what you have to do is scroll to the last page of the results and monitor that. Mostly what you're monitoring is changes to that page's content and the addition of another page of search results. It's awkward, and I only occasionally find useful results here, but Topica is still active enough that I would at least look at the lists it hosts and consider adding it to my information trapping list.

TILE.NET Lists

TILE.NET (tile.net/lists) is not a message repository. Instead it's an online listing of newsletters and mailing lists. It's also one of the oldest online resources for this kind of thing, so you know it's extensive.

You have the choice of browsing by name, description, and domain, which I don't recommend unless you have lots and lots of free time. A search engine also allows you to search between lists and newsgroups. You probably got your fill of newsgroup searching at Google Groups, so stick to lists. Make your searches single-word—`ethics`, `medicine`, `woodworking`, `Google`.

The big drawback to TILE.NET is that a lot of the lists have no descriptive information, and you can't get a sense from the title of some of the lists what exactly they are. However, for when you want to make sure you cover every available inch, and want to set up traps for every available resource, you don't want to miss TILE. There are too many listings here.

> **TIP**
>
> There are lists of categorized information as well as general mailing lists. If you're looking for academic information try JISCmail (jiscmail.ac.uk), which contains information on mailing lists for academic communities, mostly in the UK.

L-Soft List Catalog

Sometimes you'll hear someone refer to a mailing list as a LISTSERV. That's not really a correct usage. LISTSERV is a certain type of mailing list software and it's a trademark. A mailing list may run on LISTSERV, but a mailing list is not a LISTSERV. (It's like saying, "Give me a Kleenex," when you're using a generic brand of tissue.)

You might realize however that mailing list software would have to be pretty darn popular to become a common usage noun. And you're right. The L-Soft List Catalog (lsoft.com/lists/listref.html) contains information on over 58,000 mailing lists—and those are just the publicly available ones!

There are some unusual ways to find lists here (**Figure 9.14**)—you can search by country and search by lists that have over 1,000 or over 10,000 subscribers. You can also do a keyword search for lists.

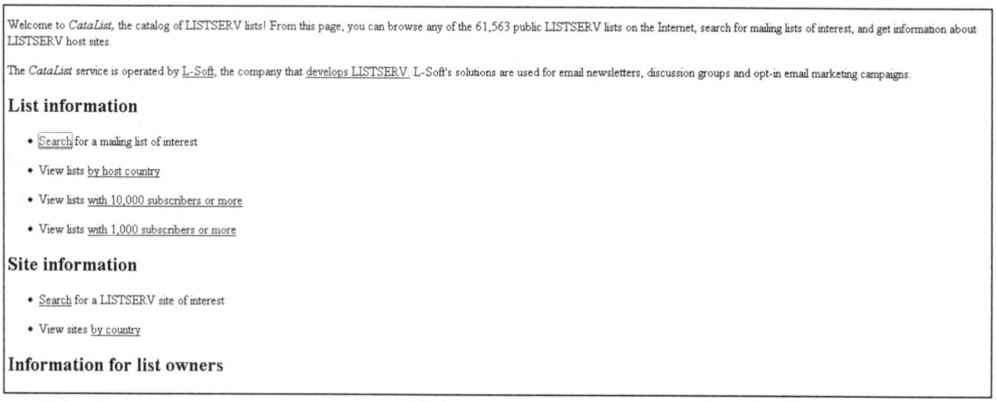
Welcome to *CataList*, the catalog of LISTSERV lists! From this page, you can browse any of the 61,563 public LISTSERV lists on the Internet, search for mailing lists of interest, and get information about LISTSERV host sites.

The *CataList* service is operated by L-Soft, the company that develops LISTSERV. L-Soft's solutions are used for email newsletters, discussion groups and opt-in email marketing campaigns.

List information

- Search for a mailing list of interest
- View lists by host country
- View lists with 10,000 subscribers or more
- View lists with 1,000 subscribers or more

Site information

- Search for a LISTSERV site of interest
- View sites by country

Information for list owners

Figure 9.14 Several different list search options at L-Soft.

The list search offers several different options. You can search for keywords within the list name or list description (which is what I recommend) or within the host name. You can also limit your searches to only those lists that have a Web-based archive (useful if you want to review list archives before you subscribe). Beware using the Web-based archive search limitation—a search for autism found 12 results, but when the search was restricted to only those lists with Web-based archives, the same search found only 6 results.

By now you know: there are hundreds of thousands of mailing lists out there. But guess what? That's not the only way to have a conversation online! In fact, there's another way to have open online discussions and that's via online boards.

Searching online conversations

There are software programs (and some hosted services) that allow people to put up online boards or discussion forums. The advantage of those is that they allow conversations to be centered on one site. The disadvantage of course is that unless you publicize the heck out of 'em, forums can be hard to find and hard to build traffic for. A secondary disadvantage is that sometimes online forums become irresistible target for spammers and trolls (people who want to start arguments and fights online).

But if you can get past those problems, you'll find a lot to love in boards. Generally they evolve into a community, so if you find a good community that acts courteously toward itself and exchanges good information, you can anticipate the entire forum to generate good information even as it moves forward into new topics. Generally, moderated boards (forums that have a manager control the postings) are better than unmoderated boards, but in both cases the information quality varies across forums.

I can recommend two places that will help you both find forums and find messages on forums.

Building Queries for Forums

You thought building queries for mailing lists and newsgroups was different? Building queries for online forums is even more different. In my experience, forum discussions are fairly disjointed. The community I mentioned above also means that the group develops its own vocabulary, history, and so on. For best results, I recommend monitoring the front page of a forum site and watching for the keywords in which you're interested. The more general, the better. For some less-active forums you might be able to get away with just monitoring the front page and not using keywords at all.

Some of the resources outlined in this chapter allow you to search many boards at a time. In that case, again, stick to more general keywords and monitor search results pages.

Big-Boards

Big-Boards (big-boards.com) tracks and provides information on the largest boards and forums on the Internet. And when I say largest I mean hundreds of millions of posts by hundreds of thousands of users. There are over 1,800 boards listed in this directory. Very information-rich trapping areas, as long as you can keep the information flow to a usable level!

You may browse available forums in a subject index or search by keyword. Each forum listing has an information page that provides a description of the board, as well as a screenshot and number of monitors. Each listing also has a stats page that graphically shows the number of members and the number of posts per day, and gives a text listing of the number of users and the average number of posts per week.

You will not be able to monitor forums directly from Big-Boards, but it will point you to a lot of potential trapping areas.

Yuku

Yuku (yuku.com) is not a board posting search engine. Instead it finds the forums themselves. It's up to you to go to them and decide what you want to monitor, but Yuku does provide a lot of information for you.

Use general to slightly-less-general search words—think of Yahoo Directory's top level categories and then maybe a category or so more specific than that. If you get too many results, carefully get more specific. I find it's way too easy to end up with nothing. Your search results are very informative—you get the name of the forum, description, total visits, total posts, average daily visits, and average daily posts. That should give you enough information to decide if you want to monitor the forum.

What you find when you decide to visit a forum will vary a lot. Some forums require membership to even view posts. Some forums require membership to post, which means you can monitor them without having to have a membership to the board. The Search Results page for a forum search looks like **Figure 9.15.**

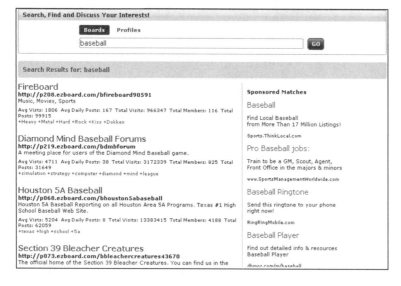

Figure 9.15

38 average daily posts? You can handle that. 167? You may want to watch specific board sections with a page monitor.

Pay attention to the average number of daily posts! If traffic in the forum is light (less than a few dozen messages a day) you may wish to monitor only this front page. If the traffic is heavier, you may wish to pick a section or sections in that discussion forum that are most relevant to your interest and then monitor those using a page monitor. If you're very interested in singular topics, you can choose to be notified of topic updates via e-mail—just look for the "Click to receive email notification of replies" link. You don't have to be registered on the board in which you're interested to get notification of updates to topics. (This can lead to a lot of e-mail but we discuss that in the next chapter.)

As you can see, searching tags and online conversations is quite different from searching full-text search engines. But if you take the opportunity to use these resources for general searching, you'll add a whole new dimension to your information trapping.

10

Filtering
the Inflow

For the last several chapters we've looked at how to get information, such as alerts, notices, and updates about the topics in which you're interested, flowing toward you.

It's a little intimidating, isn't it? You've set all these traps, now what are you supposed to do with all this information?

The RSS feeds can be organized in your RSS feed reader and kept until you're ready to look at them. E-mail, on the other hand, has a distressing tendency to pile up and hinder you from getting to the information that you really want to deal with.

This chapter addresses the other side of information trapping—what to do when you get start getting the e-mails full of the information you wanted. Do you save them, filter them, or forward them onward? Do you hide under your desk? You've learned to make your queries comprehensive and manageable; now we'll take the first steps to make the flow manageable as well.

I have a spectacular disadvantage in writing this chapter. There are billions of ways you could have your e-mail set up. You might use Outlook, Thunderbird, or Eudora. You might be using a corporate setup. There's no way I can cover every possible e-mail permutation. For this reason, I'm going to introduce you to a free online e-mail service and teach you how to filter using that service. Because the service is compatible with POP forwarding, you can use it as an initial filter and still get e-mail to your regular mailbox. So you can think of this service as your first filter point for information trapping.

Introducing GMail

GMail (gmail.com) is a free e-mail service from Google. Now you may be wondering, "Why did Google, which is known for search engine technology, start offering an e-mail application?" You've got me. However, GMail does marry useful e-mail reading with excellent searching functions, as you'll discover later in this chapter. It also offers an enormous storage limit—over 2.5 gigabytes, as of this writing, and increasing all the time.

GMail's many advantages

GMail offers a huge number of advantages for information trappers:

▶ **A lot of storage space.** You won't have to keep clearing out your old traps (unless you've set eight or nine thousand!).

▶ **Great filtering capability.** Keep the stuff that can wait, forward the important stuff to your wireless PDA or mobile phone. (There's also some fun address kludging you can do, which we look at in a minute.)

▶ **Spam-filtering.** GMail's spam and virus filtering is very keen— perhaps a little too keen—in that you'll sometimes find something you wanted in the spam trap!

▶ **Great searching ability.** GMail offers a huge number of special syntax that lets you zero in on the information you're seeking.

> **TIP**
>
> Keep in mind that you can also apply all the hints and tips I provide in this chapter to your own e-mail program, if it offers filtering like GMail does.

Getting a GMail account

GMail accounts used to be by invitation only. As of this writing, however, Google is offering GMail invitations to those who are willing to accept an invitation by text message. So if you've got a cell phone that can accept text messages, you can sign up at google.com/accounts/SmsMailSignup1.

If you don't have a mobile phone, check and see if GMail is offering free accounts yet. If it isn't, you can request a GMail invite (that will let you open a new account) by sending an e-mail to informationtrapping@gmail.com.

You can also check out 43things.com/things/view/70590 for a list of other folks offering invitations to GMail accounts.

Once you have an account and you're signed in, your onscreen mailbox will look like **Figure 10.1**.

You see that the folders are on the left side. Beneath them are some labels— you'll use those when you filter (more about that in a minute). At the top of the screen is a search box for both the Web and your mail, and, of course, in the middle of the page is where actual content appears.

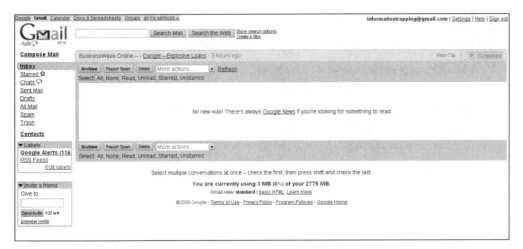

Figure 10.1 A lovely empty mailbox at GMail.

If you're used to using offline e-mail readers like Eudora, you might find the way GMail organizes messages a little odd at first. Instead of listing individual messages in a list, it gathers similar messages into a thread, and displays them in your inbox as one message. This means that many of your alerts and updates will gather into one message thread. There are other ways to group messages, as you'll see a little later in this chapter.

> **TIP**
>
> One potential use of GMail is as a "jump-off point" for your information filtering. You set up all your alerts to go to the GMail account, and then you set a series of filters that moves the information into the appropriate places, such as to your mail account, to a cell phone, or even to the archives to be viewed later. You can also use this same idea if you have a group of researchers working on the same project. Simply set up your GMail account to accept all the information traps, and then filter them so that they forward to the appropriate people, after which they're archived. That way everybody gets the appropriate information on what they're working on, but at the same time all the information traps are being gathered and archived in one place.

Address construction in GMail

Now let's talk for a minute about what's going to go into your mailbox. You'll be receiving alerts, updates, notifications about changed pages, and so on. The good thing about these types of e-mails is that they're computer-generated. What's so great about that? They have patterns that you can filter on. But before we get to the filtering part, let's first look at how you can control the address where the alerts are delivered.

What? You have only one address on GMail? No you don't. Even if you don't have more than one account, you have far more than one address.

In fact, you have practically an infinite number of addresses, thanks to GMail's *plus-addressing* and *dot-addressing* capabilities. For simplicity's sake, stick to one or the other. I recommend the plus-addressing.

What plus-addressing means is that you can append a text string to your e-mail address, and GMail will deliver the e-mail to you. So if your address is **informationtrapping@gmail.com**, you can use a plus sign (+) to put a string between **informationtrapping** and **@gmail.com**, like this:

informationtrapping+hello@gmail.com

And you can even use several plus signs in a row, like this:

informationtrapping+I+went+to+Quiznos+for+dinner@gmail.com

That may be a silly example, but what it shows is that for every service from which you get an alert, such as GoogleAlert, Trackle, Watch That Page, and so on, you can set a unique address using plus-addressing. Which makes filtering very simple: as soon as the filter hits the address, it performs the action you specify. (And incidentally, if you start getting spam to one of those addresses, you'll know where it originated and you'll be able to dump those e-mails right into the bit bucket.)

> **TIP**
>
> For some reason, if you go into your GMail account and try to send yourself an e-mail using plus-addressing, it won't work: the e-mail will bounce. So if you want to play with this feature, be sure to send yourself an e-mail from outside the GMail system.

Of course, filtering won't work every time. Sometimes you'll be looking for keywords. Sometimes you'll be looking for where an e-mail came from. And sometimes alert services (like Google's e-mail alerts) don't support e-mail addresses with plus signs in them. In these cases, you need to look at more of GMail's filtering options.

Filtering with GMail

Before you get into the filtering, take a look at the e-mail you want to filter. What can you filter on? For example, Google Alerts have "Google Alert" in the title and the keywords for which you're searching. EZBoard notifications come from EZBoard.com. In those cases, you can filter on the Subject and the From lines. And, of course, if you created a unique e-mail address with plus-addressing, you can filter on that as well. Keep an eye out for patterns in the header; they're easy to manage.

To access GMail's filtering, choose the "Create a filter" link in the fairly tiny type at the top of your page. A screen displays that looks like **Figure 10.2**.

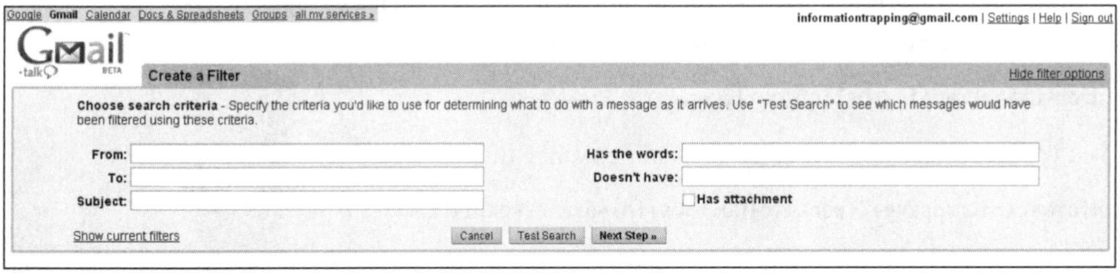

Figure 10.2 The first step in using GMail to construct filters.

Note that here you're only specifying what to filter for. What happens when the filter is activated is for the next panel.

If you're filtering by From or To addresses and don't want to filter on an entire address, search for the strings on either side of the at sign (@). For example, if you're filtering on **theexample@example.com**, you could filter either for **theexample**, or **example.com**.

If you want to filter by subject line, bear in mind that you don't have to have the words in the same order as the subject line. So if you want to filter on the subject **Google Alert - Monty Python** you could filter for **Alert Google Monty Python** and it would match.

You can also filter for the presence or absence of keywords, and whether or not the e-mail has attachments. (I have yet to find this feature useful for information trapping, but I do find it useful in this age of viruses that come in attachments. If you're very nervous about receiving attachments, you can have a filter that moves any e-mails with attachments straight into the trash.)

> **TIP**
>
> Speaking of match, notice the Test Search button at the bottom of the filter setup screen. If you click this button, it will run your search against your current inbox and show you what things match your search. I recommend doing this early and often. Test your filters as you're building them, and you won't get any unpleasant surprises later!

I recommend keeping your filters as simple as possible. If I'm getting a Google alert for autism developments, and the Subject header is **Google Alert - Autism Developments**, I might only filter for the words **Google Alert Autism**. If that's my only Google Alert (extremely unlikely, but possible), I would filter only for **Google Alert**. That's because the simpler my filter is, the less likely it's going to break because of the title changing, the subject getting cut off by the mailer, or some other odd happening.

If you set up enough e-mail alerts, your filters will break at some point. However, if you match the minimum amount of information to make the filter work, your filter has less chance of breaking.

Once you have a filter set up and you've tested it, you want to click the Next Step button. A page displays showing you the actions that can happen once an item hits a filter (**Figure 10.3**).

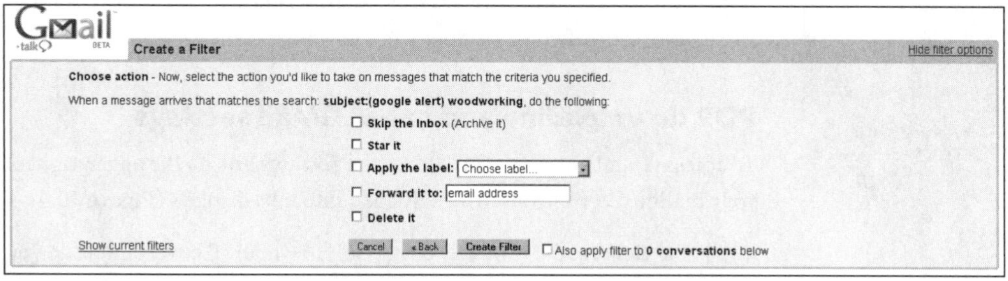

Figure 10.3 You can choose any of the five actions shown here.

Options include the following:

▶ **Skip the Inbox.** Drop it directly in your archive, bypassing the Inbox and putting the message in the All Mail inbox. Handy when you want to keep an eye on a certain subject, but you're not interested in immediately reviewing every item that comes your way.

▶ **Star It.** Put a star on it so that it grabs your attention and also moves it to the Starred message list.

▶ **Apply the Label.** Labels are for dividing up messages. Think of them as message folders, or as tags for your e-mail. From this action list, you can also generate new labels. I recommend one label per topic.

For example, maybe you're monitoring PubMed and Google News for autism. You're more interested in the scientific research from PubMed. So you'd label both of them `autism`, move one to the archive, and star the other one so that it gets your attention.

TIP

Yes, you can apply multiple actions to one filter. You can't do two things that would cancel each other out, such as move it to the archive and then move it to the trash, but you can move it to the archive and apply a label, for example, or apply a label and then forward the mail to a different e-mail address.

▶ **Forward It.** Forward the e-mail to a specified address. Note this is not the same as using a POP client to download your GMail—we'll cover that momentarily.

▶ **Delete It.** Throw it away!

With regard to information trapping, filters are probably GMail's most important feature. But there are other settings on GMail you may want to tweak, especially if you want to download your e-mail.

POP downloading and other GMail settings

To access GMail's other settings, click the Settings link on the upper-right of your mailbox. A page of settings divided into tabs displays (**Figure 10.4**):

▶ The **General** tab is mostly cosmetic. How many Conversations do you want to see per page, do you want e-mail snippets showing or not, etc.

▶ The **Accounts** tab lets you use a different From address on your e-mail (you will have to verify that address before you can change it).

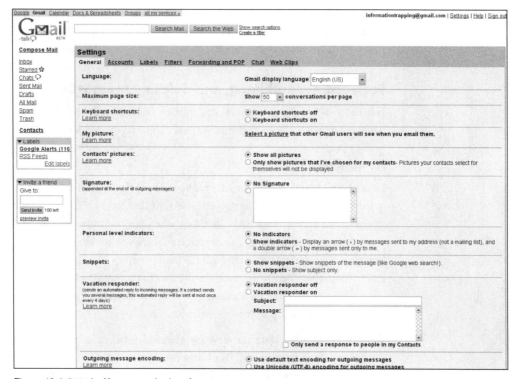

Figure 10.4 GMail offers several tabs of settings.

▶ The **Labels** tab lets you generate new labels, rename labels, and remove labels.

▶ The **Filters** tab lets you filter your messages (we've looked at that already).

▶ The **Forwarding and POP** tab lets you either forward *all* your e-mail (and either archive or trash GMail's copy) or download your e-mail from GMail (and either trash or keep GMail's copy). Note that you have to enable POP forwarding before you can use it. It's disabled by default.

Should you enable POP or not? If you'd rather keep your e-mail archived on your own computer, either for security reasons or because your own e-mail program has a more sophisticated filter, you should probably enable POP and then delete your messages from GMail. If you instead work from several different computers and never know where you'll be getting your mail next, make sure you're not using POP and are just accessing your mail from the Web.

You know your situation better than I do, so take a few minutes and adjust the GMail settings in the way that works best for you. From there we get into serious stuff: saving, moving around, and deleting messages.

Forwarding, archiving, and deleting messages

How do you know what to forward, what to archive, and what to delete? And how do you keep all that stuff you want to save without going crazy?

Forwarding

Here's how I handle it: For e-mail that I consider important, I set up filters to forward those messages to my cell phone, while keeping them on GMail so that I can act on them later. That way, when I'm not in front of a computer, I can keep a heads-up idea in mind of things I should really address immediately. I don't try to answer all my mail from my phone—I use it just as an alerting service. Of course, if I'm monitoring something for friends or clients, I usually end up forwarding a lot to them, too, although I wouldn't do this via a filter without their permission.

You should be a lot more conservative about forwarding to other people than forwarding to yourself. You know how much information you can handle. On the other hand, you don't want to flood your Mom or best buddy or client with a bunch of information they don't have time to review.

Archiving

GMail offers you over two gigabytes of storage. There's no real reason for you to throw anything away. That doesn't give you carte blanche to just dump your messages in there every which way. Use the organizing feature GMail offers: Labels.

Labels are located on the left of the main page. You can edit them from there or from the Settings page. You can also use filters to automatically apply labels to certain e-mails as they're coming in.

I strongly urge you to take a little time and think of an organizing theme for your labels now. If I were monitoring several topics, I might create a label for each topic. If I were just monitoring one topic, I might either put everything in one label or break out my labels by the services I was monitoring (Google Alerts, Watch That Page, and so on). It doesn't matter what you choose as long as it makes sense to you and you can apply it consistently as you generate filters.

Now, knowing Google, you might suspect that GMail has a very good search offering. And it does. Knowing that, you may wonder why it's important to organize your mail. Can't you just search for what you want after the fact?

To search for what you want, you have to know what to look for, and sometimes you just can't remember the right keyword. In this case, you have to browse through your e-mail until you find what you need. If you've organized your e-mails as you go, however, this is so much easier. There also will be times when you don't need to search but just need to browse through the e-mail to get a sense of what you've got. Having the mail organized into discernible topics makes it easier. And organizing your e-mail means that making sure it stays pruned and limited is less important.

Deleting

I'm not saying never delete any e-mail. There always will be times when you come across a false positive or a bit of junk or something that will otherwise have nothing to do with your e-mail. But GMail's amount of storage means that, if sufficiently organized, you can store and easily move through huge amounts of information. Two gigabytes' worth of text is an awful lot of text!

Of course, you won't always find what you're looking for by browsing. That's when you've got to search.

Searching

With GMail, the best way to search is using the Advanced Search form. It doesn't take up a lot of room, it's easy to understand, and there are a couple of features that make it easier to search from the Advanced Search form. Look for the "Show search options" link at the top of your mailbox page next to the query box.

The Advanced Search form looks like **Figure 10.5**.

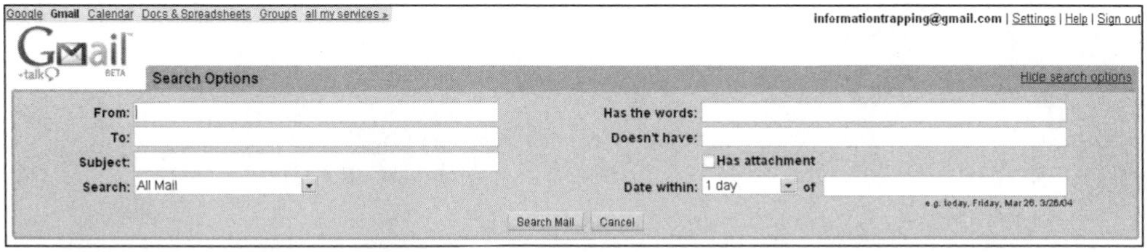

Figure 10.5 GMail's advanced search options.

Going from RSS to E-Mail

Yes, e-mail is great for alerts, but you may not have realized that it's also great for getting RSS feeds!

Many people prefer to keep their RSS feeds separate from their e-mail. They see it as a different tool requiring different attention. Other people don't want to have to learn yet another tool, get their information from yet another place, and would rather look at their RSS feeds at the same time using the same tools and their e-mail.

These viewpoints aren't right or wrong; they're just viewpoints. You may find that you prefer reading your RSS feeds in e-mail. In this case, I have two sets of tools for you to try. One is for Outlook, and one is for any kind of e-mail program.

You may also want to take a look at GMail's RSS feed offerings. Not all of GMail's accounts offer RSS feed readings, which it calls "Web Clips." To see if Web Clips are offered by your account, click the Settings link and look for a Web Clips tab. Web Clips are shown across the top of the inbox, one at a time, and therefore aren't suitable for heavy-duty information trapping. But if you're looking for a way to casually keep up with one or two feeds, this might be worth a try.

Reading RSS Feeds in Outlook

If you use Outlook, you're in luck. Outlook is by far the most popular e-mail program and therefore has a lot of add-ins available. If you want to try reading your RSS feeds in e-mail, take a look at the following:

- **intraVnews** (intravnews.com/) version 1.12 (as of this writing) is free for personal use or for use within charities and non-profits.

- **Attensa** (attensa.com) looks to be fairly new, but with lots of developing going on. The features for this Outlook-based feed reader include integration with the tagging site del.icio.us.

Non-Platform-Specific RSS to E-Mail Services

Don't have Outlook? Want to try reading RSS feeds in GMail? Great!

- **RSSFwd** (rssfwd.com/), a free service, asks you to provide the feed to which you want to subscribe. Then it shows you what the feed will look like, asks you for an e-mail, and confirms the e-mail. You'll get new items as they're added to the RSS feeds.

- **RMail** (r-mail.org/) has a slightly different format. You enter an e-mail address and the URL to which you want to subscribe, and you'll be added to the list. You can also see the most popular feeds that are already being subscribed to. Also free.

There's no law that says you have to receive all your RSS feeds by e-mail. There may be a few particularly important ones that you want to receive via e-mail, or even a few really important ones that you want to receive via a message on your cell phone. (You can find more information about mobile information trapping by registering your book at www.peachpit.com/title/0321491718—see the Tip that follows.) If the idea of reading RSS feeds via e-mail intrigues you, try viewing a few and see how you like it. You might want to switch completely to e-mail!

> **TIP**
>
> By registering your copy of this book at peachpit.com/title/0321491718, you can access additional chapters on mobile information trapping, RSS tools, keeping up with your traps, and more.

As you can see, the form is pretty straightforward. You can search by the To and From headers, by subject, and by what words are and aren't in the message. You can also search by date and whether or not the message has attachments. The drop-down menu lets you limit your message to a particular part of your e-mail, including labeled e-mail! This is just one more reason to make sure to organize your messages; it makes them much easier to search.

Let's consider a searching strategy for your messages. Because you're most likely going to be searching titles and snippets that have been e-mailed to you from alert services, you want to take a more general approach to the search than you would with a full-text search engine. However, you should take advantage of the special syntax whenever you can to help narrow your search. Are you sure it was a Google alert? Include **Google** in the subject. Are you sure that it had the word "green" in it? Search for the word **green**. Use as many of the small clues as you can remember, and then remove them one by one, because your memory may not be exact.

If you're used to using client-side e-mail programs such as Eudora or Outlook, GMail will take a little getting used to at first. But if you move around a lot and access your e-mail from several different computers, I think you'll appreciate the ability to access GMail from pretty much everywhere. The filters and spam filtering are very useful, too.

GMail has attracted a lot of interest in the online community, both for its affiliation with Google and for its large storage capacities. Many developers have made their own useful tools and gizmos to use in association with GMail. Some of these you might find useful; let's take a look.

A GMail Toolbox

Lots of outfits have come up with various GMail tools to help extend or change the GMail experience. Some of these tools are offered by Google, but most of them are not. The following are just a few of the tools you can add to your GMail experience, and a couple of Web sites that will keep you up to date on new ones:

▶ **GMail Notifier** (toolbar.google.com/gmail-helper/). This tool sits in your system tray and pops up a little notifier whenever you get an e-mail. Created by Google, GMail Notifier must be downloaded. It requires either Windows 2000 or XP or Mac OS X 10.3.8 or later (including Tiger).

▶ **GMail Loader** (marklyon.org/gmail/). Maybe you like GMail so much you want to switch ALL your e-mail to it. And now maybe you're wondering how you're actually going to do that. You're in luck. The GMail Loader will work with several types of e-mail programs and get them into GMail. This is a downloaded product; you have to be fairly computer-savvy to work with it.

▶ **GMail Drive** (viksoe.dk/code/gmail.htm). What's the point in having over two gigabytes of storage if you can't use it? GMail Drive lets you treat GMail like another drive on your computer. You have to be somewhat Windows-savvy to use this add-on.

▶ **GMail Preview Bubbles** (persistent.info/archives/2005/08/20/gmail-preview-bubbles). If you use Firefox and Greasemonkey, this is the extension for you. This Greasemonkey extension displays a popup "bubble" of message content when you mouse over it. If you need to quickly scan through messages, this tool provides a very cool way to do it.

▶ **gMailto Bookmarklet** (sippey.typepad.com/filtered/2004/06/gmailto_bookmar.html). Bookmarklets, small bits of JavaScript in bookmark form, perform all sorts of handy functions. This one gives you a one-click way to open an outgoing message in GMail. Surfing around, see something interesting, and want to e-mail a friend about it? No problem! That's what this bookmarklet is for.

▶ **GMail Tools** (gmailtools.com/). GMail Tools is a blog that keeps up with the latest tools and tricks—and sometimes available invites—for GMail.

▶ **GMail Tips** (http://gmailtips.com/). Whether you're new to the world of Web-based e-mail or just want to learn how to use GMail as efficiently as possible, you'll appreciate GMail Tips. It offers over 40 tips on how to use all aspects of GMail more effectively. If you want more in-depth instructions on how to make the most of GMail, this is the place. Wow, a whole chapter on GMail!

Other E-Mail Options

Of course, maybe you're not interested in using GMail. Maybe you don't think it's that great. Maybe you're not interested in Web-based e-mail readers. Maybe you want to try something besides GMail. I don't want to leave you out in the cold, so let me make a few suggestions.

For the most part, you have two e-mail options—Web-based (everything happens on the Web, so it doesn't matter which computer you're using or what operating system it's using) and client-based (the e-mail program sits on your computer and therefore you have to be at that computer to access your e-mail). Sometimes a solution can be both, especially if you use different computers between work and home. You can access your mail via the Web, and then come home and download it to your computer.

Web-based e-mail

Gmail isn't the end of all available Web-based mail services. In fact, it's barely the beginning. Several search engines and many, many independent companies offer Web-based e-mail. Take a look at Yahoo's mail offering, and then check with your ISP.

▶ **Yahoo Mail** (mail.yahoo.com). Yahoo doesn't offer as much storage as GMail does (as of this writing, it has only 1GB of storage) but it does offer spam and virus protection, as well as the ability to send Yahoo Alerts to your cell phone. And while you can only set up to 15 filters, you can block up to 500 addresses.

▶ **Your ISP**. Check and see if your ISP offers the ability to read mail online—most of them do. Your ISP's home page should let you know whether it offers this feature. Often it's linked from the front page (**Figure 10.6**).

I find this useful for when I'm away from home and I've just got to check on something. I go to a secure computer, log in to my e-mail, log out, and feel secure in the knowledge that I haven't deleted my e-mail—I've just looked at it. The message I looked at will still be there when I go to my main computer later and download my mail.

Figure 10.6

EarthLink lets you check e-mail from any computer.

Client-side e-mail

It seems that the most popular client-side e-mail reader is Outlook, based on the number of tools that are developed for it. But there are other readers available as well:

▶ **Eudora** (Eudora.com). One of the granddaddies of e-mail programs, I've been using it for well over ten years. It has integrated protection against spam and phishing, and a fairly powerful set of filtering tools. The downside is that it's less popular than Outlook and has fewer people developing for it.

▶ **Thunderbird** (mozilla.org/products/thunderbird/). If you're already using Mozilla or Firefox, you may want to take a look at Thunderbird, brought to you by Mozilla. It's a free, open-source program and, like Outlook, it has a lot of developers writing for it. You can get an idea of what extensions are available for Thunderbird at addons.mozilla. org/extensions/?application=thunderbird.

▶ **Pegasus** (pmail.com/). Though the Pegasus mail program is not as well-known as other e-mail programs, it's still fifteen years old. Pegasus is an excellent choice for older computers and operating systems that might not be able to handle the latest and greatest e-mail clients. It also has an extremely powerful filter system, and it's free. If you want very strong filters or you want an e-mail client that gives you more opportunity to look under the hood, Pegasus is for you.

Moving On. . .

Obviously, finding and setting up the information streams you need is the first part of information trapping. But the second part, which we've gotten into with this chapter, is management. How do you organize what you find? How do you make sure it gets your attention? When do you delete it (or should you ever delete it)?

Your e-mail box will be an important part of managing the information as it flows to you. Though Gmail is a free service, it offers a variety of filters, features, and add-ons that will help you track, and keep, the information you want.

But when you use a Web-based or client-based e-mail service, you're sitting in front of a computer. What do you do when you're on the road, with no laptop, no WiFi, nothing but your phone? If you want to learn how you can be an information trapper on the go, register your copy of this book at peachpit. com/title/0321491718, where you can access additional chapters on mobile information trapping, RSS tools, keeping up with your traps, and more.

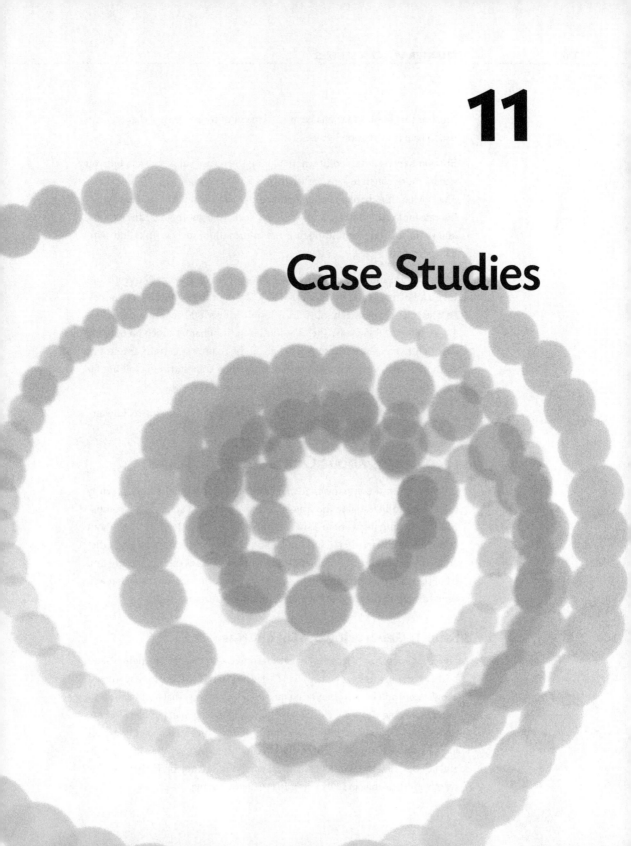

11

Case Studies

Most of this book so far has been discussion of tools—things that you can use to trap information better.

But you may be at the point where having the tools is all very well, but you need a more concrete sense of when and how you might want to use them. That's what this chapter is all about. We look at two hypothetical case studies: one for finding external information, such as news, reports, discussions, and so on, and one for finding internal information, such as links and critical comments.

As you might imagine, setting up a thorough set of information traps can take a lot of hours and touch on as many as two or three hundred resources. In one ongoing research job I do, I monitor over 800 separate pages and 1,500 different RSS feeds. The case studies in this chapter touch on only the highlights, or mention resources that might require a certain amount of caution or query revision. If you find your own trap-setting involving far more resources than the ones in this chapter, good for you!

Let's start with Fred, who needs to learn more about outsourcing to Taiwan.

Fred Learns about Outsourcing to Taiwan

Fred works in a company that makes computer parts. His boss recently asked him to investigate the feasibility of outsourcing some of his company's manufacturing work to Taiwan. Fred realizes that what he knows about outsourcing to anywhere could fit in an ant's lunchbox. So while he's discussing with his boss and others in the company what their needs are and what they hope to accomplish, he sets up several information traps that will keep him up to date and inform him about outsourcing.

Step 1: Generating useful queries

Fred decides to go to a fresh information source—a news search engine—and begin experimenting with query words. He heads over to Google News (news.google.com) and begins generating queries. He discovers that a simple search for **outsourcing Taiwan** yields about 100 results—very manageable—but the first ten were published in the last couple of days, meaning he could expect five stories a day from this search alone. Fred thinks that may be a little much, and besides, the stories don't actually fit what he's looking for. He narrows his search a little using **outsourcing Taiwan manufacturing**.

Bingo! He's halved his results, the first ten results were generated over a couple of weeks, and a cursory glance at the page summaries shows that these stories are exactly the sort of thing he's looking for. So he saves that search. After some more experimenting, he also settles on the phrase **"outsource to Taiwan"**, as well as the queries **"DRAM production" Taiwan**, and **DRAM outsourcing**.

Fred has generated two searches that address specifically what his boss has asked him about. But beyond that he has also generated a search that will give him ongoing information about the whole issue of outsourcing to Taiwan in the first place, as well as a couple of searches that remove Taiwan from the equation and look at the whole issue of computer manufacturing and outsourcing in general.

By monitoring these information traps, Fred will be able to both directly answer his boss's question and perhaps make a few suggestions of his own! (Maybe Fred will discover that Taiwan is not the best place to outsource some of its manufacturing—maybe it's India, China, someplace else, or nowhere at all.)

With these queries, Fred begins building his traps by starting at a news search engine.

Step 2: Using news search engines

Fred ponders how urgent his need is to get this information. He finally decides that he will have the Google News updates delivered to his cell phone, just to give him constant feedback about Taiwan and outsourcing in general. The rest of the searches he'll set up as RSS feeds and specify a certain time every morning to go over what's been delivered to him.

He stays at Google News, reruns the searches, and takes advantage of the option to send the results to his cell phone's e-mail address. Then he goes to Kebberfegg (researchbuzz.org/tools/kebberfegg.com), chooses the News option, and one by one generates OPML files for his queries. He then imports these files into his newsreader of choice, which happens to be NewsGator, and deletes the Google News feeds since he's already getting them by e-mail.

Fred now has the cornerstone of his information trapping—fresh information being delivered to him from two or three different angles. He will use the information that he gains from these searches to tweak his queries over time. Perhaps a new company pops up in Taiwan that does what his company is interested in—he may want to monitor them. Perhaps a new advocacy group arises—he'll want to monitor its activity and news. Fred knows that he's off to a good start, but he also knows that he may have to change his queries and direction over time.

Fred's next stop is to see if anybody out there is talking about outsourcing in Taiwan besides his company.

Step 3: Doing group and conversation searches

Fred begins his search at Yahoo Groups. By doing a general search for **out-sourcing**, he discovers 508 groups are available! He narrows the search a bit to **outsourcing manufacturing**. He finds a few interesting groups and reviews them. One of the groups looks so relevant to his interests that he subscribes so that he can read it in its entirety, noting that it has relatively low traffic (only a few posts per day). The other two groups are sometimes relevant, but not so much that he wants to read them all; they're pretty busy. For those he runs a few searches based on his original queries, and saves the results as RSS feeds when that's an option, and when it isn't, he notes the URLs so that he can send them to a page monitor.

In other situations, Fred might have found that the groups in which he's interested were private. In these cases, he would have had to subscribe using his Yahoo account. But he was lucky enough to find that all the groups in which he was interested were publicly available.

From there, Fred heads to Google Groups. (As you may remember from the earlier chapters, Google Groups is a combination of Usenet, a very large set of public discussion lists, and Google's own discussion groups.) A search of Google Groups' entire index for **Taiwan outsourcing** brings mixed results. On one hand, he's finding some good results. On the other hand, he's finding too many of them and too much spam. Fred decides to look for individual groups instead. If Fred had found a satisfying and relevant number of search results, he could have chosen to have search results for the entire index delivered to him as e-mail alerts.

One step forward...

Fred remembers that Google Groups offers far fewer lists than Yahoo Groups does, and risks a search on a single word: **outsourcing**. He finds just 150 results, and after some investigating picks five that he wants to monitor.

All the groups that he wants to monitor are extremely relevant to his interests and have a low number of members (fewer than 50 in each group) so he picks up the RSS feed for each group and adds it to NewsGator.

So far Fred has not deviated very much from the original queries that he picked up from his news searches. That's because he has been searching mostly for groups, and not for conversations within those groups. Now Fred is moving to search online message boards (Web sites that contain online discussion forums), and may discover that his searches will have to be altered for conversational style.

Fred goes to Yuku (yuku.com), a search engine for online message boards. He cautiously starts his search using the word **outsourcing** but gets no results. He searches for **Taiwan**, but gets only a few results that don't seem related to business. A search for **business** brings hundreds of results, all far too general.

Fred ponders. How would he pose the issue that he's investigating in an online bulletin board? After a few moments he comes up with this question:

`How do I begin outsourcing in my computer manufacturing business?`

. . .two steps back?

From that question he developed a new query: `"begin outsourcing"` and tried that. This query, while admirably specific, provided no results. He gave up and moved on to a different search.

Not all resources will provide useful traps to all researchers. Fred tried his original queries and then generated some new ones that seemed more appropriate to his research. While his results were better—a key indicator that his query revision was working—they were still not useful to his search. At this point, he could decide to let things lie and move on to the next resource, or continue to revise his query. In this case, he decided to move on.

Fred has a couple of choices. He can either try to search Google or Yahoo for more forums, using his query words and words that will be more likely to find forums and mailing lists (words like **forums**, **posting**, **thread**, **earlier**, and **later**). Depending on how much time he has to set up his traps and how much time he has committed to reviewing them, he could decide to stick with the "big two"—Yahoo Groups and Google Groups—or try to find more forums related to his interests.

At this point, Fred has a flow of news stories related to his interest and a somewhat more limited flow of discussion groups talking about his interest. His next task is to find Web sites dedicated to the topic in which he's interested and set up page monitors.

Step 4: Monitoring pages

Fred knows that most of the news sources he's monitoring are general. His next task is to find Web sites that are more oriented toward outsourcing specifically and see if he can integrate any of them into his information traps.

He starts with the Yahoo Directory (dir.yahoo.com). Knowing that Yahoo's directory is not a list of sites and is more of a subject index, he starts again with a single-word search query—**outsourcing**. He finds the relevant category and looks at the list of available sites. He finds half-a-dozen that seem to have potential and spends some time reviewing them. In some cases, he decides to monitor the front page. In other cases, he decides to monitor a different page on the site. And in one case, he decides to monitor three different pages on one site—the front page, the news release page, and the page of a journal relevant to outsourcing that is hosted on the site.

From there he moves to the Open Directory (dmoz.org) and tries the same thing, finding a few more useful pages. He doesn't feel, however, that he's getting full coverage of the outsourcing industry, especially as it relates to Taiwan. So he goes to Google and tries a specific search based on the search that failed when searching forums: **"begin outsourcing" advice**. He gets 371 results and is able to narrow that down to 10 pages to monitor what he did not find through the directory. He's now more comfortable that he's getting complete coverage.

Many information trappers might stop here, believing they're well on their way to becoming informed. In Fred's case, however, there's one more category of resource that he wants to cover.

Step 5: Monitoring stocks

In his research into outsourcing, Fred sees some publicly owned companies whose names are coming up over and over again. These companies have made decisions about outsourcing to Asia—some of them are including it in their strategies, some have pledged never to do it, and so on. Because Fred is interested in outsourcing as a possible direction for his company, he's interested in the fortunes of these companies.

Fred wants to monitor a specific type of data that's found on the Internet. In this case, it's stock performance. Perhaps in your case it will be something else. Fred probably has done various kinds of stock monitoring before. Perhaps his company even subscribes to an information service. If it does not, Fred could go to Yahoo Finance, for example (finance.yahoo.com) and either set alerts for certain companies or subscribe to their RSS feeds. In any case, such a specific type of information doesn't have to be part of the information trapping process, but it's relevant to Fred and his strategy.

Fred's future strategy

At the conclusion of his work, Fred has 75 or so feeds in his reader, several e-mail alerts set up, and a hundred or so pages in a page monitor. He has made his boss aware of his traps and will be spending an hour or so in the morning reviewing them before proceeding with the rest of the day's work. Fred has a base of constantly updating data to sift through as he builds his report about outsourcing in Taiwan. How long he uses this information depends on when his report is due, whether or not his boss wants him to treat his report as an organic, ever-changing document, the directions his research takes him, and so on.

In the case of Fred, most of the information he's looking for is external—it's not directly related to his company. In Ethel's case, however, there's a need for tracking more internal information.

Ethel Tracks a Blog

Ethel has a blog that she wants to use to make herself better known in the community. She understands that she'll need to create good content, make sure she's publishing an RSS feed, and submit her site to search engines. Beyond that she wants to see who is linking to her site and what is being said about her site.

Unlike Fred, who is monitoring information for a report that will one day end (ostensibly), Ethel is setting up her information traps to be monitored on a more-or-less perpetual basis. And unlike Fred, Ethel will be looking at resources like blogs, so she will probably have more luck with discussion groups, and may not need to monitor news at all. However, like Fred, her first step will be to figure out the backlinks and keywords for which she should be monitoring.

Step 1: Determining backlinks and keywords

Ethel's blog is a consumer advocacy site called "ICalledandAsked.com." That's both the name and URL of the site. The name is unique enough that she'll be able to use it in her trapping. If she had gone with a different name—**"I Don't Know"**—she might have had to confine herself to monitoring only for her blog's URL. If her name is uncommon enough, she might be able to monitor for that as well. **"Ethel Mae Potter"** is probably unique enough.

Ethel has three main things she can monitor: the name of her site, the URL of her site, and her own name. Is there anything else she should add? It depends on what's on her site. If she has a tool that other sites might link to—a dictionary, a featured article, a database of information—she could track that URL as well. If she doesn't, it's probably best to monitor just the URL of the home page.

Now that Ethel knows what she's looking for, she has to figure out where to look for it.

Step 2: Choosing resources to search

Fred, seeking external information, had a good sense of where that information was located. He was looking for credible information, data, and experiences. It was easy for him to determine where to look.

Ethel, on the other hand, is seeking internally focused information—links to her blog, mentions of its name, and mentions of her name. Where she looks is based on information about herself. Is she famous? Is she controversial? Is she known from some other arena?

It's entirely possible that for the purposes of monitoring information, Ethel is neutral—neither known nor unknown, controversial or not. That's the case we're going to look at here.

Step 3: Monitoring blogs

Because Ethel is not particularly famous or infamous, she decides to start her monitoring with blogs. Most blog readers read other blogs, so blog search engines are a good place to track mentions.

Ethel starts with Feedster (feedster.com), and begins the process of tracking her name, her URL, and her site's name. She decides to go with all RSS feed alerts in her blog searches—she's not interested in getting any notifications via e-mail. After she's set up these feeds, she wonders if she should be monitoring blogs for mention of her site's theme—consumer advocacy. After all, if she finds relevant blogs, she could ask them for links or begin a dialogue with them. She does a quick search for **"consumer advocacy"** and finds a small number of results scattered over a couple of weeks. Pleased, she adds these to her RSS feeds.

Continuing her search, Ethel visits some other blog search engines, such as Technorati (technorati.com) and Google blogs (blogsearch.google.com/), and generates several more feeds to add to her feed reader. With those added, she's confident that she'll be notified quickly whenever someone mentions her or links to her blog. She'll also have several chances to build her profile in the community by reading and responding to consumer advocacy posts on other blogs. If she goes a step further and registers with Technorati, she'll be able to get even more information about who's linking to her blog.

Of course, blogs are not the only place where people discuss and link to things. There's group discussion, as well.

> **TIP**
>
> When Fred was setting up information traps, he was able to evaluate his queries by the initial number of results he was getting. Ethel won't be able to do that in the searches for her name or her blog's URL. If she's only started, she might not have anyone linking to her at all! Ethel will have to set up many of her initial traps on faith and see what kind of results she gets. If she's getting too many mentions to keep up with, she may have to adjust her traps to exclude popular results (like from NewsIsFree, newsisfree.com) or try some other adjustment to cut down the flow.

Step 4: Monitoring group discussions

Ethel, like Fred, proceeds to Google Groups and Yahoo Groups to set some traps. Yahoo Groups is a tough one, because she can't search the entire database at one time, but has to pick groups that she thinks would mention her blog or her topic of interest. (Ethel can do a Yahoo Groups search for communities containing topics relevant to her blog, but she can't do searches for messages containing topics relevant to her blog.)

She finds a couple of active groups for consumer advocacy and decides to subscribe to them, both to monitor for mentions of her blog and to find bits of news that might make worthy blog items.

Google Groups is much easier for her. She sets up monitors for her name and the name of her blog, but decides against monitoring for the phrase **"consumer advocacy"** after she finds neither groups nor good search results that represent conversations in which she wants to get involved.

Ethel spends some time looking for online forums as well (using the techniques used by Fred earlier in the chapter) and does find some boards that catch her interest. Since Ethel is monitoring issues that are more consumer-level, it makes sense that she might get more use from online discussion boards. Her problem is making sure that she doesn't get overwhelmed with the number of results that she gets.

Step 5: Monitoring search engines

Ethel has to use search engines to set up some traps, but not for searching for consumer advocacy. Instead, she'll need to use the search engines to monitor for links to her site. She goes to Yahoo, Google, and MSN and searches for links to her site as well as the name of her site. She then sets these searches up as RSS feeds when that's an option, and alerts when it isn't.

Consumer advocacy is too broad a topic to include in a search engine. But Ethel could monitor for her name, as well as her blog's name. This may have to be adjusted over time if another famous Ethel Mae Potter appears on the scene.

Ethel could, if she wanted, access Yahoo and the Open Directory and find consumer advocacy sites that she could cull for news and posts. However, she wants to concentrate on blog content to build that community first, so she skips those resources. Her last big decision is whether or not she should monitor news search engines.

Step 6: Deciding whether to monitor news

In Fred's case, monitoring news was the cornerstone of his strategy. He needed fresh data and statistics about outsourcing. Since Ethel's research is more personal and site-focused, monitoring news is less of an issue for her.

There are three scenarios, however, in which she would want to monitor news:

▶ She is actively courting mentions from the media—by putting out press releases, having herself listed in expert directories, and so on. In this case, Ethel would want to monitor news search engines for her name and the name of her blog.

▶ She is trying to build journalist awareness in a more low-key way—for instance, by monitoring news search engines for her topic of interest and then contacting the journalist with comments, additional resources, or pointers to her blog.

▶ She wants to use the news search engines to find bits of interest for her blog. Using news search engines to find stories to add to the blog is better than using general search engines—the stories are fresher, flow is lower, and generally they're easier to target.

Ethel does have plans to start issuing press releases, so she monitors for her name and her blog's name. In this one case, she generates e-mail alerts and has them sent to her phone. She wants to be able to react quickly when a journalist mentions her in a story or her press release gets republished. All her other monitoring is done strictly by RSS feed.

Ethel faces the future

Ethel's needs are somewhat more basic than Fred's, but she will also have to be ready to tweak and change her traps in the future. She may become well known for her commentary on one particular topic, in which case she'll need to monitor that topic. She may develop a positive (or adversarial) relationship with a retail company over its consumer-relations policies, and decide she wants to monitor its press releases. It's even possible that a particular iteration of her name becomes prevalent (Ethel Mae P., for example) and she'll have to adjust her traps to accommodate that. As she realizes her goal of increasing her profile in the community and the blogosphere, her traps will have to be adjusted to reflect that.

At the moment, Ethel is committed to review her traps three times a week, with ongoing updates to the traps as necessary. Her timeline is open-ended; she has no plans to end the monitoring at all.

Different Strokes

As you can see from these two case studies, different needs are going to use different resources. A resource that's essential to one trapper may be all but useless to another. That's the first thing to remember. The second thing to remember is that your initial set of traps is not static. To keep up with the changes in your topic, be it internal or external, you will have to change them over time.

In a perfect world, you would be able to monitor all traps indefinitely. You would never have to back off, or do other things, or drop your topic, or anything. In that world you could let everything putter forever. But it isn't a perfect world, so in addition to knowing what to look for and how to look for it, you also need to know how to shut things off.

Shutting Off the Flow

The project is done. Or another project is coming along and you're drowning in work. Or some emergency has occurred and you need to stop monitoring your traps right now. In the cases where you have to put your trapper hat aside for the moment, there are several different ways you can back out of information monitoring, depending on what you're monitoring.

Shutting down RSS

Shutting down RSS, if you're using a feed reader, is no big deal. Just stop reading the feed. Preparing it so that you have a way back in is a little tougher. A lot of news is going to go by while you're preoccupied. Consider using Blogdigger (blogdigger.com) to save old posts from RSS feeds, but remember it's not a panacea—if you leave an RSS feed unread for more than 30 days or so, you're going to leave some things unfound and unread no matter what happens.

Shutting down e-mail

You have two options for shutting down e-mail, and they both involve filters.

The first way is to filter all your mail straight into an archive. That way you'll have it when you need it. However, some old alerts, especially for news searches, will get too old to be found in 30 days or so. Most news search engines don't keep archives for more than about 30 days, and most online news outlets also have a limit to how long they keep their stories online.

The second way is to filter your alerts straight into the garbage. If you're sure that you won't be able to read your alerts for a long time, or you're not quite finished with the topic (so you don't want to unsubscribe from the alerts completely), filter into the garbage.

You might be thinking, "Ah, that's not much different from just deleting them from my inbox!" It is. You'll find that the unused, unneeded alerts will drown out the current work you're trying to do. Go ahead and take the time to remove the alerts from your main e-mail. It will make it a lot easier to pay attention to your current tasks.

Shutting down page monitors

If you are using WebSite-Watcher or another client-side page monitor, shutting down your page monitors is as easy as never activating that software again. This simplicity comes with a tremendous disadvantage, however. You can't keep track of page changes as they occur over time.

With Web-based monitors that send you results by e-mail, it's different. You can filter those just as you filter e-mail. And you can keep track of several changes that appear over time. But like regular e-mail alerts, be sure to take the time to filter the unneeded alerts where they need to go—either into the garbage or into the archives.

Branching Out from These Basic Patterns

The purpose of this chapter has been to give you a bird's eye view of how people in two different situations might use the tools that we've discussed so far in this book. While you don't have to follow these steps exactly (and, indeed, lots of references to smaller resources have been left out) this should give you a basic pattern on which to base your own trapping strategy. Build on it from there.

12

Organizing
What You Find

Are you this type? You go to the grocery store. You're a whiz at doing the shopping, finding all the bargains, and reading all the nutritional labels. But when you get home, the groceries end up sitting on the counter forever because you never quite get around to putting them away.

This chapter is for you.

The most intricate set of information traps in the world will not help you if you're not able to put your hands on the information you need, and organize the information you find in a compelling way. In this chapter, we're going to look at strategies—lots of different strategies—for putting your information together and saving it. And because most of these strategies involve setting up client software on a single computer, we're going to start with a really basic, portable strategy. From there, we'll look at computer-based organizing solutions as well as Web-based solutions.

A Very Simple, Portable Strategy

Most of this chapter is going to cover software that you install on a single computer. That'll suit most people but not be particularly useful to those folks who have to move around between computers or check information traps in several different places. There are Web-based options as well, but for reasons of access or security you may not want to use those. The strategy I'm going to outline here is really step one—a ground-level option to help you get started. Later we'll get into more involved options.

The beauty of using a text editor

The most basic, extremely simple organizer is just a text editor. Its big pro is that plain ASCII text files are compatible with just about everything (and they stay compatible—ten years from now you will still be able to find a text editor for your ASCII files). Furthermore you can fit a lot of information in an ASCII file, and such files are very portable. The big disadvantage is that they only store text—they don't store multimedia, and they don't store fancy formatting (though they will store HTML files; you'll just see the formatting tags instead of the formatting itself).

Text files are how I do most of my initial information organizing. I use a program called UltraEdit; it's available at ultraedit.com. (In fact, I'm using it to write this chapter right now!) It allows you to open several different text files at a time. What I normally do is create one file for whatever I'm working on at the moment, leave it open, and toss in information as I find it. That way I know that everything I need is in one file at any particular time, and from there I can write up a Web page, a report, or an e-mail, and copy-and-paste it where it needs to go.

The ability to copy-and-paste my text and not have to worry about formatting weirdness is the primary reason I use this method of organizing information instead of setting up a Microsoft Word file or some other program that uses non-ASCII formatting.

And text files are usually small because, well, they're just text. And even when you have a big text file they're usually manageable. I've thrown multi-megabyte files at UltraEdit and they've been handled fine. When I need to take text files somewhere, I put them on a flash drive (a very small portable hard drive; you often see them on keychains or lanyards). I can carry them knowing I don't have to worry about special configuration files or whether or not a different computer has a particular program. (If worse comes to worst, Firefox will open a text file!)

UltraEdit isn't free; it costs $39.95. But if you want to try something a little less expensive, there are lots of free text editors available, including EditPad Lite (editpadpro.com/editpadlite.html), NoteTab Light (notetab.com/ntl.php), Cream (cream.sourceforge.net), and Metapad (liquidninja.com/metapad/).

Another portable option: wikis

The ability to toss a text file on a flash drive and head out the door makes keeping data text-based very useful to me. But there are other portable information options as well. There are wikis, which are structures that allow groups of people to add content collaboratively. (You can get more detail about wikis and their history at en.wikipedia.org/wiki/Wiki.) Can you imagine if something like that was portable? TiddlyWiki, also known as WikiOnAStick, is available at tiddlywiki.com. It allows you to set up a wiki that's portable on a Flash drive, and which you can open and edit in a browser. In fact, the instant you open the TiddlyWiki home page, you've downloaded the software (**Figure 13.1**).

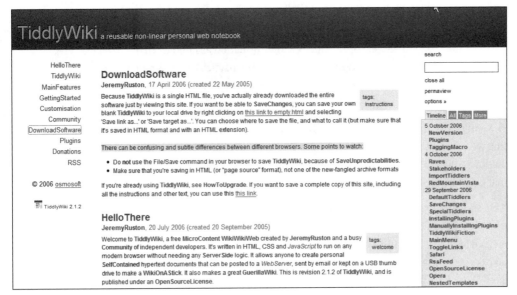

Figure 13.1 TiddlyWiki allows you to create outlines of information and carry them on a flash drive. Acquiring it is as simple as visiting the home page.

Maybe you're not sure about what browsers will be available on a computer when you get to where you're going. In that case you may want to also put Portable Firefox (portableapps.com/apps/internet/firefox_portable) on your flash drive. Portable Firefox is a version of Firefox designed to be as portable as possible. It takes your cookies, bookmarks, and other browser information with you as you move around.

If you don't want to use client-based software, or at least software that you can't put on a flash drive and carry with you, your organizing options are going to be limited to what you can find on the Web, which may carry with it security and privacy implications. You won't have to worry about being around your computer all the time, but how you can manipulate your data will be limited.

Let's look at options beyond simplicity now, starting with more extensive client-side software options.

Organizing Information on a Single Machine

If you're going to be doing all your work on a single machine, the advantage is that you're going to be doing all your work on a single machine. And that means you can can "pull back" from the idea of just organizing the information that you're gathering and focus on a bigger idea—indexing the contents of an entire machine! From there you can "zoom down" to organizing information on a project level.

It wasn't too long ago that trying to search an entire computer was very tedious. Windows offers tools that allow you to do it but they're slow and sometimes the search results don't give you the information you need.

But now Web-based search engines have begun offering tools that allow you to index the contents of your computer (though not all contents—more about that shortly). These programs go through your computer rather like a search engine "spider" goes through a Web site, and builds up an index of your computer's contents. They then allow you to search the content by keyword, getting results that sometimes include a preview of the item, when it was created, and so on. The search engine technology offered by these indexers allows you to do deeper and faster searching on your computer than you can usually do with the Windows search utility. We'll take a look at three of the search engine desktop searchers here, from Ask, Google, and Yahoo.

What's Getting Indexed and by Whom?

Unfortunately, these search engines on your desktop can't index everything. If you're using some super-specialized, very rare software that saves files in its own proprietary format, these search engines probably aren't going to be able to help you.

What do I mean? All indexing programs can take a survey of what's on your computer—just a list of files—and build an index from that. So if you're just searching by filename, a desktop indexer will probably be able to find the filename no matter what kind of file it is. However, a desktop indexer will not be able to go into every kind of file and index every single word. So if you're looking for a phrase within the contents of a file ("Dear Aunt Sally,") a desktop indexer will be able to search only a limited number of the files on your computer to find it. It's kind of like the difference between searching the Yahoo Directory—where you're searching only file names and descriptions—and searching Google, where you're searching the entire contents of Web pages.

So which desktop indexers support which files? I'll note that as we look at each of your options.

Search-engine indexers for your computer

Warning! These indexers are, for the most part, Windows-only. I suspect that as the Apple brand has gotten very popular (thanks to the iPod, iTunes, and other Applesque innovations), we'll be seeing a greater effort to support those folks who use a Mac. Watch the offerings from the search engines to see if they take the lead in offering Mac support for their products.

Ask Desktop

Ask Desktop (sp.ask.com/docs/desktop/) requires Windows 2000 with SP3 or Windows XP on a computer with at least 500MHz and 128 MB RAM minimum.

Once you've installed Ask Desktop, as with any other indexer, you'll have to wait for it to finish indexing your computer before you make the most of it. When you first install it, Ask will open a browser window and show that it's indexing your computer, along with a notification of the last files indexed and how many files total have been indexed. How long the indexing takes depends on how large your hard drive is and how good your computer's processor is. My experience is that it usually takes an hour or so. Ask keeps refreshing the number of files that you have indexed.

Once your hard drive is indexed, you can search within your browser, or you can open up the client interface. (I prefer the client interface, as it gives me access to the preferences for the program, allows me to download the latest version, and lets me set the indexing speed for slow or fast.) Searching is by simple keyword; you can search the computer, the Web, or your e-mail (Outlook or Outlook Express e-mail). When you run a search, your results will be divided up into tabs (**Figure 13.2**).

Some types of files can be previewed in the right pane. The first tab will have all the results, but the other tabs will be divided into folders, pictures, applications, and so on. On the left of the screen will be results, while on the right is summary information about each file as you click on it. Some files, like audio and graphics files, will actually preview in the right side of the screen (sounds will play, you'll get a thumbnail of images, and so on). Double-click on the filename to open the file itself.

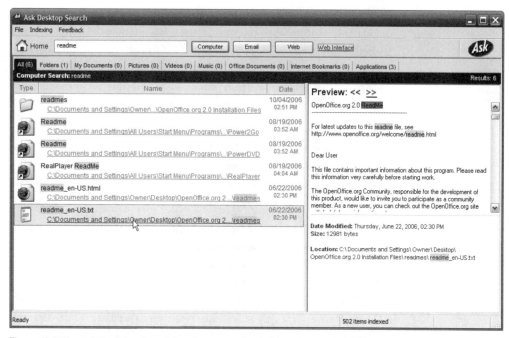

Figure 13.2 The Ask Desktop Search breaks up search results across several different categories.

Ask Desktop supports Microsoft Office versions 2000 and higher (this is what Ask claims, but I found that the Desktop Search also indexed files made with Office 97), Outlook, Outlook Express, PDF and ZIP files, image files (.jpg, .gif, and .png), music files (.mp3, .wma, and .wav), video files (.mpg and .wmv), several comment formats, HTML, and TXT files.

Ask does not offer esoteric file format indexing; it's actually pretty limited in what it does index. On the other hand, Ask has a small file footprint and won't put a strain on a slower computer. If you have an older computer and you want to index documents that are mostly from Microsoft applications, start here.

Google Desktop

Google Desktop (desktop.google.com) requires Windows XP or Windows 2000 SP 3+.

It just happens to have a desktop search engine, and also offers "gadgets" for desktop information, as well as the ability to index the contents of your

GMail account. Because of this, you'll have to supply a little bit of additional information when you start up the application; you'll need to specify whether you want to index your GMail information (assuming you have GMail) as well as whether you want to get Google "Gadget" content (little programs that you can set up on your desktop) and whether you want to use Google as your default search engine in Internet Explorer.

You'll also have to specify whether you want usage information to go to Google or not. Google uses the information you send it to personalize the kind of information that displays in the sidebar, but if you have privacy issues, you can choose not to send information to Google (and thus disable some of the advanced features).

Once you have answered these questions, Google starts indexing your hard drive (giving you an estimate for how long it will take) and displays your sidebar, which includes things like photos, news, weather, and a little scratch pad where you can save notes. If you want more, there are literally hundreds of Google Desktop Gadgets available at desktop.google.com/plugins/. By default, Google Desktop will only index items when your computer is idle. You may choose to start indexing immediately, but it could slow down your computer.

Google Desktop's search search is rock simple because—surprise!—it looks just like Google's regular Web search! Google Desktop's search runs inside your browser (**Figure 13.3**).

Figure 13.3

Google Desktop's search looks just like Google's regular search.

Searching is by keyword, and the search results look as Googly as the search page. Search results show the name of the file and its location (and a snippet if Google can index that file), as well as when it was indexed and an option to open the folder in which the file resides. You can sort your results by relevance or date (since Google's indexing your desktop, it can determine the file dates of items). All items are presented by default in the search results, but you can also choose to see only e-mails, files, Web history, chats, or other files.

There may be a little additional information depending on the type of file being returned in the results. Image files have thumbnails in the search results, while text files have caches.

You can use Google Desktop as just a simple search, but you do have some other options that you can see in the preferences. The Desktop Preferences link is next to the query box on the Google Desktop home page (**Figure 13.4**).

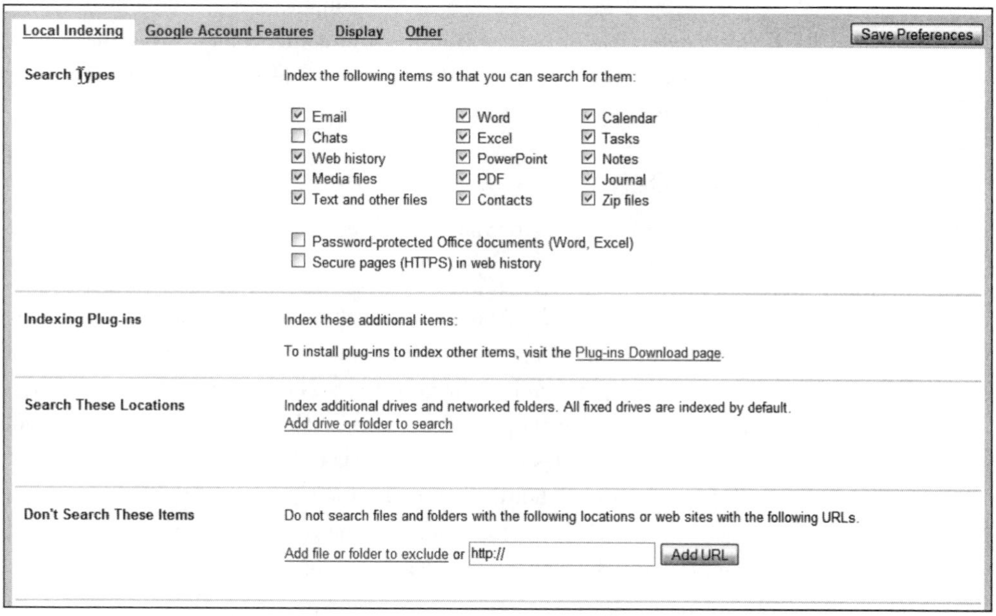

Figure 13.4 Control what's being indexed via Google Desktop's preferences.

Preferences are set up in tabs and include specifying which file types you want to index and whether you want to add any other filetypes for indexing. (Google has a subset of its gadget page at desktop.google.com/plugins/c/index/all.html?hl=en that will give you access to lots of additional indexing plug-ins, from Belkasoft's ICQ plug-in for GDS Pro to Larry's Help File indexer.)

You can also add or remove files and folders from your indexing, as well as encrypt your index and data files (though this will impact your computer's performance). Finally you can choose to have your desktop's indexed files available for search across several desktops. Because Google stores your files on its servers, you can search your files via your Google account from no matter where you are. This has serious privacy and security implications; think carefully before you decide to do this.

Google Desktop supports a variety of formats including Microsoft Office, MSN and AOL Instant Messenger, Google Talk, PDF, music, images, and ZIP files. In addition Google, as previously mentioned, also offers dozens of plug-ins for searching more obscure file types.

Google Desktop not only offers lots of plug-ins for extreme flexibility, it also offers the ability to index across computers, if you do your trapping from more than one place. However, this ability comes with some privacy and security risk, as your data files will be stored away from your computer. Think carefully about using it.

Yahoo Desktop

Yahoo Desktop (desktop.yahoo.com) requires Windows XP or Windows 2000 SP 3+.

When you download Yahoo Desktop, you not only get the application, you also get the Yahoo Toolbar, which is an installation option when you first install the program. When the program has been completely installed, you also have the option of logging in with your Yahoo account so that Yahoo can index your Yahoo Messenger conversations and Yahoo address book contacts. If you don't have a Yahoo account or don't want to share that information, just click Cancel. When you first launch Yahoo Desktop, you get the should-be-familiar-by-now search on the left and preview on the right (**Figure 13.5**).

Unlike the other two desktop indexers, Yahoo Desktop has a client interface and doesn't work through the browser. Furthermore, Yahoo Desktop defaults to showing just results from your e-mail. You'll have to view the All tab, furthest to the right on the results page, to see all your results. Otherwise, the Yahoo Desktop results page is excellent, showing Microsoft Office documents in preview mode and even playing multimedia (**Figure 13.6**).

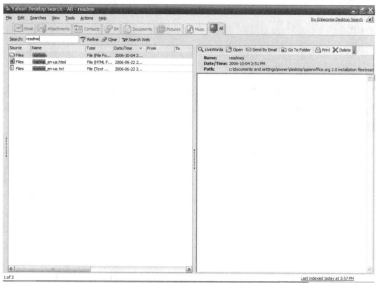

Figure 13.5

Yahoo uses a client application instead of a browser and filters to search for keywords.

Figure 13.6

Yahoo Desktop previews a variety of documents excellently, including HTML.

A handy Refine button lets you easily narrow down searches further by a variety of factors, including date/time, size, and path. I found both the searching and the indexing to be very quick; you can increase the speed and effectiveness of the indexing by choosing Tools > Options from the main menu and then choosing Indexing Priority from the Options screen. While you're here, you can also choose some other options for indexing and searching with Yahoo Desktop.

Yahoo supports several different kinds of files, including Outlook, Outlook Express, Thunderbird, Microsoft Office, PDF, and, of course, plain text and HTML files.

Yahoo also has a free downloadable expansion pack that allows indexing of an additional 300 file types. You can download the pack and get a full list of the additional file types at desktop.yahoo.com/filetypes.

You'll want to spend some time in the preferences menu that I mentioned above. It was here that I had to do a little additional tweaking. For example, I had to set as a preference that media files (such as music files) would play automatically in the preview pane. Without doing this, I would have to launch them manually every time I found a music file. Yahoo Desktop Search also has a More Indexing option that shows you exactly how much is going to be indexed on each folder of your hard drive (**Figure 13.7**).

Figure 13.7

Be sure to check the indexing options to see what Yahoo Desktop is actually getting in its index.

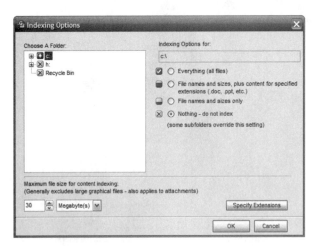

Yahoo Desktop seems to not index the contents of your Program Files directory by default. If you've installed programs in that folder, and the information generated by the programs is also kept in that directory, you want to make sure that at least specific subfolders within the program folder are being indexed. This is doubly important if you have programs there that are critical to your information trapping.

Also, be sure to check the default indexing for e-mail clients. It appears that Yahoo Desktop does not index e-mail by default. If you're sharing a computer or have security/privacy concerns, this is probably a good thing. However, if you have a computer to yourself and you're doing a lot of collaborative searching that's coordinated by e-mail, you definitely want to make sure it's being indexed!

Fleshing Out Client-Side Options

Computer-level search engines are a good start when you want to make the information on your machine findable. But from there you actually need to organize the information relevant to your topic, and computer-level search engines are not going to help you stash away the stuff that you find while you're browsing the Web. For that you need an information organizer. I've got three for you to look at: Net Snippets, Surfulater, and Onfolio.

What these programs do, for the most part, is work with your browser. As you're browsing you might find a story you find interesting, or some text, or a page. These information organizers allow you to take what you come across and put it into a format that makes it easy to organize. They range from free to over $100, and they all have a bit of a learning curve. If you use Internet Explorer, you'll have no problem using any of these offerings. If you use Firefox, you should be able to use them with no trouble, but you might have to install extensions. However, if you use Opera you're probably out of luck: I found that, for the most part, these programs were not Opera-compatible.

Net Snippets

Net Snippets (netsnippets.com) comes in a free and a couple of paid versions, and works with Firefox and Internet Explorer. If you want to use Net Snippets with Mozilla or Firefox, you'll have to install a Net Snippets button, which you can learn more about at netsnippets.com/mozilla/install. asp. Once you've installed Net Snippets (and the button if you're using Firefox), you'll see a little Net Snippets button on your toolbar. Click it and you'll get a little sidebar next to your browser (**Figure 13.8**).

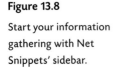

Figure 13.8

Start your information gathering with Net Snippets' sidebar.

Here you can create a set of folders to organize your content (which I recommend if you're covering several different topics). If you want to add the contents of a page you're viewing, right-click on the page you want and choose Add Page to Net Snippets. You'll get a popup window where you can specify the importance of the save, make notes, and modify the page to a certain extent by removing formatting, converting to text-only, and so on (**Figure 13.9**). Once you're finished, you save the page to Net Snippets.

This is a useful tool, but you do have to use it—if you only save half your pages you're going to end up frustrated. Net Snippets does allow you to do keyword searching as well as look at the pages you saved within the last 7 or 30 days.

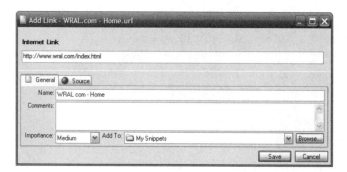

Figure 13.9

Once you "snip" an item, you can set its importance and add notes.

There is a free version of Net Snippets and two pay versions; standard for $79.95 and professional for $129.95. You can get more information about the different versions of Net Snippets at netsnippets.com/compare.htm.

Surfulater

Surfulater (surfulater.com) is also available for Firefox and IE. Once you've installed it, and installed the extension for Firefox if necessary, you'll see that you get a lot of functionality just from the right-click menu while you're browsing.

As you're browsing, you may find some information you want to keep. Right-click in the body of the page you want to keep, and you'll get options to save the page, to save the article plus the page, or to just add the article. When you've done that you'll get a window that shows you what you've saved. Note that if you highlight text on the page before you choose an article to save, you'll end up with a lot more information saved in Surfulater (**Figure 13.10**).

If you look at the left side of the screen you'll see that Surfulater saves its pages in an outline format. You can set up several different folders and organize the information you want that way. If you're monitoring and gathering a lot of information on several different topics this is pretty much critical; while you can search Surfulater by keyword, organizing your materials at the onset makes it easy to browse as well.

Surfulater costs $35 but a free trial version is available.

Figure 13.10

If you highlight text before saving an item, Surfulater will grab more text.

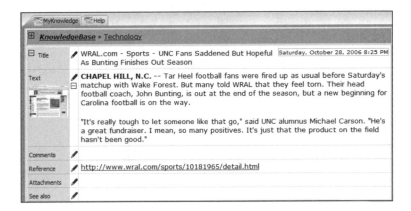

Onfolio

Onfolio (onfolio.com) used to be an independent company, but in 2006 it was purchased by Microsoft and is now a free download that's incorporated with the Windows Live Toolbar.

To use Onfolio, you'll have to install the Windows Live Toolbar (available at toolbar.live.com/) and then install the Onfolio button (which you can get at onfolio.com).

Onfolio is accessible from the browser in two ways. you can right-click and get the option to save a page or a site to Onfolio, or you can click on the Onfolio button in your Windows Live Toolbar. Onfolio launches as a browser sidebar (**Figure 13.11**).

Again, right-clicking brings you a lot of options in Onfolio; when you choose to save pages, you're given a popup window to enter any notes you want to enter, name the page, and save the page as either a link or as an actual local copy of the page. I save actual pages whenever possible, realizing that there's no telling how quickly a page might vanish off the Internet. If you have space limitations, however, you might want to limit yourself to saving URLs only (**Figure 13.12**).

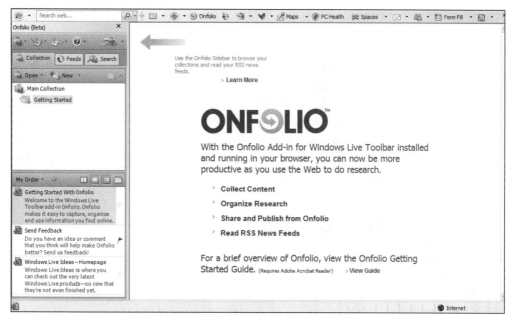

Figure 13.11 Onfolio is part of the Windows Live Toolbar (above) but launches in a sidebar (left).

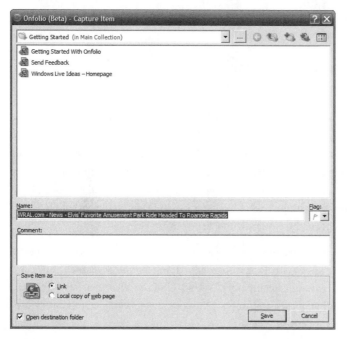

Figure 13.12

Onfolio's options for saving a page.

In addition to having the option of saving a single page, you also have the option of saving an entire Web site. Now as you might imagine, this can be a very extensive, not to mention time-consuming, thing to do. My site, ResearchBuzz, has thousands of pages. So when you open the save site dialog you get a window similar to the save page window, but it asks you how many "levels down" you want to save. Be sure to use the "Advanced" dialog, which lets you specify what kind of files you want to download (just Web pages, or PDF files, .doc files, etc.), the maximum number of files you want to download, and how you want Onfolio to respond to timeouts (**Figure 13.13**).

Figure 13.13

Be sure to use the advanced options if you save an entire site! You'll want to set limits on how much you download.

Like Surfulater, Onfolio offers the ability to organize your saved materials into folders, and again they're keyword-searchable. Right-clicking on an item you've saved gives you the option to do a variety of things, including flagging the item with one of many colors, editing comments, exporting the contents, or even "blogging" the item you've found (**Figure 13.14**). (You need to configure what blog you use in Onfolio; supported platforms include Blogger, LiveJournal, and TypePad.)

I can't imagine too many scenarios where you'd want to save the entire contents of a Web site. Perhaps if you're doing competitive intelligence and want to go through a company's Web site and see what they have, or if you find an online library and find all the contents very relevant and very useful. If you save entire Web sites, be sure to put a maximum page download limit, lest you discover that the site you're targeting has a secret stash of press releases and you're going to be downloading for the next two days.

Figure 13.14

Once you've saved a page, you can edit it, flag it, even blog it.

Choosing the best program

Which of these programs do you want to use? If you want something fairly simple to use, try Surfulater. If you're looking for something that has the capacity to download large files, look into Onfolio. And if you're looking for something that offers a full package, from getting the information to turning it into a nice report, try Net Snippets.

I've presented you with some pretty heavy-duty offerings for client-side information organizing. Software like Onfolio and Net Snippets can take an information-monitoring project all the way from the gathering to the publishing stage. And that's as it should be; all the information is installed on your computer, pages can be saved in their entirety, and you're operating from your own "workbench."

But you may find that a client-based organizing solution is not for you. You want to be able to do your searching across several different computers, or create a place of organization that several different people can access. Unless you're all in one room together, that's hard to do from a single computer! In this case, you might want to use Web-based organizing solutions, which I cover next.

Web-Based Organizing Options

The intention of this type of solution is the same as client-based solutions—to help you organize the information you find. But in execution, Web-based solutions are a little different. There may be a limit to how much you can have stored on a site. With your speed of access there may be only so much you want to access at a time. You may have security or privacy concerns.

Like going from plain text files to something really extensive like Onfolio, you have your choice in Web-based solutions, from the really basic to the really extensive. We'll start with the basic and then get more complex.

When I say simple, I mean simple. I mean what are basically bookmarks online. For just saving a list of URLs and sites, I like using tagging sites like del.icio.us and RawSugar.

Tagging sites

We have discussed tagging earlier in the book. Now let's look at it briefly from a user perspective as opposed to a researcher perspective.

Tagging sites allow you to save pointers to Web sites with both descriptions and tags. And as we've seen earlier, if enough people participate in a site that allows tags, then soon you develop a very large and active collection of resources that are searchable by keyword.

Because it is currently the eminent tagging site and because there are so many tools to make using it easier, I'm going to cover del.icio.us here. But I'm going to also mention other tagging sites that you may want to check out.

For all that I love about del.icio.us (del.icio.us/), I can't stand the name (I can't seem to stop typing it incorrectly), so as you've probably already noticed, I call it Del instead. To use Del, you'll need to register, which requires a user name, password, and e-mail. Once you've confirmed and set up your account, you have a couple of options.

The first option is to take ten minutes or so and try out some keywords, see what other Del users have bookmarked for the keywords in which you're interested. This will potentially give you some new resources to put in Del, as well as some ideas as to what keywords you should be using to tag your resources.

The second thing you can do is start surfing and dropping things into del.icio.us as you find them. There are a lot of tools available to make this easy.

Del itself offers one at del.icio.us/help/buttons; it's a bookmarklet to both see your Del bookmarks and to add bookmarks to your Del site. Quick Online Tips has a bunch of alternate bookmarklets that add a little more functionality at quickonlinetips.com/archives/2005/02/absolutely-delicious-complete-tools-collection/.

There are Firefox extensions to make posting to del.icio.us easier at addons.mozilla.org/extensions/moreinfo.php?application=firefox&id=527 and polarhome.com:753/~pwlin05/delic123/. And if you get a little crazy and post so many things to del.icio.us that you lose track of whether you've already posted them or not, there's Familiar Taste, which is a Greasemonkey extension that lets you check to see if you've already added an item to your del.icio.us bookmarks. It's at blackperl.com/javascript/greasemonkey/ft/.

If you're concerned about keeping your research and your URLs private, Del may not be for you. It's really designed as a site that aggregates bookmarks and interesting sites. If your overwhelming concern is keeping your bookmarks private, try Boz at sandbox.sourcelabs.com/boz/, which encrypts your bookmarks on your browser.

The following are some other bookmark/tagging sites you might find useful:

▶   **MyBookmarks** (mybookmarks.com) is free and gives you the option to make bookmarks publicly available.

▶   **Furl** (furl.net), which is brought to you by LookSmart, lets you not only save a link to a page but also a cache of a page. The window for adding a link to your archive includes the option to rate the page as well as mark it private and to assign to it one of several categories.

▶   **Yahoo's Bookmarks** (bookmarks.yahoo.com/config/set_bookmark) is good for people who already have a Yahoo account and don't want to do more than manage and keep a set of bookmarks online. It's not heavy-duty, doesn't offer a lot of tagging and saving features like some of the other utilities in this chapter, but it's a good basic bookmark manager, especially if you're already using Yahoo Directory to start with.

▶   **Simpy** (simpy.com) looks similar to del.icio.us, but offers a pull-down menu to specify whether an entered bookmark is public or private. You also have the option of sending a link to other people at the time you're adding it to your directory of bookmarks. Simpy also allows you to sync the bookmarks in its service with del.icio.us.

▶   **RawSugar** (rawsugar.com) is a tagging resource like del.icio.us, but is rather newer. In addition to the tagging option, RawSugar users can see the latest links added to the site and do regular Web searching via Google in addition to the tag searching of RawSugar's archives. (If you search for something that isn't found at RawSugar, it automatically reruns the search using Google.)

The sites I just mentioned here are basic bookmark/tagging sites. But we can get a little more extensive than that, by looking at Web-based resources that are designed to act more like a research partner for you. If you tend to move around between several different computers *and* you don't have much in the line of security concerns, online organizing resources can be very useful as they're accessible all the time and from anywhere. They come in several different flavors, from page keepers to free-form databases to wikis. We'll look at several different examples.

Extensive Web-based organizing sites

Maybe you want something that's more extensive than just bookmarks, but you want to be able to access it from any computer. In that case you might want to consider a Web-based organizing site. These sites offer the ability to extensively organize information yet access it from any computer. Most of them have a bit of a learning curve, though, so be prepared to invest some time in getting used to them.

eSnips

eSnips (esnips.com) is a service of Net Snippets, which we covered earlier in this chapter. The differences are that the service is online, and you get 1GB of space to hold the snips of information from the Web or from your computer that you want to save.

Registration is free. Once you've confirmed your registration, you're invited to download an eSnips toolbar (which works in Internet Explorer, Firefox, and Netscape). You can also get an extension for Firefox. The eSnips toolbar "floats" on your desktop, giving you a quick way to save snippets you find to your online eSnips account. If you want to save lots of "bits" of information and are less interested in whole pages and sites, eSnips is quite useful.

OnlineHomeBase

OnlineHomeBase (onlinehomebase.com) is a "free-form" information keeper. Instead of having to figure out how you'll bookmark something, or structure it so it fits into an existing infrastructure, you can use Online-HomeBase to create collections of free-form information, in addition to organizing the people who need the information.

OnlineHomeBase is a subscription service costing $2.95 a month, but a free 14-day trial is available. Once you've registered, you'll be taken on a quick tour. Take the tour; it's worth it. You'll then have the option to create your new HomeBase; you have several different layout options, including three columns with a calendar and even a daily diary which you update by sending e-mail (**Figure 13.15**).

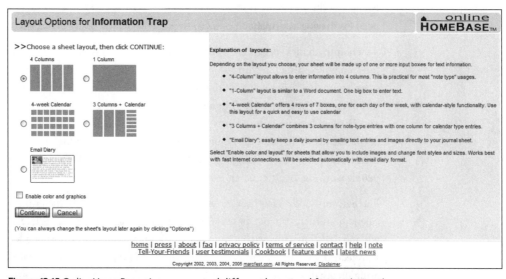

Figure 13.15 OnlineHomeBase gives you several different layout and formatting options.

The HomeBase consists of two large parts; an online calendar and an online notepad. Don't be put off by the word "notepad"; you can actually upload images and links into the notepad. (Note that some of this functionality works best with Internet Explorer.) There's also a calendar where you can put events and reminders. If you don't mind using a little geeky formatting (a couple of semicolons) you can actually e-mail yourself reminders of events. With a little more text formatting you can e-mail other people reminders of events, and actually get reminders on your cell phone.

OnlineHomeBase is not the ideal solution if you're a) married to Opera or another more obscure browser; b) needing a start-to-finish infrastructure for keeping your information and developing your reports; or c) concerned about having to do a little text-formatting geekery. But if you're in a small group of people and you want a basic tool for collaboration, and a tool would come in handy, this is useful. And it's very inexpensive. Note that the service does include only 10MB of online storage, which nowadays is pretty paltry. Don't choose this service if you're going to upload a lot of graphics and files that'll eat up that space!

TWiki

No no, not the little robot from Buck Rogers. TWiki (twiki.org) is a wiki developed for sharing information between a group of people across an enterprise.

As an information-organizing solution, this is probably the largest and most complex thing I'm going to mention in this chapter. It's actually a free, open source software solution that's being used on many corporate sites (the Web site lists a variety of clients that use it, including Yahoo, Motorola, and Disney. For obvious reasons most of these sites use TWiki behind a corporate firewall). Since the whole point of a wiki is that it's editable by any member of a team that's using it, this is great when you have large groups of people working together on an information-gathering project.

Furthermore, TWiki has been extended by a large set of plug-ins, including a calendar and access to databases and RSS feeds. While this software is free, it will require a huge investment in time and training to make the most of it for a project. If you need an enterprise-size solution for your information gathering or organizing, I urge you to try TWiki. Independent researchers and those working in small groups in the same place will likely find it overkill.

Backflip

Backflip (backflip.com) is another information manager that's more about gathering and managing pages than it is about gathering and managing small bits of information. Like many of the other resources mentioned in this book, it's a free service. Unlike some of the other resources mentioned in this book, it's not designed to share bookmarks. Backflip bookmarks are private by default; this is idea for a solo researcher who doesn't want to share his or her bookmarks even inadvertently.

When you've registered, you'll have the option of importing your bookmarks as well as generating some general-level folders for organizing your bookmarks. For the information trapper who wants to use these tools to organize a few different topics, most of these folders probably aren't necessary.

There are also other ways to view your pages as well, including looking at your most popular pages as well as your most recently added pages. Backflip has a bevy of tools that you can add to your browser to make "backflipping" pages easily; however, if your browsing isn't proving very inspirational, you can also check out pages that are being backflipped often, as well as the contents of publicly available folders (remember, Backflip bookmarks are private by default, but there is an option to make them public).

This chapter has covered just some of the solutions you can use to gather, share, and organize your information. There are lots more. To find more resources to experiment with, try searching Google or Yahoo for online bookmark managers or information organizers.

Sticking to a Strategy

The most important thing is to have some kind of strategy for how you're going to accumulate your information (and share it if you're working within a group). Maybe you'll settle on something simple, like the multiple-tab text editor that I use. Or maybe you need to work with several different people across a huge company, and you need an elaborate solution like TWiki. No matter what you finally choose, stick with it for at least a month. It takes that amount of time to develop a habit to save the information as you trap it. Don't say to yourself, "I'll find this later," or "I'll remember where this is." I promise you: you won't. Trap as you go. (For what it's worth, I have to remind myself of this all the time too!)

Accumulating and organizing the information you find is only the second step in your three-part process. The first part is to find and monitor the information. The second part is to accumulate and organize it, and the third part is to reuse and republish it, which we'll look at in the next chapter.

13

Publishing Your Information

In the last chapter, we looked how to organize the information you gather. In this chapter, we look at how you go about publishing it.

Is there a difference? Definitely. As you might have noticed in the last chapter, a lot of the options for organizing and gathering your information are designed to be private. While you're gathering, polishing, or just thinking about how all the bits fit together, you may not be ready to make it available to the public. The publishing aspect is when you have pulled something together—an article, a report, a book—that you're ready to unleash on the world.

Of course, some of you might be doing research that's not designed for perusal by the entire world. In this case, there may be a private arena—an intranet, perhaps—where the information can be stored. Or maybe the information is just for you. I find in this case that making an effort to summarize it—even if it only amounts to writing a rough article or an e-mail to myself—helps me understand the information I've gathered together and maybe even gives me a few more insights. Even if you only want to share your information with a small group of people, it's critical to discover a good way to make sure the information gets where it needs to go.

You might think that when publishing information online you're pretty much limited to one option: create your own Web site and publish your pages there. Seven or eight years ago, that might have been the case, but these days you have lots and lots of options for getting your information online.

I'm going to cover just a few broad categories here and not get too much into the details. The creation, care, and feeding of a Web site or another online publishing solution is way out of the scope of this book. I'll recommend books and other resources as we go along.

The first option is a possibly unexpected solution—a plain old Word or PDF document!

Publishing a Word, PDF, or Text Document

It may seem counterintuitive to focus on "office" documents when we're discussing the Web, but you can easily publish the information you've gathered to generate a report and simply upload it to your corporate or institutional Web site. This works equally well for Word documents, PDF documents, or TXT documents. More obscure formatting (like WordPerfect or other word processors) might be a little harder for people to read.

Pros

▶ If you're already generating Word or PDF documents for consumption in your office, publishing those file formats directly to a Web site saves you from having to generate something else for the Web.

▶ Because you're not hampered with design or having to integrate your information into an already existing structure, making a Word or PDF document can be a lot faster.

▶ The people who find your document can easily print it out, save it to their own hard drives, or move it somewhere else to peruse at their leisure (which can sometimes be tough with multi-page Web sites).

Cons

▶ If you're not already generating a report for the offline set, this method will in fact be an extra step.

▶ Search engines, while they're okay at indexing Word, text, and PDF documents, are pretty awful at formatting them—your carefully crafted report may end up looking at bit spastic through Google's "view as HTML" lens.

▶ Standalone reports can also be a bear to update, and it's tough to inform users that you've got a report that has more information than the report they viewed last week (it's a little easier to see the updates on a Web site). As far as I know, you can't publish an RSS feed from a Word document. And in my experience, it's a little tougher to find a standalone document like a PDF file than it is a Web site.

Essentials

The essentials for posting these kinds of documents are pretty simple: make a document in your favorite (preferably popular) word processor and upload it to a Web site! The following tips may help you ensure your document survives the translation into HTML by a search engine without getting mangled:

▶ Use as little formatting as possible.

▶ One column beats two columns. Sometimes if you format your content in two columns, the search engine has a hard time indexing it and presenting it in a readable format.

▶ Fewer pictures are, in my experience, better than a lot of pictures. Try to reserve pictures for when illustration of a point is really necessary.

Now let's look at a more Internet-oriented solution: using a mailing list to broadcast your research.

Publishing to a Mailing List

If you're doing research that's ongoing, or you don't want to go to the trouble of creating and organizing an entire Web site, you may want to consider publishing to a mailing list. It doesn't need to cost you anything; there are plenty of free mailing list services out there to which you can publish your research.

Pros

▶   Getting your information out there is as easy as writing an e-mail message. You don't have to worry about fancy formatting, or page creation, or anything like that.

▶   People can get updates to your research in e-mail instead of having to remember to visit your site (or put a page monitor on it).

▶   You might find it easier to incorporate sending out a regular e-mail into your routine than updating a Web site.

▶   People who don't have particularly fast connections can download a plain-text e-mail far faster than they can visit a Web site.

Cons

▶   If you want to add fancy content to a Web site (like Flash media, audio, and polls), you won't find plain-text e-mails useful.

▶   It can be difficult to organize information within a mailing list.

▶   So many people have spam traps nowadays you may find that your information is not getting to them or you may be accused of being a spammer. It's amazing how often this can happen—people will forget they subscribed to a list, have someone who shares e-mail with them subscribe to a list, not want to bother to learn how to unsubscribe so they take a shortcut by accusing you of spamming, and so on.

▶   Having to administer a mailing list can be time consuming and tedious.

▶   It's sometimes difficult for someone who wants to learn more about your research to visit a mailing list archive in order to get up to speed.

Essentials

Even if you can't stand the idea of using a mailing list to publish your information, you might want to consider creating a mailing list in conjunction with a Web site or wiki. I've had a Web site for ResearchBuzz for over eight years, but many people would rather get a weekly newsletter with a summary of what's on the Web site. Sometimes it's because they don't want to visit the site regularly; sometimes it's so they can pass around interesting bits via e-mail, and sometimes it's because they want to print out interesting bits and keep them.

When you have a mailing list, you can have either a discussion group or an announcement-only list. Newsletters are announcement-only lists. Discussion groups allow the readers to discuss your research, add opinions of their own, and even contribute to what you've found. You'll have to be careful, though—leading a bunch of people in a discussion often leads to a lot of refereeing and damping down of flame wars. Unless you're creating a list for a small group of people, stick to announcement lists.

> **TIP**
>
> When you start up a mailing list, it's very important to set up confirmation subscriptions. So whenever people try to subscribe to your mailing list, they have to respond to a confirmation e-mail that's sent to your address. It protects them—it means nobody can subscribe them to a mailing list without their permission. And it protects you—if anybody accuses you of spamming them with your newsletter, you can point out that your newsletter is a confirmed subscription and that all subscribers had to confirm their addresses.

Free mailing lists

If you'd like to start a mailing list, you have some free options to choose from. There are a few pay options as well. One thing I would not suggest, unless you're a big geek with a lot of free time, is setting up your own mailing server. You'll have to deal with things like people accusing you of spamming, accidentally getting on blacklists, and making sure that your server doesn't get cracked. By using a hosted solution, you let somebody else handle all that hassle, while you can concentrate on publishing your research and getting it out there!

Google Groups

Google Groups (groups.google.com) is a free mailing list service, though you must have a Google account to create a mailing list. Once you're logged in and choose to create a group, you'll be asked to set up a group name and e-mail address, as well as a description. (There's also a switch to tag if the group should be considered "adults only.")

You have three access options: public (anybody can read and post), announcement-only (anybody can read, only the moderator can post—this is the setting for newsletters), and restricted (reading and posting are private and by invitation only). List archives are not searchable and do not show in Google Groups search results (**Figure 14.1**).

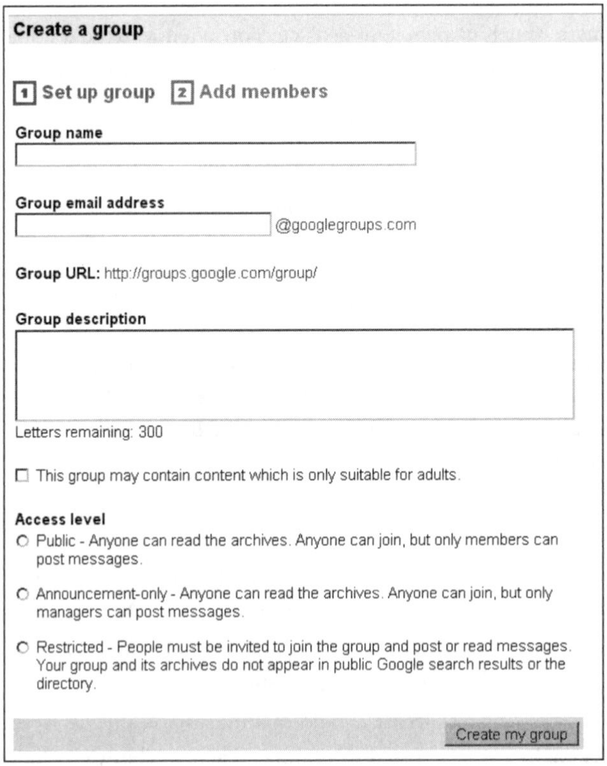

Figure 14.1

Setting up a Google Group is a one-screen process.

Yahoo Groups

You need to have a Yahoo account to set up a new Yahoo Group (groups. yahoo.com), and instead of a single-page setup like Google Groups, it uses a multi-page, stepped setup. You must specify the category of the group, which you can do by either browsing or searching Yahoo Group's directory structure (**Figure 14.2**).

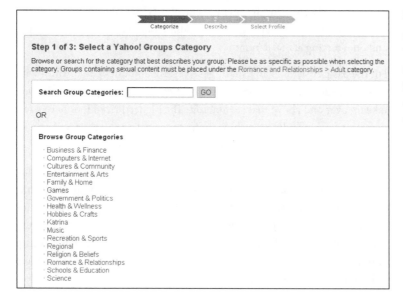

Figure 14.2

Setting up a Yahoo Group is a multi-step process, but it gives you immediate control over things like categorization.

After specifying the category, you need to name the group, enter a group e-mail address, and describe your group. (This page is the one that looks very much like the similar Google Groups page.) Then you are asked to specify the e-mail address at which you'd like to receive messages from the group and the Yahoo Profile that you'd like visitors to the new list to see. Finally, you must echo a random string of numbers and letters to prove you're not a robot trying to set up a mailing list.

Free mailing lists are, well, free, but you do run the risk of having random, unrelated advertising shoved in your newsletter. In addition, the support isn't that great. If you're looking for an advertising-free option that offers fairly good support and a little more functionality, your best bet is to go for a paid mailing list service. Don't worry though—they're not particularly expensive.

Paid mailing lists

There are lots of paid mailing list services out there. I'm going to cover two that I'm fairly familiar with, and then give you a pointer to where you can find many, many more. Let's start with NetAtlantic.

Net Atlantic

Net Atlantic (netatlantic.com) hosts the ResearchBuzz mailing list. It has three levels of service for the announcement lists that you would use to send out newsletters—one starting at $15 a month, one starting at $30 a month, and one starting at $60 a month.

For the basic cost, you can usually get a certain amount of bandwidth with which to send out newsletters. You will be charged for any bandwidth you take up over and above that set amount. The higher-priced lists have a few more features, including the ability to try to resend messages as well as send them a little faster. These features are not absolutely necessary.

While learning your way around a list interface can be a little intimidating at first, it's not that hard. Note with Net Atlantic, you can set up documents that are mailed to users when they subscribe and unsubscribe, get daily (or weekly or monthly) subscription reports, and be able to watch the delivery progress of your newsletter (there's always some address that gets hung up or otherwise blocked so you can't deliver to it). I find Net Atlantic's support folks prompt and fairly helpful.

Sparklist

Sparklist (sparklist.com) is a little more expensive than Net Atlantic. It seems to be designed for larger clients. Its packages start at $50 a month for a discussion group and $100 for an announcement list. (The big difference? Discussion lists have a maximum of 2,000 members.)

If you're interested in marketing with your newsletter, Sparklist offers a lot of tools for tracking and reporting the activity of your readers. (What they click on, when they open it, and so on. Note that these tools only work with HTML newsletters.) Like Net Atlantic, you can also get subscribe and unsubscribe reports, as well as support from real people.

Whether you choose one of these services or an entirely different paid service, be forewarned that they often make strong recommendations about how to handle your online newsletter—like making sure it's a confirmed subscription list (they may even require it). They may also strongly suggest that you keep an unsubscribe link within the body of your newsletter to conform to federal guidelines (or again, they may just require it of you). Please be sure to follow all these directives; doing so makes you a better Internet citizen and makes it easier to protect yourself if someone claims they recieved something from you they didn't want.

There are dozens and dozens more mailing list hosts available online. You can get a huge list of them at dir.yahoo.com/Business_and_Economy/Business_to_Business/Computers/Communications_and_Networking/Software/Email/Mailing_Lists/.

Publishing guidelines for mailing lists

While setting up mailing lists is very simple, sharing the fruits of your research consistently over long periods of time is not so simple. When you're considering publishing a newsletter or announcement list for your newsletter, keep these guidelines in mind:

- ▶ Pick a regular schedule of publishing and stick with it. A daily newsletter is probably too much (unless they're very short), while once every two months is probably too little. Try for either once a week, once every two weeks, or once a month.

- ▶ If you stick to text-only newsletters, you might stand a better chance of getting your newsletter delivered. Sometimes HTML newsletters are blocked because they're considered to be spam.

- ▶ While Google Groups and Yahoo Groups make it fairly easy to find the archives of a publicly accessible list, that isn't always true of paid services. If you're using a paid service to host your newsletter, make sure it offers archives of a mailing list (most of them do) and that you offer some kind of Web-based pointer to the archive—even if it's just a single-page site you post on your institution's intranet.

Other methods that work well for publishing your research are Web-based. This is what most people think of when they consider publishing their information on the Internet. However, the methods I propose may not have been the ones you were thinking of.

Hosted Blogging Solutions

Blogs are mentioned throughout this book. Short for *Weblogs*, they're very popular ways for everyone from grade school kids to corporations to share their opinions, insights, and news. You can set up a blog on your own server, or you can get a hosted blogging solution. We'll look at both of them here, starting with hosted blogging solutions. With hosted blogging, the blog software is contained and maintained on a third party's server. You can either have the blog itself at your own domain, or you can have the blog hosted on the third party's Web site.

How is a blog different from a Web site? For the most part, blogs are Web sites, but they're easier to maintain. You don't have to hand-code most blog sites; there are templates available for the standard parts of your site—parts like navigation and headers and footers. That leaves you free to concentrate on generating content—and free to change your entire site just by changing the template. If you're allergic to HTML or you're nervous about moving around and hand-coding a bunch of files, blogging could be for you (especially hosted blogging).

How is blogging different from other information structures, such as a wiki, that you maintain? A blog is ideal when you want to regularly publish news, information, and links, with optional commentary. A wiki is more for a set of information structures that you want to fill up.

For example, you might want to publish information on treatments for breast cancer. You could publish a blog that would have running pointers to news stories on breast cancer, press releases about new treatments, and commentary on personal experience or research processes. On the other hand, you could also publish a wiki, which might have pages for treatment, drugs, clinical trials, and so on. The pages on the wiki would be filled in as the publisher found information in various categories. The information wouldn't be date-based, and there wouldn't be much room for commentary.

Pros

▶   With hosted blogging, you may not have to set up your own site; the hosting site usually takes care of that for you. In the same vein, you don't have to worry about server fees.

- Posting a blog is very simple; in some cases you can also even post via e-mail.

- When your blog is part of a hosted blog site, your site will often be automatically indexed by the hosting site's search engine.

- You don't have to worry about keeping the blogging software updated and maintained.

- You don't have to worry about your software's installation getting messed up by accident.

Cons

- Sometimes visitors will take you a little less seriously if you don't have your own site, so if you do use hosted blogging, consider having the blog published on your own site.

- If something happens to the host site, it might happen to your blog, too.

- Customization of your blog will probably be more limited than it would be if you had your own site.

- If your site gets overwhelmingly popular and it's located on the blog host's site, the blog host might want to impose visitation restrictions on it.

Essentials

There are many places where you can post a free blog. Really large sites that are not more journal oriented include BlogSpot and TypePad. BlogSpot is a service of Blogger, while TypePad is a service of Movable Type. We cover those here.

BlogSpot

BlogSpot (blogger.com) is a service of Blogger, which is brought to you by the folks at Google. Blogger actually allows you to create blogs for your own site or to host them on Blogger's servers. We'll look at hosting items on Blogger's servers here, and at hosting them on your own server in the next section.

The first thing you'll need to do is sign up for a Blogger account, which is free. Once the account is set up, you can start making blogs. Yes, multiple blogs—you can set up more than one. I don't recommend doing this, though, unless you're publishing information on topics which are very different—heart surgery and ratites, for example. It's easier to keep up with posting and maintaining one blog.

Once you've registered and signed in, look for the Create Your Blog link. Clicking it produces a multi-step walkthrough that includes naming your blog and choosing a template. When you're finished, you're taken to the composition area where you can write your entries (**Figure 14.3**).

Figure 14.3

Blogger has a composition area that lets you preview posts and insert HTML.

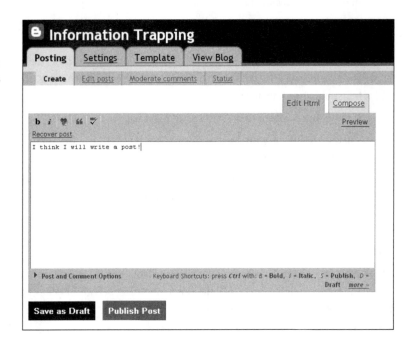

Blogger has a lot of little tricks to it; for hints and updates to features, check out Blogger Buzz, the official Blogger blog, at buzz.blogger.com/. In the meantime, here a few hints you might find useful.

▶   **Play with the templates.** There are lots of Blogger templates to choose from. Experiment until you get the one you want, and the one you think your audience will want. Some of the templates are very stylish, but maybe you want something easy to read or easy to scan for information.

- ▶ **Consider comment moderation.** Blogger offers a variety of ways to make sure that the comments on your blog do not get overrun with comment spam (people or robots coming in and posting fake comments which are actually just attempts to get links back to a Web site). Be sure that if you have comments on your blog (although you don't have to provide this option), you turn on comment moderation.

- ▶ **Post regularly.** You don't have to post every day or every hour like some people seem to. But do post regularly; otherwise, folks might forget to come visit. (Sure they could use your RSS feed, but not everyone wants to do that.) Think of the people who might discover your Web site via a search engine, only to find that you haven't posted in a couple of weeks or longer. Do you think they'll bother to get your RSS feed?

- ▶ **Publicize your RSS feed.** Blogger has Atom feeds available, but they work in RSS feed readers. Unfortunately, I haven't seen any of the templates show the feed by default! The feed is always the same file name; it's atom.xml. So if you have a BlogSpot blog at example. blogspot.com, the URL of your feed would be example.blogspot.com/ atom.xml. Make sure you link to that URL on your site's home page, so that all your readers know where to get your RSS feed.

BlogSpot is a great place for people who aren't very Web-oriented and who just want to quickly put up a Web site for their research. For people who want to get under the hood and do a little tweaking, a TypePad blog might be a better choice.

> **TIP**
>
> BlogSpot and TypePad are for all kinds of blogs, while other sites are designed more for diary sites and online journals, which is a little outside the research republication we're talking about here. Two examples of that would be LiveJournal (livejournal.com) and Xanga (xanga.com).

TypePad

TypePad (typepad.com) is brought to you by the people who do Movable Type. It is a hosted solution. There are three levels of hosting here: $4.95 a month for Basic, $8.95 a month for Plus (which allows you to have up to three blogs and customize your design), and $14.95 a month for Pro, which allows you to have multiple authors (for collaborative blogs), as well as full

HTML editing and an unlimited number of blogs. There is also a free 30-day trial available.

You have to create an account and provide the name of your blog, as well as the preferred URL for the blog (you can have a URL at blogs.com or typepad.com). Once you've signed up, you've got a lot of choices to make! You'll have to choose your blog's layout, a design style, and most importantly how private your blog is. You can make it freely available, freely available but not publicized to the general public, or completely private and accessible only through a user name and password, If you're looking for a way to publish a blog for a limited group of people, the latter option is a good way to do it. If you do choose this option, you must immediately specify a user name and password.

When you're finished, a control panel opens, where you make your posts, edit the way your blog looks, and make lists (**Figure 14.4**). Lists? Yes, you can specify lists of things like people and music and have them show up in your blog. You can also set up photo albums.

Figure 14.4

TypePad is a little more complicated, but also more flexible.

Everything for TypePad is made available through the control panel that lets you do a variety of managerial tasks, including banning IPs from making comments, seeing how many page views your blog has gotten, and uploading files—you have 500 MB of file space for your TypePad account. While TypePad is not as simple as Blogger, it offers far more in the way of easy tweaking and customization.

For those of you with limited Web-building experience, hosted blogs are a great choice. They don't require server maintenance or hosting, and they're very easy to interact with. However, those of you who want to try different software, or want to do more tweaking than is offered by a hosted service might want to host a blog on your own site.

Your Own Blogging Site

The difference between blogging on a hosted service and blogging on your own site is that if you do it on your own site, you host both the software and the blog. You may have to get up to your elbows in technical stuff, but it also means more freedom.

Pros

▶   Blogs and sites on their own domains tend to be taken more seriously.

▶   You may not like your "neighbors" on the free blog sites; on your own domain you don't have to have any.

▶   You can install all the plug-ins and add-ons that your ISP will permit.

▶   You will have many more software options than the free and hosted services offer.

Cons

▶   Hosting your blog on your own site is much more technical.

▶   Sometimes the hosting and the domain name registration costs more than a hosted service.

▶   If you're not careful, you can get hacked. (Well, you can get hacked on a blog hosting service, too, but at least then you have someone to yell at.)

▶   Generating content and maintaining a site can be much more time consuming than just generating content on a free hosting service.

Essentials

There are two ways to have a blog on your own site: you can use a hosted service that publishes the blog to your site, or you can install the software on the server yourself.

In a way, the former option is the best of both worlds. The technical work is at a minimum, while you still have the freedom of your own domain. We'll look at both options here.

> **TIP**
>
> While we'll look at options for blogging software to put on your site, we're not going to look at all the intricacies of finding a Web host, registering a domain name, learning to use FTP, and all those little bits of knowledge that go into maintaining a Web site. For a good book on that, check out *Blogging in a Snap*, from Sams Publishing.

Using a hosted service to publish your blog on your site

In addition to hosting a blog on its own server, Blogger also allows you to publish a blog to your own site. To publish a hosted blog to your own site, however, you'll need to know how to transfer files to your site via FTP (File Transfer Protocol). Your Web host's support section should have more information about that.

To use Blogger to publish a blog to your site, you'll still need to have an account. Actually the setup works very much like hosting a blog with BlogSpot, except you'll need to choose the Publishing tab in Settings (**Figure 14.5**).

There you'll need to specify your FTP server, the path where blog files should be kept, and your blog's filename and URL. After that, setting up the blog proceeds as it did for blogs hosted on Blogger.

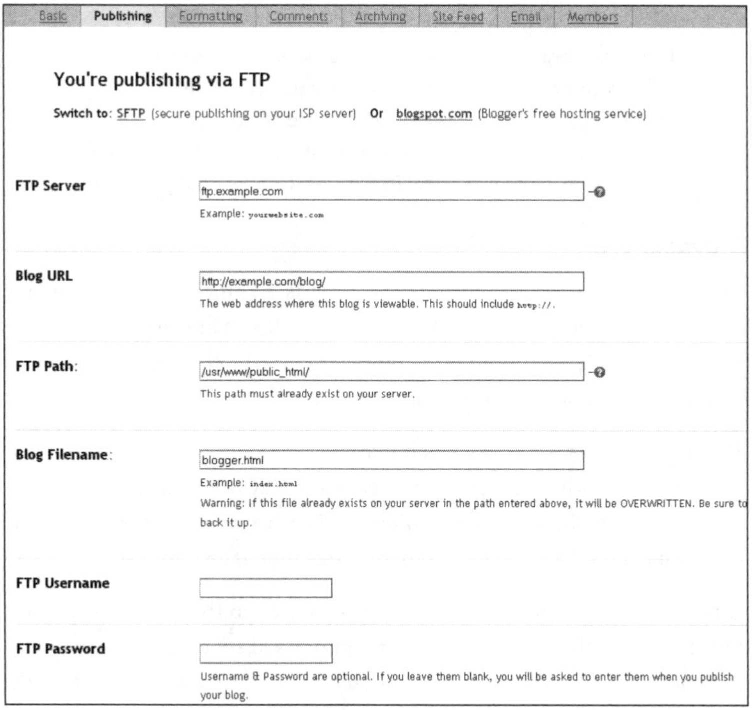

Figure 14.5

If you want to publish to your own site in Blogger, you'll have to set it up here.

Installing software to host your own blog

In addition to using hosting services, there are several packages that you can install on your own servers. Some of these packages are free, while some of them cost money. The ones I'm covering here are fairly low-cost. There are content management and blogging packages that could run into the thousands of dollars, but those'll be overkill for information trappers who are just trying to share their knowledge. Let's see what's available on a smaller scale.

This space is still developing, but we'll look at two popular packages—Movable Type and WordPress—and I'll give you pointers to some other packages you can investigate.

TIP

If you're a librarian or someone who's working on Web space within a company or institution, be sure to clear it with the IT people before you start installing software. In your case, the IT folks might actually prefer that a software package is installed on the site instead of an external FTP connection touching the site.

Movable Type

Movable Type (sixapart.com/movabletype) is a complex application, and sometimes it can be frustrating, but its flexibility is amazing. In addition, Movable Type is supported by a large community of people who are constantly developing plug-ins and add-ons for it.

Pricing. Movable Type has several layers of pricing, ranging from a personal version with no support for free, all the way up to an enterprise-level version that you have to contact Movable Type to get pricing for. There are discounts offered for not-for-profit and educational groups.

Installing. To install Movable Type, you have to go through a several-step process that includes downloading a compressed set of files, uncompressing and uploading them to your site, setting file permissions (so that the core programs that make up Movable Type will run), and then tweaking configuration files so that the program looks for data in all the right places. After that, you must log in to Movable Type, set up your first blog, and set your preferences. It's not rocket science, but it is time consuming.

Movable Type offers a tool you can download and run on your server to make sure that your server has all the Perl modules and other bits necessary to run Movable Type. If your Web site passes the test, be sure to follow the instructions step by step so that you don't later trip over some step you missed. If you're nervous about installing the software yourself, Movable Type can, for a small fee, install the software for you.

Features. Movable Type offers a lot of functionality right out of the gate. Some of the things you might want to pay attention to are the fact that some of the versions of Movable Type allow you to publish unlimited blogs on your server (again, only recommended if you're publishing information on very different topics), can accept comments (where people make comments directly on your site) and trackbacks (where people link to your page and where their links are noted on your page). Movable Type also gives you a lot of control over the way your templates look, as well as the ability to archive your information several different ways—daily, weekly, or monthly, and by category. (You can set up your own templates as well.) Posting an entry is very much like posting in TypePad (**Figure 14.6**).

Figure 14.6

Movable Type offers several levels of detail to post entries.

In addition to its native functionality, Movable Type also offers huge numbers of plug-ins that are designed to add extra functionality to the software. Some of these are very easy to install, while others are pretty complex. You can get a full directory of available plug-ins at sixapart.com/pronet/plugins/.

__TIP__

Remember, not all plug-ins for blog packages are created equal. Some plug-ins are created by the company that created the software, while others are created by third parties. Be cautious of the third-party ones. Try to stick to third-party plug-ins that are recommended or at least acknowledged by the creators of the blog software for which they are intended.

WordPress

WordPress (wordpress.org) is the blog software on which I currently run ResearchBuzz and other sites. I have fallen in love with it over time. Some of its features are a little hard to grasp at first, and you'll probably have to do a lot of experimenting before you understand the available Web site templates and WordPress's formatting language. Once you have that all in hand, though, you'll be amazed at what you can do.

Pricing. WordPress is an open source project and it's free, though it does accept donations.

Installing. Because WordPress is free, it's free for hosting companies to install on their Web sites. For that reason, you may find that your hosting service has the option to do a "one-click install" of WordPress. If it does, take advantage of it! It'll save you a whole lot of trouble. If it doesn't, you can download an installation document that'll take you through several steps. One of the steps involves creating a database within which WordPress holds its information. It's not quite a ten-minute install, but it's pretty quick.

Features. WordPress offers a "dashboard" of tools across the top of the page. Notice that in addition to providing a place to post your blog information and create an entry (**Figure 14.7**), you also have a place to post "pages"— information relevant to your site but separate from your blog.

Examples of pages you might put here are information about you/your institution/your company, an overview of your project, and feedback forms. There's also a place where you can make link lists (links in several different categories), create users, and manage comments. Everything is fairly straightforward except the WordPress "Themes"—those templates that determine what the pages look like. The default theme isn't bad and there are many WordPress themes to choose from for the completely non-artistic among us (that means me!)

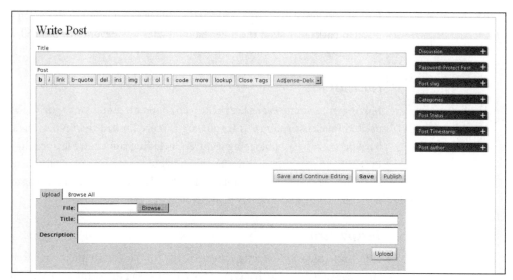

Figure 14.7 Most of WordPress's post detail is in collapsible boxes to the right of the post area. You can take advantage of it—or not.

And like Movable Type, WordPress also offers plug-ins to extend the capabilities of the software. You can get an overview of the types of plug-ins available at wp-plugins.net/, or try the list at wiki.wordpress.org/Plugin.

Other blog software packages

While Movable Type and WordPress seem to be the two blogging software packages that get a lot of press, there are many others available. Here are three more that you might want to look at.

pMachine

If you want to install your software on a corporate site, you may want to try pMachine's ExpressionEngine (pmachine.com). It's one of the more expensive packages. A commercial license is $249.95; a non-commercial license is $99.95. However, if you're planning to use ExpressionEngine on a personal site, you can download its slightly limited core package for free. It offers a variety of features that make it appropriate for a group of people or people in a company setting, including a private messaging system and support for a discussion board (sold separately). This is a very extensive and complicated package, but on the other hand, it goes way beyond the basic idea of blogging.

NucleusCMS

Moving from a more expensive package to another free one, we've got NucleusCMS (nucleuscms.org). This software is more limited than pMachine's, but offers a variety of blogging features, including some nifty features like the ability to save entries as drafts, the ability to write entries and post them in the future (handy if you want to take a holiday but you want your blog to keep updating), and a variety of available plug-ins.

Textpattern

Like NucleusCMS, Textpattern (textpattern.com) is free. It offers a markup language called Textile that is purported to be easier to use than HTML and more reliable than WYSIWIG (What You See is What You Get) sites. Textpattern offers the features that you'd expect in blogging software, including some unique twists like the ability to password-protect site sections or specific pages, the ability to close pages after a specific period of time, and more direct editing of CSS files.

There's no doubt about it—blogs are really hot right now. And if you're publishing information that's best organized by date, blogs are a good choice. But if you're looking for a way to set up an outline of information that gets filled in over time, you might want to try a wiki instead. And though you don't hear nearly as much about them as you do about blogs, there are plenty of options out there for wikis as well. For simplicity's sake, you might want to try one of the available hosted wiki options.

Wiki

As I've mentioned earlier in this chapter, wikis are best understood as containers for information—outlines that you can fill in with information as you find it. Blogs, on the other hand, are more vehicles for date-based entries and commentary. And while some blogs allow you to break your entries down by category, those category/entry listings are not usually that easy to read.

Pros

▶   Easy to expand.

▶   Handy for large groups who need to put information together.

▶   Can be set up so that it can be edited by anybody or just by a certain group.

▶   People who visit it do not have to go through a bunch of archives to zero in on just the information they need.

▶   It only takes typing a word in a certain way to make a WikiWord, giving it its own page in your wiki.

▶   Information on topics is concentrated on singular pages, which might make it easier to be found via search engines.

Cons

▶   Fairly new; it can take a little getting used to.

▶   Openness of content editing can be a disaster unless carefully managed.

▶   Not as easy to incorporate commentary; more for factual data. (Because many people edit the same pages, if you incorporate commentary, you might end up with a page full of flame wars.)

▶   It's difficult to summarize in a newsletter, compared to summarizing something more date-oriented, like a blog.

Essentials

The best example of what a wiki is all about is probably Wikipedia (en.wikipedia.org/wiki/Main_Page). This wiki is an attempt to build an encyclopedia that's fully open and fully editable. That sounds like a recipe for disaster, but somehow it's not. Let's look at a typical page (**Figure 14.8**).

Notice there are tabs across the top of the page that include Edit This Page, which anyone can click and then edit the page they're looking at. There's also a history page that shows the edits that have occurred in the past. Edits can be as simple as correcting a spelling error to as complex as fleshing out an entire article.

Does this seem a bit overwhelming to you? A wiki that's also an encyclopedia? Okay, let's look at some smaller-scale stuff. To get an idea of how other groups are using wikis, try the list at usemod.com/cgi-bin/wiki.pl?SiteList or WikiIndex (wikiindex.com/Main_Page), an effort to list all available wikis.

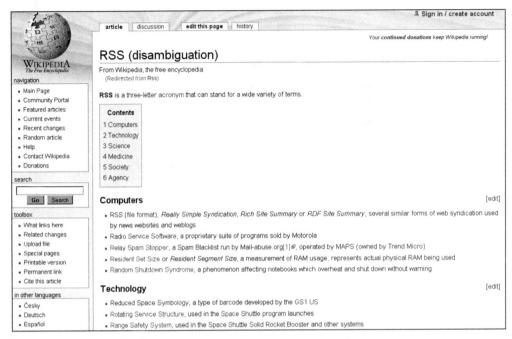

Figure 14.8 A typical Wikipedia page.

Earlier in the book, we looked at a few options that you have for portable wikis and giant enterprise wikis. There are wikis that you can install on your own server, but they're somewhat technical. If you're interested in setting up a wiki on your own server, you can get a list of wiki software packages at dmoz.org/Computers/Software/Groupware/Wiki/Wiki_Engines/. Most of them are free. For the sake of simplicity in this book, we're going to look at hosted wiki services.

Hosted wiki services

At the moment, there doesn't appear to be any premiere wiki hosting services, so here's a roundup for you to choose from, all of which have different highlights and strengths. Most of these are free; the ones that aren't have only a nominal cost.

JotSpot

JotSpot (jotspot.com) offers a lot of extras. For the most part, it's a paid service, but there's a free service available, too. Getting started is a simple five-part process: enter your e-mail address, your password, and the subdomain that you want to appear on the jot.com domain where your wiki will be set up (it'll look like this: example.jot.com). You then need to provide your name and enter a word string that shows on the page to prevent robots from setting up wikis. Once you've done all that, JotSpot will present you with your new wiki (**Figure 14.9**).

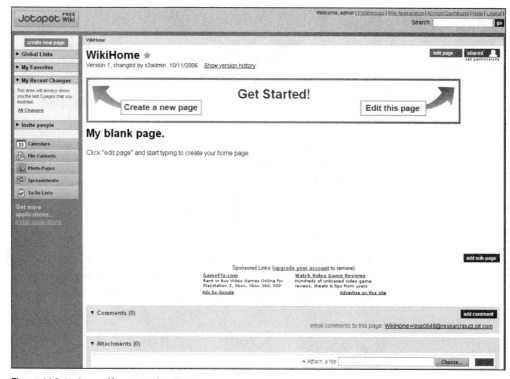

Figure 14.9 JotSpot offers a quick wiki setup.

JotSpot has instructional videos, FAQs, and a knowledge base for learning more about how to use the JotSpot service. And this will come in handy; JotSpot has a lot of additional functionality, including a variety of applications you can add to your wiki, like a calendar, RSS feed reader, company directory, and blog.

> **NOTE**
>
> JotSpot used to be a paid service, but Google acquired it in late 2006. As of this writing, JotSpot has suspended new accounts and billing for its services. I suspect that when the transition to Google is complete, JotSpot will relaunch as a mostly free service. Stay tuned.

PBwiki

PBwiki (pbwiki.com) has a simple one-step process for making a wiki. You enter the name of your wiki, and provide an e-mail address. Once that's done a URL is e-mailed to you. Click on that URL and boom, you have a wiki. You'll be asked to create a password and specify whether you want your wiki to be public or not.

PBwiki is not as slick and extensive as JotSpot, but it's not as expensive or intimidating either. Once you've logged in, you're shown the front page of your site along with some pointers to documentation. The PBwiki folks encourage you to play with the features and experiment with some of the offerings like RSS feeds and the ability to publish a sidebar on a blog. There's also a very lively forum available.

PBwiki is free, but a premium version is available for $9.95 a month with higher levels of service going up to $34.95 a month for corporate level blogs. The additional costs pay for more file space, more available designs, and more features.

SeedWiki

Like PBwiki, SeedWiki (seedwiki.com) offers accounts that are primarily free, and like PBwiki it's very easy to sign up. Accounts require a name, e-mail address, and password.

Once you've registered, you're given the option to set up a wiki or a blog—unlike the other services they're not set up for you. Setting up a new wiki means specifying a name for it, a language, a description, and a folder—in other words, the subject under which the wiki should be listed.

Once you've made your wiki, a vanilla page with a navigation bar on the side displays to help you administrate it. I like the way that SeedWiki is doing its wiki because it provides a lot of freedom to experiment. You can make a wiki, and if you don't like it or want to mess around, you can just delete it and start over—no muss, no fuss.

Wikispaces

Less standalone than a regular wiki is Wikispaces (wikispaces.com), which offers easy integration with blog tools like Blogger. Once you've registered (registration requires a user name, e-mail address, and password), you have the option of creating a "space." Spaces can be public (anybody can view and edit), protected (anybody can view, but only certain people can edit), and private (nobody can view or edit). Public and protected options are free, but the private option costs $5 a month.

Once you've created your space, you'll see that it looks a lot like a wiki, only the editing options seem a little friendlier than most. For more information on integrating Wikispace into your TypePad or Blogger blog, go into the options menu and check out the Integrate a Blog option.

Wikis and blogs are two types of Web sites, and are offered as packaging and hosting services. But while they're two types of Web sites, they aren't the only kinds of Web sites. You can also make your own site.

Making Your Own Site

When it comes down to it, an HTML page is just a text file that has certain formatting elements in it. It's not a programming language. It doesn't require compiling. As long as you have some Web space and a way to upload your HTML files, you can create your own Web site to hold your found information.

Pros

▶   You can do absolutely anything you want to with it.

▶   You can integrate multimedia content.

▶   You can experiment and try out different ways to encapsulate information.

Cons

- ▶ You have to code your own Web pages, which, while not difficult, does require a certain amount of technical knowledge.

- ▶ You'll spend a lot of time maintaining the containers for your content (the pages) as well as the content itself.

- ▶ You may have to hire a designer to make your pages visually interesting.

- ▶ You'll miss out on a lot of plug-ins and other ways that blog software and wikis add functionality.

Essentials

A tutorial on HTML is totally outside the scope of this book, and frankly I wouldn't recommend creating your own site unless you have an information structure in mind that just doesn't work within the confines of a hosted blog site or wiki, unless you already have extensive HTML skills and some experience as a site builder.

Basic HTML skills

Basic HTML skills can be acquired through any number of books. But there are online tutorials available as well. Check out the HTML Goodies page (htmlgoodies.com/primers/html/), which has a seven-part HTML primer that's designed to take one week to complete. HTML Code Tutorial (htmlcodetutorial.com/) has a whole domain dedicated to teaching the ins and outs of HTML. And if you want something really exhaustive, which when gathered into a PDF document weighs in at over 300 pages, check out mcli.dist.maricopa.edu/tut/lessons.html.

Planning a Web site

If you have an idea for a very small Web site, it might not even occur to you that you have to plan out a Web site. But take it from me, even the most modestly considered Web sites have a tendency to grow like Topsy. Making The Net Work has an overview article that gives several salient points about which you should think when planning a Web site: makingthenetwork.org/toolbox/tools/webguide.htm. An article at Sitepoint breaks down what you'll need to do, step by step, as you plan your Web site: sitepoint.com/article/site-planner.

Now if you look at these articles, especially if you're an individual or in a small group, you're going to feel like they're serious overkill. And they probably are! But at least glance over them. If you're building a Web site for an institution or a corporation, please look over the site planning articles carefully. If you're building the site yourself, it'll give you some useful guidelines. If you're not, it'll help you understand the goals and concerns of the people who are building the site.

In this section, we've looked at learning HTML, but of course that's not the only way to run your own Web site. You also have the option of learning a software package that'll help you put a Web site together. For example, you could learn Dreamweaver, or Microsoft's FrontPage. So you can either learn HTML or a software package—but the same "cons" of extra coding time, maintenance, and lack of universal plug-ins will apply.

Thus far in the chapter it's been all about content—how do you make the content, where do you keep the content? That's the place to start. But the next step is how do you distribute your content? So let's spend a little more time on RSS feeds.

RSS Feeds for Content Distribution

RSS feeds, as you learned earlier in this book, are XML documents that alert users of changes to Web sites and summaries of new content. They can get a lot more complicated than that—they can hold everything from graphics to MP3 files—but at the heart of it, RSS feeds are about providing information updates.

Making that kind of information available is critical to you, the information publisher; the more ways your Web site can be kept up with, the more likely your visitors will make the effort to keep up with it, and the more readers you'll have. So you might have a blog and a newsletter, or a wiki and a discussion group, or a quarterly published PDF and a wiki. In addition to all that, you should have, whenever it's available, an RSS feed.

Built-in solutions

When is it available? For blogs, all the time; all major blog software and services automatically create RSS feeds for you. For wikis, some of the time. When evaluating a wiki, look for syndication options. And be careful because many RSS feeds for wikis require having the user name and password within the RSS feed's URL; this is not the best idea for security reasons and should be used very carefully, and not with an information-sensitive wiki. And for mailing lists and providers, it depends on the provider you're using; Google Groups and Yahoo Groups have no problem with providing RSS feeds, while it's less available in the paid services.

If you've got an RSS feed built into the solution you're using, you've got one big thing to decide and one big thing to do. If you don't have an RSS feed, I'll give you a quick tutorial on creating one.

Choosing between full or abbreviated

RSS feeds are marked by the "full or abbreviated?" controversy. A "full" RSS feed means that it reproduces in its entirety the contents of a Web site. A blog, for example, that posted all of its entries in an RSS feed would have a full RSS feed. An abbreviated RSS feed is a feed that only contains an overview of the changes to the site—story summaries or, more often, the first 20 (or 30 or 50) words of a story. ResearchBuzz is an example of a site whose feed contains only snippets of stories that have been posted to the Web site, while Gary Price's ResourceShelf has a full feed.

Feelings run high about this. Some people think that full RSS feeds are absolutely the way to go and it's not fair to RSS feed users to use anything else. Other people are more concerned about what making full RSS feeds available would do to the distribution of their content. As you'll see in a moment, it's very easy to repurpose the content of an RSS feed and make it available on other Web sites. In other words, if you made the content of your Web site fully available via your RSS feed, it's possible (even likely, depending on your content) that someone would use your RSS feed to put your content on their site! Why? To have fresh content. To generate pages on which to put advertising. There are lots of reasons.

Now maybe your research is nonprofit or just a hobby and you don't care if your content gets repurposed to other sites. Or maybe you'd welcome the reuse of it as long as it got the word out there about your research. That's fine; publishing a full-content RSS feed would be the right step for you. (It does have its value for your readers, including the ability to keep up with your site without visiting it directly and passing on the full content of useful site additions to friends and interested parties.) However, if you're concerned about your content being used on other sites, or you're trying to make some revenue from visitors coming to your site (and therefore need eyeballs looking at your site's advertising), then I recommend using abbreviated RSS feeds.

Of course, how you have the RSS feed doesn't matter unless your visitors know about it, which brings us to the next step.

Promoting your RSS feeds

Make sure that visitors know about your RSS feeds! This is especially important for hosted services like Blogger. In my experience, the basic templates don't do a lot to highlight the fact that an RSS feed is available. So make sure that the home page has a link to your RSS feed, and make sure as well that you submit your RSS feed to at least a couple of RSS feed directories like the ones we've looked at in the book. Feedster (feedster.com) is an absolute must, as is Technorati (technorati.com).

Most hosted services have RSS feeds built in. Google Groups and Yahoo Groups offer RSS feeds. Most blog packages have RSS feeds built in. But you may be in a situation where you have to make your own feeds by hand. Okay. It's not fun, but, okay. Here's a basic lesson on making RSS feeds.

Creating your own RSS feeds

If you have to make your own RSS feeds, try to limit them to basic text information; multimedia RSS feeds can be a bit complicated. Use this three-step process to make your own RSS feeds.

Start with a template

Just like HTML files, RSS feed files have headers and footers that never change. They help tell the computer that's reading the file what it is and how it should look. You'll need to change a little bit of information on them but not much. **Script 14.1** shows a typical header for a basic RSS file.

As you can see, there are some elements that you need to address:

▶   **Title.** The name of your Web site, naturally!

▶   **Link.** The URL for your Web site. (Note this is the URL for your Web site, not your RSS feed.)

▶   **Description.** A brief description of your Web site.

Script 14.1

The header.

```
<?xml version="1.0" ?>
<rss version="2.0" xmlns:dc="http://purl.org/dc/elements/1.1/
→ " xmlns:sy="http://purl.org/rss/1.0/modules/syndication/
→ " xmlns:admin="http://webns.net/mvcb/" xmlns:rdf=
→ "http://www.w3.org/1999/02/22-rdf-syntax-ns#" xmlns:content=
→ "http://purl.org/rss/1.0/modules/content/">
<channel>
  <title>Your Marvelous Web Site</title>
  <link>http://www.example.com/marvelouswebsite</link>
  <description>Describe Your Site Here</description>
  <language>en-us</language>
  <pubDate>Mon, 04 Dec 2006 22:22:20 GMT</pubDate>
  <copyright>Copyright 2006 You</copyright>
  <lastBuildDate>Mon, 04 Dec 2006 22:22:20 GMT</lastBuildDate>
```

▶ **Language.** The primary language in which your content is generated. The above example shows American English. You can get a list of the language codes you can use in your feed at msdn.microsoft.com/workshop/author/dhtml/reference/language_codes.asp.

▶ **PubDate.** The date your feed was published.

▶ **Copyright.** Whatever copyright disclaimer you want to make about your content.

▶ **LastBuildDate.** The date your content was last revised.

At the end of your RSS feed you'll need your footer (**Script 14.2**), which is very simple. That you can leave as it is.

Script 14.2

The footer.

```
</channel>
</rss>
```

Fill in the blanks

The actual content summaries from your Web site are contained in items, which look like **Script 14.3**.

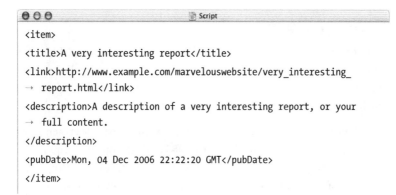

```
<item>
<title>A very interesting report</title>
<link>http://www.example.com/marvelouswebsite/very_interesting_
→ report.html</link>
<description>A description of a very interesting report, or your
→ full content.
</description>
<pubDate>Mon, 04 Dec 2006 22:22:20 GMT</pubDate>
</item>
```

Script 14.3

The items.

You'll have to customize an item for each of your RSS feeds:

▶ **Title.** Title of your item.

▶ **Link.** A direct link to the item. This can be a file or an anchor within a file.

▶ **Description.** This is a little misleading. Yes, this can be a description of your item, but it can also be the item itself, spread out over several paragraphs. If you want to include all your content in your RSS feed, put your unabbreviated content here.

▶ **PubDate.** The date the item was published.

Lather, rinse, repeat

For each bit you want to include off your Web site, you'll need to generate an item. So in a plain text file you'd put the feed's header, an item for each story you're going to include in the RSS feed, and then the footer. You can theoretically include as many items as you like, but I'd limit it to 15 or 20.

I actually did this once a week (for a couple of years!) for a Web site that doesn't generate an RSS feed. Here's how I did it: I had an RSS feed template. Every week I changed all the dates via my text editor's search-and-replace function. Then I edited each of the items to reflect new content. Since I changed the RSS feed weekly, it was easy to keep up with.

Once you've generated your RSS feed, upload it to your site. And then check to make sure that it works.

Testing your RSS feed

To test your RSS feed, use Feed Validator at feedvalidator.org. Enter the URL where you uploaded the feed and Feed Validator will tell you if it's okay or not. If it's not, Feed Validator will tell you why. I do this every week, too; here are some common problems I run into.

▶   **Unencoded characters.** Some characters have to be properly encoded before you can include them in an RSS feed. The one that trips me up is the ampersand (**&**). The proper way to encode it is by using **&**. (Most of the time I remember to search and replace the ampersand with **&** before uploading my feed.)

▶   **Smart quotes.** Sometimes I'll copy and paste something from a non-text source (such as a quote). Sometimes those quotes will include "smart quotes" instead of the ASCII plain quotes.

You can get a full list of what Feed Validator flags, as well as pointers to how to fix the problems, at feedvalidator.org/docs/.

Making RSS feeds publishable to Web sites

RSS feeds in and of themselves are just text files. Many of your users will want to read them with RSS feed readers, which is okay, but some of your readers may want to include your feed on their Web site. Or perhaps you have many RSS feeds and you want to include feeds from one site on another of your sites. There are several ways to do this, from installing programs on your server to simpler solutions. Let's stick with simpler. FeedDigest can take a feed and give you code to put your feed on a Web site.

FeedDigest

FeedDigest (feeddigest.com/) allows you to not only make a feed publishable but to format it and change its look and content. You start by just specifying the URL for your feed. From there, you'll be given several options, including how many items to show and how to sort them. Then you'll be prompted to choose the template for the digest from about ten options.

Once you've generated the feed and registered, you'll have the option to get PHP or JavaScript code to include the digest on your site, or to give to others to include the digest on their site.

FeedDigest will also show you how to edit your site to make your RSS feed easier to discover by browsers and robots visiting your site. You'll also learn about "pinging sites"—making sites that index RSS feeds aware of new content on your RSS feed, so they know when to index it.

Working Toward Manageability

Once you get into the full swing of trapping and publishing information, you'll find that you're culling a lot of interesting information and you're passing it along in various formats. You may even find that this process of finding, organizing, and passing along the information is taking more and more of your time! In a bonus chapter, which you can access by registering your copy of this book at peachpit.com/title/0321491718, I offer some solutions for making information trapping a routine, rather than a giant monster that takes over your life. I also provide tips for how to keep your keywords and search sources fresh and current.

Thanks for reading!

> **NOTE**
>
> You can access additional chapters on mobile information trapping, RSS tools, keeping up with your traps, and more by registering your copy of this book at the URL mentioned above.

Index